STEERING FROM THE BACKSEAT

SHARON SALA

STEERING FROM THE BACKSEAT

Copyright © 2018 by Sharon Sala

All rights reserved. Except for use in any review, the reproduction or utilization of this work in whole, or in part in any form by electronic, mechanical, or other means, now known or hereinafter invented, including xerography, photocopying, and recording, or in any information storage or retrieval system, is forbidden without the written permission of the publisher.

This is a work of nonfiction.

Printed in the USA.

Photo:
Erin Kanske
Artsy Phartsy Photography

Cover Design:
The KILLION Group, Inc.

At this writing, my mother, who has become known as Little Mama to all of my friends and readers on Social Media, is 98 years old, and in her fourteenth year of living with Dementia.
She's been in charge of nearly everything all of her life, and never minded letting you know it.
However, the disease that took my mother away, leaving me with Little Mama, has also taken away her memories of everything, including me.
She's been trying to 'go home' for so long, but she's forgotten how to take charge.
She often appears in the posts in this book, so I'm dedicating this book to her.

Mother --
You were the hub of our world, until the wheel fell off.
I'm praying hard for you to realize your greatest wish.
If I could, I would take you home myself, but since I can't,
Know that I'll be steering from the backseat, trying to get you there.

ACKNOWLEDGMENTS

Many thanks to those listed below, for helping me on the next step of my journey to being me.

With much appreciation to:
Pam McCutcheon at Parker Hayden Media

And to the red-head on the cover for her rendition of Driving Miss Daisy:
My daughter, Kathryn Sala

A NOTE FROM THE AUTHOR

I've been posting stories and messages from Spirit on Facebook for many years, and my friends and readers have continually asked me to please put some of these into a book. I kept telling them I would, but then I didn't.

This year I set the intention to follow up on as many of my writing promises as I could, and this is the first promise I'm getting to keep.

Know that they are all individual posts, over different years, and in no particular order. I chose them for the messages that were in them, rather than having it read like a daily log...which did not suit this purpose.

I refer to several people quite often in the posts without identifying them, other than their first names. My Facebook friends and readers are so familiar with my family, that they already know who they are.

So I'm posting a legend of sorts below, so you'll know of whom I speak.

Mother aka Little Mama, is self-explanatory.

My Daddy was a special man to me. Both of his grandmothers were

Native American. One was Cherokee, the other was Cree. But he lived his adult life with a burden. Alcohol. He fought it all through my childhood until the year my son was born. He poured every bit of liquor he had down the sink, and lived twenty more years as a sober and loving man.

He died two months before my sister passed.

Grand and Grampy are my mother's parents, and the pivotal and guiding lights of my life when I was growing up.

Kathy and Chris are my children. Crissy is my niece, who I helped raise after her mother, Diane, died. She is my other girl.

Diane was my younger sister and only sibling who lived past birth.

She died two months after our Daddy passed.

Scout is a nickname for my only grandson. He belongs to Kathy.

Ash, mentioned often in the posts, is Kathy's partner in life.

Chelsea, Logan, and Leslie are my son, Chris's, three daughters.

Destiny, Devyn, and Courtney are Crissy's three daughters, and Diane's granddaughters.

I have two ex-husbands. Their names are not pertinent to these posts.

Denise cleans my house. She's been doing so for so many years that she has become part of my family.

I had a childhood sweetheart, who I found again after my second divorce.

His name was Bobby. He was a member of the Muscokee Tribe, and the love of my life. We had eight blessed years together, and then he got sick - cancer - and died in my arms. I thought I might die with him, but it was not to be. My work here is not over.

Bobby is with me in spirit...always. I can't see him or hear him, but I feel him.

As an Empath, dreaming and knowing are parts of my gift.

He was my touchstone in life, and he is my guiding light now.

These people are my tribe.

The posts you are about to read are from Spirit, and from my heart.

I happily share them with you.

AND SO IT BEGINS...

This is a scene to quiet your mind.
　Close your eyes.
　Breathe in. Breathe out.

I am walking through a vast expanse of ripened wheat without disturbing a stalk. I pass as if I am not solid.

The earth is quiet, and I am one with the silence as I accept this is food.

A wind rises, blowing across the wheat and shaking the grain from the stalks, as if it is being threshed.

Now I hear sound, and look behind me.

Thousands of people are in the wheat and more behind them, holding out baskets for their share of falling grain, moving without speaking, without discord, taking only what they need.

Breathe in. Breathe out.

You need not be on a mountain top, to be closer to the God-light.

It is within all of us.

You need not seek a master to lead you in prayer.

You need not bow your head, or drop to your knees, as if showing those around you that your piety is greater than theirs.

Take away ego, and lift your face unto the heavens where the God-light is brightest. Open your arms, open your heart, speak your truth, and know that you are heard.

Breathe in. Breathe out.

Find the place within you that most resonates with joy, and know that sending out that feeling, links you with like-minded people all over the world. And the joy expands exponentially.

Find that place within you that most resonates with peace, and know that sending out that feeling, links you with like-minded people all over the world.

And so the peace will expand exponentially.

Find that place within you where you hide your greatest fears, take away the shields you have in place, release what is not yours, and give the rest to God.

Breathe in. Breathe out.
And so it is.

My Prayer For You

I pray for peace and grace in your life.

I pray for you to know joy.

I pray that life is kind to you in some way, every day.

I pray for you to be overwhelmed with kindness.
I pray that you learn to share it.
I pray for your days to be filled with laughter.
I pray for your peace of mind.
I pray that you find forgiveness.
I pray for your troubled heart.
I pray for your grief to ease.
I pray for trouble to pass.
I pray that you find the answers you need.
I pray that you learn to appreciate what you've been given.
I pray for you to see truth.
I pray for your good health.
I pray for your healing.
I pray for your anger to be assuaged.
I pray for your safety.
I pray for your loved ones.
I pray for you to have total understanding.
I pray for you to know mercy.
I pray that your steps lead you on the right path.
I pray that you accept your fellowman without prejudice.
I pray most of all that you walk in light.

Always remember—That which you disdain is someone else's dream.

The dissatisfaction of where you live, what you wear, the car you drive, the job you have, would be a life-long dream come true for someone else.

The fact of being alive means there will always be someone struggling worse than you, and the only time that struggle ends is when you die.

For this time in your life, even if you are striving to better your situation, accept where you are right now as a lesson to be learned, not a punishment.

Struggle is never a personal attack. Life is not about people out to get you. We are thrust into life-altering situations all the time. Our job is to figure out either how to survive it, or to do better, or both.

If you have food, shelter, mobility, clothing, and a job, you are rich in personal comfort. It's not what it looks like, but how you view it that sets your path.

If you walk out of that shelter every morning to go to your work with the gratitude that you have some place to go, you are far wealthier in what matters, than the person who can only find joy in possessing more things.

Denise is cleaning.

It's supposed to get up into the 50s this afternoon. It was in the single digits over the weekend. My sinuses don't know whether to dry up or sneeze.

I dreamed about a man with hookworms in his brain. I could see them. There was a faint red rash on the top of his bald head. Nothing that looked obvious from the outside, and then that's when I saw all of the little worms inside. He was running around trying to get someone to cure him, and it wasn't happening. Just as I was waking up, he was sitting in a corner, maybe waiting to die...or just waiting.

I think it was a message—an analogy for how I see the nation.

Everything feels sick...off center...and people are running around in panic trying to find their safe place...trying to find balance... And the fact that the man sat down in a corner may not have meant he was waiting to die...it could be that he had just accepted what was, and got out of the way of the coming chaos.

I don't know how to explain it, but I do know it was a message...and analogy of how I see what's happening.

It is an unsettling time in our country with all the threats of what may happen, and what might end, and what will be taken away, but "may happen" doesn't mean it will, or even can happen. I think the man sitting in the corner just means wait and see. Wait and see. And so I am.

We are living in a world of impatient people now. Angry because they can't get somewhere fast enough. Frustrated to have to stand in line - wanting everything now - wanting it without earning it -without saving up for it. There is a whole generation of people who don't know what 'doing without, or saving up to buy it' means.

At the same time, and growing up within the same time period, there is a generation of people who never had enough. If only the vast knowledge, and great wealth of goods and services in this land, was not owned and run by big business.

Need should be met with help, without bankrupting families to keep someone alive. Need should be available for the asking, instead of going through months and months of paperwork and red tape, only to be rejected in the end by something as ridiculous as a typo. It happens. It is a travesty. It is how this country operates. Help for some, but never for all.

God sees all.

Some may escape justice here, but you cannot escape the debt you owe the universe when you die.

It's called Karma.

That which you have given out into the world, is what you will gather in spirit.

Do it right the first time.

❦

It's cold and wet here, kind of a drizzle in the air. We need a downpour. This state is so dry. The ice storm passed me by. I am so grateful. I had already said my piece to the universe about rejecting the ice, and refusing to accept its presence (yes, I believe in positive thinking) but I also kept picturing Tyhen, the young woman from THE DOVE, which is the second book in my Native American time-travel trilogy, The Prophecy Series, up in the air above the city, blowing the storm away.

Aren't you glad you don't have to live in the world in my head. I think it would drive a sane person crazy. But since I came this way, it is sanity to me.

My mother used to read my books, then look at me as if I was a stranger and say, "I don't know where you get all this. If I didn't remember all too vividly the thirteen hours of labor I was in, and if you didn't look just like your Daddy, I would think you weren't even mine."

She was very proud of me, but she was a practical woman. Thank goodness she loved to read. For that reason I was given a pass for any bad words in the books. She would say, "I don't know why you had to say that word," referring to something a character said, and I would tell her, "I didn't say that. He did. His reaction and how he speaks does not have to fit into polite society. He murders people, Mother. Those are his words, not mine."

She'd wrinkle her brow and wander off, thinking about what I'd said.

Bobby read my books. He asked me once, in a very serious manner, if I thought of him as my hero. It made me cry. He... the only man who ever valued ME...the only man who loved me without boundaries...the man who gave my wings back, reminding me that I had always known how to fly. I told him, yes, he was my hero in this life, and forever. I'll never forget the look on his face. He had a hard life. He was such a good man. He was a hero many times to others in his life, but never acknowledged. He needed to be somebody's hero and he was mine.

Acknowledge kindness.

Never forget to say thank you.

Be aware of the people within your life.

You walk among angels, unaware.

Just for the record... it is a shame that social media has turned us all into big fat tattletales.

He said.

She said.

They said.

I won't.

You can't make me.

You're evil.

You're blessed.

Pass it on.

You're going to hell.
Dare you to deny this.
You have no heart.
My way is the only way.
The word lie no longer has a meaning.
Alternative fact.
Shaming by posting horrible pictures.
Lying about what they mean.
Blaming your neighbor.
Blaming a race of people.
Blaming one side for not taking your side.
And all of this compliments of social media.

Because it's easy to be a jerk—to point fingers—to berate—to chastise—to judge, judge, judge, to write scathing posts against one another, and then have the option to hit Send, knowing there's nothing anyone can do to stop you. Even if you're sorry later, it's too late.

Words wound, and wounds never heal.
They scab over and leave scars as reminders of what you suffered.
We all bear a few scars.
Some are scars of our own doing.
Some are scars left by others.
So today is a new day... Another chance to get life right.
Stand in YOUR truth without defiance.

You have the rights to how you feel.

Going to get a perm this morning.

It's supposed to get up to 76 degrees today. We set a record yesterday at 77 degrees. My allergies are messing with me. I'm losing my voice, and we just started February. If this is already Spring, we're due for a long, miserable season of sneezing and coughing.

The world that made me, the people who helped shape my life, the houses I lived in that sheltered me, the family who loved me as a child... gone...it's all gone.

So what do I do when I can't go home? How do I ground myself in the now, when my heart needs a place to belong, and people who know my name?

I do not thrive in a city. I can live in it, but it doesn't comfort me.

We are often uprooted by life. It's not something you can even prepare for. But it's part of the journey, and it's up to us to find a way to cope. It may not be what we wanted, but we will wind up where we need to be to continue it. Do I dwell on the past? Not a lot. But some days are harder than others to get through. It is what it is.

On the days that I am saddest, Bobby always makes his presence known.

Last night was a gift. I fell asleep surrounded by spirits, touching my face, my covers, shaking the bed just enough to let me know they were there. Like when I was little, and Mother would come into the bedroom where Diane and I were sleeping. I was awake just enough to know she was there, pulling the covers up over my shoulders, smoothing the hair away from my face, kissing my forehead and patting my back before she left.

That's what last night was like—taking me back to childhood, and being tucked into bed by my Bobby. He always knows when I am sad. I miss him. That is all. I just miss him.

You set the tone for each day of your life.
You can dwell on what's gone or what's missing.
Or you can delight in what you already have.
I choose joy.

When I was little, I wanted to make some money to help Mother and Daddy buy new tires for the car. But since I already knew they didn't have money to buy new tires, that would also mean they didn't have extra money to give me, just so I could give it back to them.

So in my infinite seven year old wisdom, I decided I could make pottery and sell it. Yes... I thought that at the age of seven...having never seen pottery being made, and knowing no one who did it...and yet I knew. So I'm from Oklahoma...land of the red man...lived on what they called The Red Hills...which were made of clay...and when it rained, those hills were slick as snot to get up, and easy to slide sideways going down.

So I dug myself up a bunch of red dirt off the hillside below my Grand and Grampy's house, and went down into our cellar with an old tin bowl, and a little pitcher of water, and made myself some clay. Oh I mixed, and kneaded, and I punched, and I stirred, until I had a piece of clay about the size of a loaf of bread, and I began making little bowls. I don't know what I thought could be put in those little bowls., they weren't big enough to eat from. I think I was counting my money by quantity not usability. But I finished, and I set them up to dry on an empty space on the shelf between quarts of green beans and quarts of mustard pickles, and then spent the next two hours trying to wash the red clay out from under my fingernails and off my skin.

Every day I went down to check on them. They were slow to dry down in that dark cellar. I was seven. I hadn't given any thought to sunshine. I just needed secrecy. In case someone else got my good idea, and beat me to the market place.

Within a week they'd finally dried—with cracks. The first one I picked up fell apart right along the cracks, and so did all of the others.

Mother came down, saw the hunks of dried mud, and told me to clean up my mess, and get out of the cellar. Chastened, disappointed, and defeated, I did as I was told.

I spent the summer with empty pockets, just like the rest of the family. My dream of buying new tires for the family car were dashed.

Two things I learned from that...that there was nothing wrong with dreaming big...because during the time of those mud bowls drying, I had hope. And after they fell apart later, I learned that it was okay to fail. I had put out effort. Worked to make it happen, and the fact that the end result was unsuccessful was minimal to the fact that I had tried.

Failure isn't about something going wrong.

You only fail when you never try at all.

I have a mission today.

Beginning today, and every day from this day forward, my mission is to do one good thing for someone else. I don't know what it will be, but I will know it and them, when I see it. I don't like how discord makes me feel, so I am shifting my personal energy from fear to faith, and from anger to empathy.

Now I'm off to leap tall buildings at a single bound.

Superman ain't got nothin' on me.

I wrote until late last night, but stopped earlier to watch the Tarzan movie that came out last year with Alexander Skarsgaard. The movie was good. I think. It was hard to focus on the story for looking at the physique of that beautiful, beautiful man. God did good with that one.

We had quite a thunderstorm come through last night as well, but it had passed except for rain, by the time I finally went to bed. We really needed the moisture but I think my friends down south in Texas got tornadoes from the same storm. It's actually too cold here for tornado weather. But the rain was welcome.

I had lunch yesterday with my daughter, Kathy, and grandson, Scout, at Logan's Roadhouse. It is always a lift of my spirit to spend time with family, even if they've begun hanging on to me when we walk, as if afraid I might fall. I'm not feeble, but I have gray hair. Therefore, I suppose I have earned the right to be dependent now and then. Especially if it makes them more secure that I'm still upright and walking.

It is becoming more and more apparent to me that I am not participating in life as much as observing it. It's what I used to do when I was little. Then I was too shy to play with kids I didn't know. Now I just don't want to. We'll see how that plays out with what's going on this year with me and travel. I never liked traveling. I was good once I got to a destination, but traveling itself is nothing but pure misery to me. I think suffering motion sickness probably colored my perception of travel being fun. I've already seen the floor of the car from close-up.

Intent means nothing without action.
But be careful how you proceed.
Harsh words can end a friendship as quickly as a lethal blow can end a life.

❧

I went out to get the Sunday paper from the end of the driveway this morning, and could already feel mist in the air. It's gray and cloudy, a hint of the rain that's supposed to come later, after dark I think, unless that's changed. I haven't listened to any news this morning. I just wanted to wake up in peace.

Other than waking and breathing and sleeping, life is different for each of us. Whatever we experience each day, colors how we react to what happens next.

Our goals are different because we each came with a different purpose. We can accomplish the same thing, but we'll come at it from different paths.

Ten people in a room can be given the same task and not one of them will accomplish it the same exact way, and that's okay. Our job was not how to do it, but to just do it, so give each other a break.

What I want is not always what I can have, so rather than be unhappy, I make concessions. I'm not choosing less, I'm choosing different. Understand? That's how you make peace with where life has taken you. And to move forward, you have to make peace with yourself, and the world around you...even if the world is not at peace, you can be at peace in your heart.

That doesn't mean you accept what's happening, but that you have made peace with the fact that it IS happening. That is so important...

to learn that one thing. When you do, you will not believe the change it makes in your life.

In the next few months, hold onto your truths and the people you love.

Live life thoroughly.

Don't begrudge, and don't covet.

What is meant for one, is not necessarily meant for another.

❧

It is neither the tropics, or the subtropics here in Oklahoma, but it is February. and there was a butterfly on a bush in the front of my house.

The Bradford Pear tree is bursting with tight green buds.

There is no such thing as climate change, right? Lord love a duck.

Ah, the exciting and luxurious lifestyle of a NYT best-selling writer.

I'm doing laundry.

I have to make a run to Wal-Mart, and then I will come home and work.

Work always means write.

Everything else is what you call it, but in this house, work is always writing.

I have a doctor's appointment tomorrow morning. I'm not sick, but my OTHER doctor insists I see this one, too. So I go. The irksome part… I got an email reminder of the appt…a text reminder on my phone, and a phone call reminder I missed yesterday along, with a phone call reminder this morning. OH. MY. FREAKING. WORD.

I am a grown woman. I remember my appointments. Talk about making a pest out of yourself. They already have a warning posted in their office that if you miss 3 consecutive appointments they won't reschedule you. Ever.

To be fair, the dentist does the same thing to me. And then wants me to fill out a survey of how they did. The Chevrolet dealer here is still sending me surveys to fill out on my last visit. They'll send them until I die, before I'll fill one out. Amazon wants constant feedback on what I order. I can't buy anything online without getting pestered about surveys. I don't care why They want them, it is a waste of My time.

I got a package delivered from the post office this past Monday, which was a holiday. I said to the postman, "I thought this was a holiday for you guys." He said, without cracking a smile, "except for Amazon...we deliver those packages regardless."

Wow. That must be some deal Amazon made with the U.S. Mail.

I want to make a deal.

I'll take whatever is behind door number three.

Life rules:
Step back.
Take a breath.
Let it go.
It is already a thing of the past. Trust the truth.
Love is the answer.
I swear.

Worked until after 1:00 a.m.
Up at 7:00.
I am too old for this.
But I'm on the downhill side of the work in progress.
My house is warm.
Denise is here cleaning, and that is good enough to jump start my Monday.

When you dream of better days, you are projecting energy toward that. But you have to act upon that dream to make it happen, and when things set you back, you don't blame yourself.

You don't say, I can't catch a break.

You don't ask, why does everything bad happen to me?

And you don't act out against someone else, trying to bring them down with you.

When you do that, you are telling the Universe that you recognize you are a failure. You just told the Universe you are a loser. So the Universe recognizes and acts upon your definition...in other words, you just sucked in a whole heck of a lot of bad energy.

We've all heard the phrases 'bad Karma' and 'bad vibes'. Well that's exactly what those are, and you asked for them.

If you want a difference in your life, than you have to make a difference, be different, speak what you want.

Don't bemoan what keeps going wrong. Talk about what's going right.

Find one positive thing every day, and be happy it's part of your life.

I cannot stress enough how important it is right now to be the light.

If you want a better world, then you have to be part of the light that will change it.

You cannot go to war every day, and expect to come home to a place of peaceful bliss, because you are bringing the darkness home with you.

Laugh often.

Forgive freely.

Revenge is not for us.

Dreaming without stress or torment, because I'm listening to CDs of Whole Tones.

I am moving through my days in a calmer way. Writing with that music playing in the background of my day, making my food, taking a quick rest. And when I finally turn it off, it's like being pulled backward into an energy storm. The moment the television comes back on, I am distracted, and start feeling the sadness and the confusion. Voices sound strident. Even though they may be smiling, or have no expression at all, I can hear the stress and anger in them. One glance at someone's face, and their distress is evident, as is their depression. There is so much negativity. I am beginning to back away from television. It makes me even more determined in this life to hold the light.

Because I am a writer, I see everything visually...like a movie scene. And because I may not know the people I am around, I see them moving about like extras in the background that is my life. I am so emotionally separated now from the discord, that I feel like I am in a pre-programmed setting, acting out my part.

And my part in the play is a small part, but it is very clear to me.

I am the lantern.

I am the street light.

I am the lamp.

No matter where I go, or who I meet...no matter how far I am away from home, my part in the play is still blatantly clear.

I am one of the lights.

No matter what's happening in your life...If you are in a time of celebration.

If your path has suddenly leveled out and clear.

Or if your time has become a time of strife.

Even if it's hard.

Even if it's sad.

Even if it is the time of finality.

It isn't ever the end of you.

꽃

There are certain things in my life that I learned by watching the people I loved most.

Honesty.

Empathy.

Sympathy.

There were unwritten rules about behavior that was never going to be okay.

Taking frustrations out on someone else.

Humiliating others just for a laugh.

Taking something that didn't belong to me.

Being mean.

The times when I disappointed myself, were worse than any punishment I might have received.

People quote the bible, book and verse, and take passages constantly trying to prove a point, to justify their way of thinking, to prove it's their way or the highway, separating us, separating themselves, putting us all into boxes and labeled US and THEM.

Such confusion. Such unnecessary confusion.

All we need is one verse to guide us through life. To be the tool with which we live side by side in this world in total harmony.

One verse...

Do Unto Others As You Would Have Them Do Unto You.

The book has been sent to the editor, which means, in my world, the baby is on the way. Hopefully it won't take 9 months for the birth day, but as with all things in life, we are not in control of Mother Nature.

We still have wind. We still have fires. No imminent rain.

My son-in-law, Ash, changed out the bulbs in my living room light fixture, (love him) I don't do ten foot ceilings.

I'm making chocolate chip cookies for Scout to take on a camping trip. Yay. That means I get to eat one for test purposes.

I think it's time to eat something. I haven't had food since 5:00 o'clock yesterday. I didn't go to bed until 2:00 a.m. because I was still editing, and then I slept in a little, and got back to the final read through today. I'm past the hunger stage, but I have to eat because of blood sugar issues, so I'm off to scrounge. As it is every time I finally send off a book, my kitchen is bare. I have not taken time to replenish anything, so guess what I'll be doing tomorrow?

Grocery shopping.

Today I choose joy.

Today I choose bounty in my life.

Today I choose once more to keep the door to darkness closed.

Darkness is always in the world in one form or another, but letting it in is always a choice.

I don't call acquaintances my friends. They are just people I know.

My friends are chosen as someone I trust to respect me, just as I respect them and their ways, and what I need to feel safe in this world. That means, even if we are on two different walks with respect to a way of life, that I still value their friendship, because they respect and value mine. That's what it means to live together without conflict.

That's how we must be to end the hateful rhetoric that exists.

If someone is so juvenile and immature, that the only way they know how to behave is by slander and mud-slinging, then so be it.

Just know that they do that out of fear.

They have lost control of what makes them feel safe and so, like children, they lash out or call each other names.

It is not our path to correct them. It is not our business to judge them. But it is our right to remove ourselves from that presence.

Just remember:

You school people in how you want to be treated, by what you allow them to do in your presence.

Today I'm going through edited revisions of a LIFE OF LIES... one of my romantic suspense stories that I write for Mira Books, an imprint of Harlequin Publishing Co.

I don't mind edits. Just another chance to revisit the people I left behind.

That's how I feel when I turn in a book. Like I've moved away from some people I spent a long time with, and I always miss them at first until I am forced to move on to the next new world, with new people who come to me wanting their story told. I am forever grateful to be a storyteller.

My Daddy was a storyteller. My Grand, who was my mother's mother, wrote short stories when she was young, and sold them to magazines. My Auntie, who was Mother's sister, wrote poetry and short stories, and sold them to magazines. It comes from both sides of my family.

My gift is how my stories come to me. Like a movie and in my sleep, or sitting before a computer screen with my hands on the keys. That's when the movie starts playing in my head. I see it. I see them. I hear their voices. My task was learning how to put down on paper what I was seeing. And once I did, I never looked back.

This gift is my connection to people, which is part of my path.

Each book is a stone I set into the road upon which I walk, to carry me forward to the next. Each book—each stone—keeps me from sinking, from drowning, from faltering. It keeps me upright and on my path.

Know when you read my stories, you are reading the history of me.

You set the stones in your own path daily, by every blessing you give to another, by every laugh you share, and by the example you set for others.

Cold again. That rain that was supposed to come in last night didn't arrive, and all we have is more wind and temps in what feels like the 30s or 40s. I sure hope we get rain sometime today.

Had a hard time falling asleep last night.

I'm going to bake something in a bit.

It will warm up the house and fill up my soul along with it.

I am listening to Whole Tones healing and meditation music by Michael Tyrrell. Haven't had television on much anymore, unless I watch someone remodel a home, or cook. That's about all of the drama I care to handle.

Fifty-two years ago this March, I was waiting for my first baby to be born. He was due the 12th. He arrived on the 25th.

I named him Christopher, after my Grampy. Christopher is a family name that goes back in the Shero/Wray/Wible families for centuries.

Chris followed up his later arrival, by being late for almost everything now. He is teased about it, but he doesn't care. He gets there, which is more than some people can say. He is faithful to the core, and I love him to the moon and back. I am blessed by the good people my children have become. All three of them...even if I didn't give birth to Crissy, the last one who is my niece, she's been my girl, too, since the day she was born.

The brain controls our movement. but the heart controls our joy.

Some days there's more joy than others, but if you look for it, it will be there somewhere, waiting for the eyes to see.

❧

My son, Chris, is not adventurous with his food. When he was little, he would only eat three things for a really long time, and nothing I did on God's green earth ever changed that. It was a fried chicken leg, green beans, and steamed potatoes cut up into chunks. Not mashed. And the food could not be touching on his plate. No gravy or sauce ever.

I fed him everything when I was feeding him baby food, and he ate it, but when he began feeding himself, that was it.

He was my little man, and where I went, so did he. My first marriage ended three months before he was born, and I remarried when he was almost a year old. If I was in the garden working in the summer, he was nearby playing. One year I thought if I let him have a spot in the garden where he could plant his own seeds, and see the vegetables growing and he could pick them himself, then he would want to taste them.

He was all for the idea...raked and raked his little spot, dug the rows, and he wanted to plant English peas because I was planting English Peas, too. Then he wanted to plant some green onions, because I was planting green onions, and he planted one tomato plant because I was planting tomatoes.

And every time I worked in the garden, he worked in his, and by golly his stuff came up, and it grew little pea hulls that slowly filled out with fat green peas, and his onions popped up out of the ground with long green shoots, almost ready to pull and eat, and his tomato plant bloomed and set little green tomatoes.

One day it was time to pick the peas, and I showed him how to take them off the vines without pulling up the plants, and how to pull up the onion without disturbing the ones next to it that weren't quite ready. I was so proud of myself. I just knew I had him finally on the side of tasting what he'd grown. He tromped into the house carrying his little crop in a big red plastic bowl. He washed onions as I washed onions, and sat beside me on the couch and shelled his peas, and when he was done, he poured all of them into my bowl, so pleased with himself.

He said, "There Mama, peas for you."

I said, "But honey, those were the peas you grew. Don't you want to taste them and see how good they are?"

He had such a frown on his face. "No, Mama, you know I don't like 'dem' peas," he said. "I grew them for you."

Outwitted…outfoxed…by a four year old.

We come into the world as babies, and everything we do from that moment on relates to learning, trying, doing.

Then we become adults, and get set on a path that becomes a rut.

Never think for one minute that your time has passed.

We're never too old to learn something new.

So Happy First Day of Spring.

The high today is supposed to be 93.

That's weather for July.

Mother Nature is having a hot flash for sure.

Laundry to do today.
More writing.

We all make decisions based on what will keep us safe.

People tell themselves their decisions were based on what would make them happiest, but the underlying reason for almost every decision we make is safety.

Is that food safe to eat?

Is that car safe to drive?

Are the people I love safe here?

Is this job going to pay me enough money to keep me safe?

Is this neighborhood safe to live in?

But true safety is nothing more than a state of mind.

You could make yourself nuts trying to control the world around you, and still never be certain you were doing all you needed to protect.

Eventually, it comes down to two things—instinct and faith.

Instinct is the same thing as self-preservation. It's what makes us get out of the way of a speeding car, or not go into a dark and dangerous place.

Faith is the knowing that no matter what choice you ultimately make, you will not walk it alone.

You are forever in the presence of angels, and your soul is forever safe with God.

I forgot to set my alarm last night and woke up at 10:15 a.m.

I have no plans today other than to make the most of what life brings. I said a prayer for my Little Mama last night to find her way home. Lord knows she's been packed long enough. I have to move the stacks of folded clothes in her room, just to find a place to sit. She folds them and refolds them, and moves stacks from the chair, to the bed, to the floor, and back again. It makes sense to her, and I can tell by how many stacks of clothes there are, just how angry or sad she was that week, because when she gets angry and wants to go home, she begins packing...thus the stacks of clothes. Lots of stacks...bad week. However, she did that during the ten years I kept her in my home, and is still doing it four years later at her memory care center.

Alzheimer's is forgetting everything, including how to breathe. Dementia is living in a world of hallucinations that get worse and worse, the more memory they lose
.

Be diligent in all things.
Leave nothing important undone.
Be thankful for what you have,
Even though it may not be all you want.
Want and need are two different things.

❦

I am going to lunch and meet up with two Facebook friends who also read my books. I'll post pictures afterward, but I am looking forward to meeting them. It's a mother and daughter, (Janice and Megan) making a trip back to Oklahoma, because the Mother used to live here.

I will enjoy my time with them at noon, and batten down the hatches here in the afternoon, because more rain and storms are predicted, but this time for the whole state.

We'll see how the weather plays out today.

I asked them where they wanted to meet, and sent them a whole list of places to lunch. They picked Cracker Barrel. I love it. That's the closest to home cooking anywhere around, and the choices are many.

I was given a most beloved gift yesterday. It was messages from my Bobby through a very special lady, Leslie Draper, a psychic/medium who talks to angels. As a Native American man, he always spoke in words that had rhythm...and with such depth of meaning...and he still does.

All of the messages yesterday were for me alone, helping me, reminding me, strengthening me...but there's one I will share because it was so beautiful when I heard it that it made me cry.

"I am with you always. No matter what you are doing, or where you are going, or if you are in the house all alone. Know that if you take but one quarter of a step and then you fall, I am there. You will fall with me."

It is my promise to know I am never alone.

None of us are.

Regardless of how short our paths, or how long we must endure the journey... we each have an angel.

Even if you don't want one...even if you don't believe...it doesn't change the fact that they are there.

ॐ

I dreamed I was being chased by a bear, I spent half the night running. You can't hide from a bear, and you really can't out run them either, but for some reason I stayed just far enough ahead not to get caught. And then I began to get tired... the bear was catching up to me, and just as it was about to swipe at me with those deadly claws, a plastic bag suddenly appeared in the wind, blew right past me, and onto the bear's head.

And then I woke up, heart thumping, and worn out.

People are supposed to rest at night, but I can't mind my own business and just sleep. I have to spirit walk myself all over creation and half of Columbia, (My Grand's favorite saying) and now I'm exhausted.

I don't know where Bobby was in that dream but I could have used his help... OR... maybe he was the one who tossed the plastic bag over the bear's head.

Gaaah! I need a nap to catch up on rest.

Do Not Feed The Bears.

No Bears Allowed.

Ran errands this morning and came home with some Easter stuff. I miss not having little ones to hide eggs. I miss making little rabbit cakes for them. I miss sticky fingers, and true sugar sweet kisses. But I had my time with that, and now there are other things for me to do.

Some days are for making new memories.

Some days are for remembering the old.

It's cold and rainy. Central Heat is on.

I have a heavy heart, but this too shall pass.

That's how life works.

We go along thinking we've settled into the status quo, and then life will pick you up by the ankles, turn your world upside down, and shake you real hard to make sure everything you were holding onto falls out of your hands.

Then it's up to you to pick up what didn't break.

Sometimes you have to start over, and sometimes you just need to move forward. Either way it doesn't matter, because the change had to come.

Like school. Once you've learned all there was to know in that grade level...teachers move you up a grade.

So it's the same way with life. Once we've mastered certain soul lessons, we are moved up a grade. Even when it feels like we failed, and were held back, in truth it is just the opposite. It happens that way because humans are a species that can get caught up in a rut, and the only way to shake us out of that rut, is to drag us out kicking and screaming in protest.

Don't look at life as success and failure.

That's human thinking again.

We are light. We are energy. We are eternal beings who volunteered for a mission, and while we're on this earth, everything we do, and whatever it is that happens to us, is because of the free will we were given to perform that mission.

Some souls stick to the lesson plans.

Some don't.

The best thing we do as humans is love.

When that is gone, all of the rest of what we're doing fails.

And so we begin anew, striving to get it right before our time is up.

But even sadness is an affirmation...because if we did not love, our hearts would never be sad.

Empathy for others is a lesson learned.

Good morning to the Social Media hen house. And this includes my male friends too. There's always a rooster or two in among the hens.

I dreamed and woke, and went back to sleep and dreamed the same dang thing, and woke again. My covers looked like I'd fought the bed. It felt like it too. I got up disgusted that I couldn't let go of that dream, and changed the sheets on my bed in the middle of the night, because it was all I knew to do to make it stop. I told myself I was rolling up that dream in the flannel sheets so tight that it couldn't come back, and I put on cotton ones instead, even though they were a little bit chilly at first to roll up in. And it worked.

Now I'm washing those dreams away this morning doing laundry, and I won't have them back in my head again. I'm not talking about what it was, because Bobby always said speaking words aloud gives them power to manifest, and that dream does not need to be told.

Had a surprise visit from Chris yesterday afternoon. He called to tell me he was in the area and was coming by. He also asked would I order him a pizza, because he hadn't taken time to eat lunch...he'd been out of the office checking fields. He works for the State Farm Service agency. So I took it upon myself to finally make that cherry cobbler for his birthday that I didn't get to take to him because of storms.

So he ate pizza, and we laughed, and talked, and had a good visit. His cobbler was still hot when he left to go back by the office, but I was finally satisfied in my mind that I had observed my firstborn's birthday. Things like that are important in a mother's life, you know.

Just because you have known someone all your life, does not mean they belong in your life.

We all walk different paths, and being in a place you do not belong, with people who do not have your best interests at heart, is a very dangerous choice to make.

Be wise in all things...even who you choose to call friend.

※

In my dreams, I carried my Little Mama in my arms all night. She couldn't talk anymore, and couldn't walk anymore, but I knew what she'd ask me to do. I was trying to get her home. I don't know why I dreamed something so irrational. I can't take her where she needs to go. That has to come from her free will, and it was a nightmare. I am worn out this morning and sad. I will be writing all day, holed up in my house away from people until later. I was around way too many scary people in my dreams to cope with real ones today.

I need to shed all of this before this evening. Have plans with family.

Blessings to all of you.

Think about where you are in life today.

Ask yourself..."How did I get here? What choices did I make that put me here?"

If you are unhappy with your health, or your job, or your life in general, do something about it. Make one new choice today that is about something beneficial to you...even if it's nothing more than stopping what you're doing to have a cup of coffee...giving yourself time to breathe.

Maybe start that job hunt you've been thinking about.

You won't thrive if you are unhappy, and that won't change until you change.

You have to think of how many years you spent getting to where you are today, and know it won't change overnight.

Don't let yourself be used.

Do what you do because you want to.

Because it serves your purpose to do be doing it. And don't use lack of money as an excuse.

You can't buy attitude, and it is your attitude that sets goals, and setting new goals is what's going to help you change.

❧

My grandson came to spend the night.

I call him Scout as a nickname. He calls me Grammy.

Scout: I'm gonna stay up all night playing Call of Duty.

Grammy: Okay... see you in the morning.

Then I went to bed.

I woke up at 8:30, got dressed and went to the kitchen.

Scout came flying out of the hall.

"Hi Grammy!"

Surprised he's already up, I ask, "Did you stay up all night?"

"No. I went to bed about 1:30 in the morning."

"So I'm guessing you're hungry for breakfast?"

"Yes."

"The same?" I ask.

He nods.

And so I make two eggs over easy...the way he likes them...with no crunchy edges...no toast...no bacon.

He stands and eats them at the kitchen island.

"Thanks. Grammy," he says, and disappears down the hall to the game room.

"You're welcome," I said, but he was already gone.

Boys are so much easier than girls.

We've all heard the phrase—walking a fine line.

It refers to someone who is on neither side of an issue, but not 'on the fence', not ignoring the issue, just walking a fine line between right and wrong.

I have always believed that is a polite way of saying someone is deceitful. Placating people on both sides...making them believe you are wholly on their walk, and then turning around and saying the same thing to the other side, hoping you aren't found out.

I've never been on that path. I've fallen off of mine many times as I grew up, but I always knew where I belonged.

I don't believe in walking that fine line between a truth and a lie.

I don't believe in walking that fine line between right and wrong.

I don't straddle those fences...I pick a side.

What I don't do always do is advertise it.

I do what my elders showed me.

I live by example.

It is my choice.

My path.

My way.

Small rant happening.

For the past four years in a row my homeowner's insurance has gone up from just under two thousand dollars a year annually, to the point that it's now over four thousand dollars a year. Even though I have never filed a claim on anything! So when I got the latest notice a couple of weeks ago informing me what my NEW rate for the year was going to be, it was my "Oh hell no" moment. This morning I have gathered up both my car and homeowner's policies, and I'm going shopping for insurance.

Change happens whether we like it or not.

I'm going to have to find a new hair stylist. Mine is moving to Oregon.

One of my publishers knocked me down from my usual three-book contract to a one book contract. Like I'm on probation or something after twenty-five freaking years with them. Likely a change will be coming there, too. I don't accept other people's decisions when they do not coincide with mine. There are other avenues I am free to choose.

Then there's the slap-down from my insurance company which I'm dealing with today.

The world in which I live is imploding, and I find myself being called upon to be even stronger and more steadfast...to work harder...to shine brighter...when all I wanted was to coast back home in my aging years.

People I love are in a state of free-fall.

Lives are turned upside down...jobs are changing...families shifting out of balance...

It's all part of the shift Earth is in.

Where there is growth, life will blossom.

What was broken will be left behind.

I am many things, but I am not broken.

I learned a long time ago how to move through grief.

Bend with it—letting it take you as far as you need to move—as low as you need to go.

And when you grow weary of the hibernation, your own spirit will lift you up. and set you on your new path.

We change.

Accept your path and see what life still has in store.

🐚

Easter Blessings.

Today is a day to walk in peace.

I dreamed I was two people last night. One was quietly walking her path, while the inner me was at war. I think in a way that is many women. We do what is expected of us far more often than we should for the sake of peace, but we are ever vigilant, ready to stand up for what we believe is right, and to put ourselves between danger and those we love.

There are many ways to live with honor.

Baking ham for dinner at noon. Made potato salad yesterday. Making a big green salad today and green beans. Kathy, Ash, and Scout are my guests today. She is bringing broccoli-rice casserole (a request from Scout) and deviled eggs. My niece, Crissy had to work, and her daughters, Destiny, Devyn, and Courtney are spending the day with their Dad. The impending chance of storms today, and part of the family working, also keeps my son and family home.

In the grand scheme of things, we do not have to be together to love each other, and it's better to err on the side of safety. We can always eat together another day.

Right now, the sky has no depth or height. It feels so low and heavy that when I went out to check, I could almost feel the weight of it on my shoulders. It is an ominous and building thing of great energy. I pray we miss tornadoes and hail.

The movie, Australia, with Hugh Jackman and Nicole Kidman is on TV. I was watching it earlier and now I still hear it in the other room. That movie holds a special memory for me. I took my Little Mama to see it when it was new. Even though she had so many problems with the ongoing Dementia, she loved to watch movies. Sadly, I realized while we were in the theater, that it would be the last time I took her to one. She could not hear well enough to know what they were saying, and she couldn't remember enough of what she'd seen to follow the story. I took her because it was set during WWII, which was the war waging when she was a young woman. Finally, about half-way through the movie I saw her give up, and lean back in the seat, watching the screen without understanding. I reached over the arm of the seat and took her by the hand. Her little fingers curled around mine, and she relaxed.

That was the day I realized I had become her anchor.

No matter how old you get, if your childhood was a happy one, you will always yearn for the days of your youth. The people who once made up your world have either become your responsibility, or they have already passed. Getting older isn't a burden. It is a privilege.

And it's nothing I ever fear.

It is my blessing—taking me that much closer to going home.

Went to get my nails done Saturday. The shop where I go had three different flat screen TVs for customers to watch, and I just happened to be sitting in front of the one they had on a sports channel. And, they always have the text running at the bottom of the screens because the sound is muted. SO... I look up at the text and it's all in text-speak..."Wstbrk nds 2 cnsdr whts cmng up." Took a second for my brain to read it because...well... I still know how to spell. What they meant was "Westbrook needs to consider what's coming up."

The dumbing down of America continues.

We're going backwards anyway...

Emojis are to us, what hieroglyphics were to Egyptians.

Someday some explorer is going to sift through the remnants of this time in history and find emojis on everything. I wonder what they'll make of the little pile of poop emoji.

That's Scout's favorite.

A little thunderstorm blew through at 5:00 a.m. More due throughout the day. All I want to do is sleep, and there is no time. The story of my life has become on phrase. I have to finish the book.

As a child I saw everything in color, as varied as a box of crayons. Nothing was impossible to me.

As a young woman, the colors had become muted.

Life had crushed my dreams, often muddying my view.

Now there are too many people who see life only in black and white. They see the world as a negative of the reality, where everything that is white appears black, and all that seems black is white. But to see the true image, you cannot have one without the other.

And so it is with humanity. We are varied and beautiful, and shared and mixed, and we are the glorious product of our Creator.

We're the ones who messed it up by muddying our truth.

We are not separate.

We are the human race.

And that is all.

I just finished putting fertilizer on my front lawn. I am sweating like a field hand, and don't take that as a prejudiced comment in any way. I am a farmer's daughter, and I spent 31 years of my married life as a field hand, so I know how much they sweat. It's supposed to rain today. I'm counting on it. Otherwise, I'll be out there next watering in the fertilizer I just spread. argh.

I miss living in the country. There I could have more green weeds than green grass in my yard, and no one noticed or cared, because it mowed the same. I miss feeling comfortable on my own property. Between HOA rules, and not being able to stand outside in an oversized t-shirt and nothing else as I watch the stars, my life is stifled. However... I am blessed to have once known such a life. Once I did that and freely, so I won't complain. Instead, I will reminisce.

There is freedom in choice. I claim my power by choice.
And claiming it gives me the freedom to use it.
I am a woman.
A single woman.
A dominant woman. A powerful woman.
My body can be hurt.
But my spirit will always be whole and mighty.
I did not come from this Earth.
I am part of the energy...the light...the power of the Universe.
I came from the stars.
I am part of the God light and so are you.
Hold that knowledge close.
Knowledge is power.
There's nothing hard about being nice.
It will not hurt you to be patient.
You do not have the right to always be first.
Considering someone else's feelings is easy.
Just think of yourself in the same situation.
Then react in the way you would want to be treated.

How many times a day do you think, "There but for the grace of God go I?"

Do you know how many paychecks stand between you and homeless?

If you lost your job today and couldn't find another in time, would you have a place to go? If you do, then you are one of the more fortunate people in this world, because a very large portion of the homeless population in this country got that way because of a lost job. And what do we do?

We scramble around talking about homeless shelters, and food drives, and donating clothes, when we should be helping them find a job that will support their families and themselves. Helping them into a transition house to be self-sufficient.

They want help, not a hand-out.

I live in a city with an institution that houses the mentally ill. They keep them only until their insurance, or state aid runs out, and then they turn them out onto the street, at which point they are not only homeless, but lost and confused. They are everywhere, and it hurts my heart. Those people can't hold down a job. They can't hold onto their own sanity, and what do we do? Keep them until they are no longer financially worthy to the institution, and then throw them out with the garbage.

Are you the person wearing a cross for a necklace, with a Christian symbol on the back of your car, attending church religiously, who turns your nose up at the dirty man on the street who talks in shrieks and curses? Are you the one who looks away from a beggar? Do you justify your unwillingness to help by stating with great impunity, that they'll only take the money and spend it on booze?

Let me share something with you now.

You help them because your heart knows it is the right thing to do. What THEY do with the money is on them, but you know in YOUR heart that you gave for the right reason. They're all hungry. But sometimes the pain of their situation is greater than the pain in their bellies.

My Bobby always gave. "Because once, I was one of them," he would say, referring to his years as an alcoholic, and so it is that I give with love, in remembrance of him, and the love he had for those on the streets.

"Criminals go to prison, but it is the homeless who do the hard time."

※

Took lunch to Scout at school today. It was a treat I do from time to time, and the last one of this school year. He wanted Caine's fried chicken strips, coleslaw, and un-sweet Iced tea.

Stopped by to check on Kathy. She's getting over back surgery. She and both dogs were in the living room by the fire. Yes, it's cold here today...in the low sixties and always with the dang Oklahoma wind, which means the wind chill is most likely in the mid-fifties. She's healing well, and taking care of business, which means doing what the doctor ordered.

Just got another random call from a credit card company. If they are so excited to give me a lower interest rate on the card I already have from their company, I don't need to talk to them. They just need to lower my rate, and put their workers to doing something else by making all of these cold calls.

Here's a thought guys.

Surprise me on my next bill with a cheaper interest rate.

Then I'll be happy to hear from you.

Going to make lunch, then follow through on Kathy's schedule, and maybe take a nap. It's a day for snuggling under covers here. I can write later.

Every night I dream of trying to finish tasks and making choices. Awake, I feel like I'm living in the middle of a breath...like the Earth inhaled, and I'm waiting for the exhale.

I am so ready for this Earth shift to be final.

From the first moment we made a choice to live another life on Earth, we have been making decisions. Even as a baby...what will I swallow...what will I spit on the person with the spoon?

From then to now, our life has been about making daily choices. Regrets are bound to occur, but just remember nothing is final until we're gone, so if you have regret, accept the fact that you can't change the past, and remember the future is wide open to anything you choose.

❧

Kind of a gray sky this morning and of course, the wind, which is as much a part of Oklahoma as tornados. There will be storms in parts of the state today, and moving farther toward where I live as the day progresses. As per usual, it will likely be in the middle of the night here, when I can't see what's coming.

Thank goodness for the state of the art radar systems we have. The latest ones show the number of lightning strikes per minute in any given storm. It can separate rain from tornadoes, shows the wind beginning to spin, which creates the right set up for a tornado, and can show hail cores within each storm. Each of those weather systems shows up as one mass on the screen, but in different colors. Black with white are hail cores. We had one last week that was ten miles long.

That is at least ten miles as the crow flies and a HUGE hail core within an even larger storm. The storms show up red...lightning strikes are little white x marks. Yellow is yet another aspect of the storm. When you look up and see all that on the screen and know it's coming your way, or already on top of you, that's Okie for 'get below ground.' So we shall see how this day goes.

Nothing can prepare you for loss.
    But you should not live your life in fear of that happening.
    Live with joy.
    Go through each day with a fierce will to get all you can from each moment.
    Laugh often.
    Rage against injustice, but don't make it your war.
    Don't forget to love.

Don't forget to find time for silence.

Stop at least once a day and look...really LOOK... at what you're doing.

If it's important, then do it right.

Otherwise, step away and get back on your path.

Be present.

Let the world know that you are in it to grow light, not fight.

ஓ

Kathy and Ash came over a few minutes ago. Ash changed out a battery on one of my smoke detectors for me. With 10 foot ceilings, I have mentioned this before, I change nothing in this house. Not batteries, not light bulbs, nothing. I like the high ceilings, but they are not convenient for stuff like that. Kathy is doing really well from her surgery. It is my joy to be able to say that.

Take yourself out of the drama of your own life by doing something for someone else. If for no other reason than to get your mind off of what has you troubled.

Hold good thoughts close.

What you give out into the world, you will get back.

If you imagine yourself in a downward spiral with no way out, that is what you will receive, because the Universe interprets that as what you want.

If you need a change in your life, first change how you think.

ஓ

I could never live in a house without books on shelves.

It's like doing away with windows.

I like looking at them in the bookcases across the room. I like remembering what's between the pages. They are friends, waiting for me to revisit.

With the level of dementia my Little Mama is at, she can no longer read to enjoy a story. Even though she sees the words, she either doesn't remember what they mean, or recognize them as anything she knows. And yet when I visit her in her memory care center, I often find her sitting in her easy chair in her room, with her feet up on the footstool, sound asleep with an open book in her hands.

She has forgotten her life. She has forgotten all the deaths within it. Many times she has forgotten me. And most recently, she has forgotten chocolate. But reading was always her favorite thing to do, and while she's forgotten the meanings of words, and can no longer follow a story from one page to the other, it is still the comfort of holding a book that calms confusion.

Our loss of humanity toward one another is what's really wrong in our world.

We have subtly been divided over time by the questions we fill out at doctor's offices, job applications, and all of that is recorded nationally by census records, like age, race, religion, and education. We are given a number, and for the rest of our lives, we are registered everywhere by that number. We look at where we fit into someone else's opinion of what's best, and then not only judge ourselves, but we judge others.

We are herded, like cows with ear tags, some to work, and some put out to pasture, and finally left to die by refusing to provide their need for shelter or health care.

We are all children of God.

We are more than our age.

We are more than the colors of our skins.

We are more than the numbers of our mass.

We all exist.

We all matter.

We are here.

Life is about change. About evolving from one thing to another. We grow from babies to children, from children to teens, from teens to adults.

The seasons of being adult feel endless when you're young, but the older you get, the swifter the seasons pass. When things feel out of our control, we panic, or we begin trying to rein it all in, and wind up in a far bigger mess than when we started.

What you need to understand is that nothing is really out of control.

It is, instead, the immediate destination where life has taken you.

Once you realize that you aren't being punished, and that God has not forgotten you, you settle in and ride it out, because that's how life works.

We live purpose-driven lives.

We came here to learn, and if nothing changes, we learn nothing.

The accidents, and the illnesses, and the losses, and grief go along with the passion, the love, the joy, and the pride of an achievement.

We evolve because it is our purpose.

No matter what is happening in your life, wherever you are at this moment, is exactly where you are meant to be.

I ran errands this morning. Took a trip to Homeland, and then Wal-Mart, to get everything I needed, but I'm home. Almost waited too long to eat, (Type 2 diabetic) and had to stop unloading groceries and eat something before I could finish putting them up. I kept thinking...I'll do it as soon as I do this...or do that...and then my blood sugar dropped so fast I almost fainted. Next time I'll take the time to make a protein shake and take it with me. I know better. Stupid stunt. Bad me.

Last night ended with me barefoot in the back yard, dancing under starlight with Bobby. It's a long story I'll keep to myself, but love is magic, and time is endless if you believe.

I called to check on Little Mama. She is 98 years old now. They said she was walking around this morning, ate almost half her noon meal, and is watching TV with others. So she's the same. I guess the answer to her persistence to life is that when you don't know how old you are, then you aren't.

The good days, the bad days, the days of fear, the days of broken hearts. The days of failure. The days of learning The days of success. The days of love. The days of hate. Even the days of waging a personal war—they all add up to a life well-spent.

It doesn't matter what others see when they look at you.

What matters is how you see yourself.

I like ice cream, but I love frozen custard.

The first time I ever tasted frozen custard, I was thirteen, and Bobby was fourteen, and we were at the Muskogee State Fair as part of a 4-H meat judging team. We participated in the judging events all day, and at night, got to walk the midway at the fair, seeing the sights.

We walked up on a small kiosk in the middle of the midway that was selling something called frozen custard. Neither one of us knew what that was, and we wanted to try it.

They were selling for twenty-five cents apiece, and between us we came up with enough money for one cone.

Bobby handed the vendor the money, took the cone and started to offer me first taste, and then he stopped, looked straight into my eyes, and took the first bite before he handed it to me.

It wasn't until I had my mouth on the same spot where his lips had been only seconds earlier, that I realized what he'd done, because he was smiling.

"How do you like it?" he asked.

"I love it," I said. "Better than ice cream," and handed it back to him, but he just leaned down and licked the drips melting onto my fingers, and then pushed it back to me.

"You can have it," he said.

"But don't you want any more?" I asked.

"I'll take another taste when it's gone," he said.

He was always talking in riddles and analogies, and I laughed.

"How are you going to taste this if I already ate it?"

"Like this," he said, and kissed me.

My lips were still cold, but not for long.

"So sweet," he said. "Just like you."

I'm sure I finished the cone. But I couldn't tell you what it tasted like after that.

All I could remember was him.

He was a charmer with those bottomless chocolate eyes, and brown skin.

Even then, I had already given him my heart.

The calmer I have become in these trying times, the more battle I have in my sleep. Darkness fears light, and the brighter mine grows, the harder I have to fight to keep it burning.

I made a conscious decision to stand firm in my beliefs without causing strife.

That choice is threatening to those who use war to gain power.

I won't put hateful words into the energy of this earth.

I won't begrudge.

I won't accept prejudice.

I will not add fear to ongoing destruction.

I will not blame.

I don't have to.

There is a war being waged in the Universe between light and darkness, and we are being played like game pieces...pawns being moved around from shock to horror...from rage to revenge. And the louder we scream and cry, the more powerful the darkness becomes.

The most deadly blow I can deliver to that mindset is a smile.

Scout invited me to lunch today. We're going to Applebee's because we can both get healthier choices there. It was a Weight Watcher favorite place to go when I was on the program, because they have calorie counts, and heart-healthy options marked. And he likes the food and so do I, although I struggle with finding anything anymore that doesn't have meat, or too much heat. There is nothing more disappointing for me than to order food that looks and smells so good, is served in an appealing manner, and then take that first bite and feel like my whole mouth is on fire.

As Scout used to say when he was little, "that's just stupid."

Don't be angry in this world about your situation in life.

The place you are right now is because of choices YOU made.

As long as you are still breathing, you have the choice to change.

The softer the voice, the more gentle the touch, the easier it is for your purpose to be understood.

People who faithfully follow God's word rarely preach it. They just live it, showing who they are by being a living example.

Tell the Universe what you need, just as you might request a meal. You cannot be fed, if you don't ask for food.

I am baking bread this afternoon.

It is calming for me, and I will share.

It answers my need to feed the world, by feeding a few at a time.

❧

Celebrating Saturday because I can.

Just realized something the other day. If I lived to the age of …oh, let's just say 80, for the sake of argument…I would have lived through only 80 days that fell on June 17th. One day a year it is June 17. 80 years. 80 days for that day only. 80 days to have celebrated a birthday. 80 times I had celebrated a Christmas. It certainly puts what you call "a lifetime" into perspective.

Makes the 'big picture" of trying to accumulate power and riches very unimportant, and highlights what a brief time we have to complete the task we came here to do.

It also highlighted for me, what a waste of time it is to squabble about race and religion, when our time here is limited to a blink of the Universe.

Basically people, you have completely lost focus on what life means, if you're wasting it at war.

&

We never really know each other's hearts, not even close family, no matter how many years we've been friends, because we are all separate souls on separate journeys, and whether we were born into a family, or have accumulated friends as family, there are parts of ourselves that we do not share.

We should never let people into our worlds that can fracture the whole of who we are.

It's hard to heal a heart when the soul has been broken, too.

Look to the joy in life.

Look away from what has passed, and look to the future.

Ask for forgiveness, then live knowing you are starting off on another foot.

What was, is forgiven. What is, has yet to be.

Make it something of which you can be proud.

I heard powerful words last night that can benefit us all.

Don't take the tragedies of this world as your own.

Because you read it, or you heard about it, that makes you a bystander, not a victim.

Do not add all of that trauma to your life, and then give it even more life by repeating, and raging at what you heard.

The pain is not yours to bear.

Instead, say a blessing for strength and healing for the people involved. Say a blessing for the rescuers who go into the aftermath. Say a blessing for the healers who try to put victims back together. Then say a blessing of forgiveness for the perpetrator, and you are done.

By hanging onto the drama of what happened, even though you weren't there, you are sending even more negative energy into the Universe, which only adds to what's already there. You are giving life to the darkness, which was the intention of the attack. And every time you comment, you keep that anger alive and growing.

It is the blessings from God that shift dark to light.

It is the blessing from one to many, that spreads exponentially in love.

It isn't hard to say God bless all of you.

I send you love, and peace, and grace.

&

Opportunity.

A chance.

Are you paying attention to your life, or are you just living it?

Are you missing the messages the Universe is giving you?

When you feel an urge to do something positive and ignore it, you are missing the opportunity—the chance to change.

Remember...change is growth.

Growth is good.

Sometimes the answer to a problem is already there, and we don't see it.

We don't see it because we're still locked into looking at our lives through one window only.

We live in a house with many windows, which is an analogy for the opportunities we have in life... many windows...many choices...often requires change.

If the street you've always walked to work on is suddenly gone...broken up and hauled away, you assume you now have no way to work because the street is gone, and miss the whole point of the life lesson. There are always other ways to get to the same place.

And sometimes the answer is not trying to find a new road to the old job.

What if you took the break in the rut of your life as opportunity to try something new? What if you expanded your horizon, and looked outside what you already know, and changed not only the street you took to work, but the kind of job you were doing?

What else do you know how to do?

How can you turn a hobby into a job?

In this day and age, the opportunity to work from home is huge if you have a skill set to activate that chance.

.Life threw you a curve.
Learn something new
Don't take it as defeat.
Look at is as your chance.

※

Life is happening.
A baby was born
Some are being laid to rest. Some are sick.
Some are healing.
A marriage will happen.
A divorce will be final.
Someone will lose their job.
Someone else will find one.
A person will get lost.
Another will be found.
Accidents will happen.
People will be rescued.
Some will be saved.
Others will not.
Life is happening.
It is not meant to be perfect.
It is meant to be lived.

※

Denise had to clean house around me today. I woke up early knowing she was due soon, and my body said... "Naaah, you're not done sleeping, girl. Get your patootie back in bed. So, I did. Sent her a message to come on in and clean around me, that I was going back to bed. And she did.

I vaguely remember hearing the vacuum, that's about it. Woke back up at 10:00 a.m. Feel 100% better, and already knee-deep in the day.

I remember all of the days when my kids were little, and when I was still a farm wife, or working a job out of the house. None of that could have happened. Sleeping in, is one of the perks of getting older.

Today I am wrapping myself in light.
If you wonder how to do that, these work.
Think positive.
Remember things that make you happy.
Do unto others as you would have them do unto you.
Don't talk bad about people.
Don't make fun of people.
Understand, don't judge.
Visualize a future where conflict does not exist.
Road rage is not an acceptable emotion.
Be patient.
Be kind.
Don't begrudge other's successes.
We are all on different paths.
That's how life works.
And this is how you grow your own light.
Then watch it spread.

What am I doing today?

Oh yes...writing. Another book.
And this evening checking out the bread and butter pickles I made yesterday.
And maybe having lunch with Kathy...
If we both don't give out and decide we'd rather sleep.
I've been awake since 5:40 a.m.
I stayed in bed a couple of hours trying to sleep, but it was one of those mornings when my thoughts would not turn off.
I wish I could meditate, but I cannot.
I do not mentally visualize anything.
No stairs...no light at the top of the stairs...no candle...no nothing.
The moment my eyes close and I try to clear my head, images and emotions come at me like June bugs dive-bombing porch lights. Like a

psychedelic nightmare of what might happen, what can't happen, what will happen, what already happened...

I told Bobby I was tired of being in charge.

I'm pretty sure I heard him say..."You are never in charge."

"Tell that to the IRS," I muttered.

So, I got up, changed the sheets on my bed, started a load of laundry, got the paper, got online and found another bill to pay for Little Mama...and that's the start to my day.

The good part was sitting down to talk to you.

The message for today is that nothing is new except babies.

Don't lose focus on being positive.

Don't panic unless it's your house that's on fire.

And remember Bobby's words... "You are never in charge."

You came with a plan.

You have guidelines.

They call them the Ten Commandments.

So go do your thing.

Meanwhile, back at the ranch...

I've been outside watering plants before it gets too hot. Finished up with that, and hooked up the sprinkler to water the back yard. I'll do the front yard later this evening.

Watching that big water spray come spewing up from the sprinkler head made me wish I was a kid again, running and squealing through one side, while Diane ran through the other, jumping and playing like puppies, feeling that blessed cool water coming deep from our well, cooling hot, sunburned faces peppered with freckles—never knowing that those moments would become the jewels of our past.

I stood on my patio remembering, felt a tinge of nostalgia and knew she was standing right beside me. I could just hear her...

"Jump, Sherry, jump. Like this...do it like this."

I'm doing it honey... in my heart.

Sometimes a person goes through such tragedy that the only thing you can say to them, is "I love you," and that is enough.

When you hurt, whether it's physically or emotionally, knowing that you are loved is a reminder that you matter to your friends and family. We cannot suffer it for you. We cannot grieve it for you. But we can hold you in our hearts through it.

So for those in need...whatever it is... "I love you."

If a person prays for something desperately needed in his/her life and then it comes to them, we rejoice for them. But then we notice that gratitude doesn't last long. Another issue will arise in that person's life that gives sustenance to their need to always be the victim. It is a lifestyle. They don't know when it began, but it has become the only way they know how to live. Throughout their lives, there will be one crisis, after another crisis, after another crisis, in which he/she is the target...the victim...and they will bemoan, and pray, and weep, and challenge you to see their plight. It is what feeds their lives. They cannot see how this repeats in their lives. They need this to be who they think they are.

And for some, it will never change.

It's too painful to look inward.

To find what's broken.

It's not easy to turn loose of the only thing that grounds you, even if it's pulling you down.

But until they quit fighting with life and learn to just live it, that circle of constant desperation will never end.

☙

My last birthday present of the day came early last night.

A hard, soaking rain.

I would have loved for it to have rained all night, but was so grateful for what we received.

Plants look a bit bedraggled this morning, because some pretty strong winds came with it, but they will perk up just as I have.

Humans are like plants.

When we don't receive enough sun, we fall into depression.

When we experience lack of moisture, our skin reflects the sere, drying heat.

In the fall when plants start shedding leaves, and the sap slows down to a crawl inside the stems and branches, so does the life force in us. Our desire to grow and harvest is slowing, we begin stockpiling food and supplies, preparing for the down time in winter, just like the trees and bushes. Even though we continue to move about and function, like the plants...a part of us is sleeping.

Life is life...no matter what shape it has taken., or what color the leaf, or what color the skin. No matter its purpose, or how it interacts with the world, if it wasn't meant to be here, God would not have created it, or us.

Don't live your life believing that, because you are human, you are more important than what's around you.

Don't live your life believing that because of where you live, and what your lifestyle is, that you are more important than others around you.

Don't live your life believing that the education you received, the job you hold, the church you go to, the size of the car you drive, the house you live in, or the color of your skin gives you precedence in God's eyes.

In the world of plants, what we consider weeds have purpose.

Think about it...in the world of plants, what kinds survive best under the harshest conditions?

The strongest ones. The hardiest ones. The ones that learned to adapt.

We're the ones who've named them as unworthy.

We're the ones who pull them out of our yards and kill them because they don't 'fit' our view of what's right.

Can't you see?

Do you not yet understand?

We live how we live because when we were little someone told us this was how to do it.

If we had never been schooled to judge, it wouldn't happen.

Prejudice in any form is not innate.

As a human, when push comes to shove, and our lives become a struggle, we will need every aspect of that lowly weed—its strength—

it's hardiness—and its ability to adapt, to pull ourselves out of the strife.

I want two bumper stickers.

One on my front bumper that says, BE THE WEED.

And one on the back that says BE THE STORM.

A life lived in a valiant struggle will leave a mark when it is gone.

❧

Winston, the new fur baby at Kathy and Ash's house, is afraid of the dark.

Kathy takes him out at night before going to bed, and he won't get a foot away from her, or the bottom step. She has to keep talking to him, and walking with him a little way out into the grass before he'll do his business, then he cries to be picked up. And of course she does, because Kathy never let a baby of any kind cry in her presence.

I still have left-over homemade ice cream, and some of the fresh strawberry cake in the fridge. I wish it wasn't here because I can't ignore it. I hear it calling my name. ack.

Someone posted, asking what are we most thankful for, and the first thing that came to mind over and above friends and family, is that I am thankful I learned to persist.

I don't know when it happened.

I don't know if it was being sexually molested when I was 14, or being cheated on in my first marriage, and verbally abused in my second, or if it was losing Daddy, and then my sister, Diane, within 2 months of each other. I don't know if it was losing my Bobby, or after my mother came to live with me, and watching her slowly lose her mind, and then herself. But somewhere in the chaos that was my life, something clicked. I was reminded that I did not have to be a victim. Yes, I endured plenty of sadness and hard times, but so does everyone else.

I wasn't any different than countless other people enduring all that, too, or worse.

Somehow, I came to realize after rebounding from each personal tragedy, that I would persist—that I hadn't quit, but oddly, had become stronger, in both my faith and in me.

I reject failure in myself.

I have accepted that I will accomplish whatever I need to do.

I have faith in God, and I have faith in me.

God would never be able to do enough to heal or rescue us, if we only saw ourselves as victims.

You have to believe in yourself, and trust the Universe that, whatever the outcome, it was meant to be, and that you will survive it and move on. Maybe with less, maybe with more, but wiser for it.

I am in the midst of a cooking project. Will post a bit later. Bet my kitchen is gonna smell better than yours.

Remember my motto.

Be the Weed...sturdy and tenacious.

Be the Storm...raging against injustice.

Be the Light so that the lost might see.

2:34 a.m. Woke to thunder, wind, lightning and rain. Turned on TV to make sure it was just a thunderstorm, then rolled over and went back to sleep. There is nothing better than sleeping when it rains... IF YOU HAVE SAFE, COMFORTABLE SHELTER.

If you do not, rain is not a welcome visitor in the night.

Proof that there are always two sides to a story.

Yesterday was weird.

So much turmoil. Energy that wasn't necessarily good.

I battled all day against feeling defeated...that's why I finally posted my award from Romance Writers of America for having published 100 books. I did it in defiance of how the energy was trying to pull me down. Didn't mean for it to come across as a big pat on the back for me, but more as a message to the Universe that I do not break when life sits heavy on my shoulders, so back off, dang it.

There is a space around all of us that is not meant to be interrupted unless invited within it—like when you shake hands, or give someone a hug and a kiss. That's that personal space people talk about...but it's also visible to some and they call it an aura.

I think of it as light from my spirit, and it doesn't matter whether anyone can see it or not, but it matters if they can feel it.

I try at all times to keep my light bright and warm by feeling positive, and staying happy with what is. I don't always like my days. They're often hard, sad, and frustrating, but I refuse to be pulled into my own emotional drama. Sometimes I'll just stop what I'm doing, and give myself a good talking to, then laugh and remind myself I tried that stunt when I was thirteen, and it didn't get me any further then than it did now.

What I'm saying is that for the time we are here, we are all human, which comes with human frailties and faults. We have to live within the parameters of what constitutes a 'good life', even if others choose another path. It may appear that the others are gaining ground on you, becoming richer, living in bigger houses and driving fancier cars...and they don't seem to have the financial woes and health issues that you have. BUT...as hard as it is to hear this, you have to accept that has nothing to do with you. You did not agree to come here just to be a dissatisfied person who's wants will never fully be filled, unless you are working out bad karma from a previous lifetime. It was not your purpose to live with anger and jealousy. It IS not your purpose ever to take what belongs to someone else just to fulfill your selfish desires. Not by word or deed... which means you do not take credit at your job for someone else's work. That's called stealing. THOU SHALL NOT STEAL, remember? You should. You were created with that knowledge as a tiny bright light at your Father God's knee.

Lesson for this Sunday... do not invade other peoples' space as a means of control, because in doing so, you have unintentionally put yourself on their paths, which then takes YOU down the wrong road, rather than the one that you were already on. Once you've done that, you're going to find yourself lost, and in more ways than one.

There is nothing to be said about evil that hasn't already been said...but I know from experience that the more it is mentioned, the stronger it grows...the more outrage it can cause, the more chaos it can create.

So instead, I pray for the families who have been impacted, and tomorrow I will spread my light farther, and burn it brighter, and deny the power darkness gained today.

I pray in light.
I walk in light.
I am a light.
This is my path.
It is part of my job.
I do it gladly in the name of all that's holy.

You cannot live your life without changes happening...even to your physical self as you age.

So when changes come in life, like divorces, job changes, loss of loved ones, recovery from illness, we either adapt to what's happened and move on...or we dig ourselves a hole and crawl in, too afraid to see what else is out there...not trusting ourselves to do something different.

Here's the deal... whether you want it or not, whether you're ready for it or not., life is going to change, because you are changing.

In this time in history, people of a certain age are not venerated, or looked upon as people with answers. Even though they have already experienced and survived many things, they are not even a consideration when people go seeking help or advice.

When I was a young mother, I always took my babies to the pediatrician when they were sick. They had medicine for me, and reassurances that if that didn't work just come back and they'd try something else. It never occurred to me at the time that, that answer sounded like someone who wasn't sure...someone who didn't know. My first pediatrician for my brand new baby, Christopher, spent nearly six months trying to help me find a baby formula that he wouldn't throw up. He was losing weight, not gaining, and cried all the time. Finally, I called my Mother, who knew immediately who to call. She called her Aunt Gert, who had raised six babies during the 1920s and 30s, during the hardest of times, without benefit of doctors, or store bought medicines. After hearing what was happening, my Aunt Gert said..."Oh bless Sherry's heart...I know that baby is worrying her silly. You tell her Aunt Gert says, add a tablespoon full of white Karo syrup every time she mixes up formula, and stir it up good. That will set him straight."

I heard... and I obeyed...and it was the first full bottle of milk that my baby kept down. After that, he thrived. I have never forgotten that, and it reminded me throughout the rest of my life, to look for the people who've already lived it, for advice as to what to expect.

Now, through sheer stubbornness and perseverance, I have become a family elder. In this age of Google everything for answers, I don't often get asked for advice, but I AM often the one they come to talk to. Maybe just hearing my stories of what I endured, and how I survived, have helped them formulate their own answers. I hope so. That's what knowledge is for... to be shared.

Today I feel the need to pull love close, and the best way to do that when you are alone is to remember the people who love you, even the ones who are gone.

Even now, just writing those words sends images flooding through my mind. Seeing the laughter on my Grand's face, remembering Daddy's booming laugh, remembering snuggling close to my sister when we were little after Mother put us to bed, because everything was cold...the house, the weather, the sheets—and then slowly feeling the warmth of each other's bodies.

I remember climbing my Aunt Jewel's apricot tree, and then looking down from the branches, my hands sticky from the juice of the ripe fruit, and seeing the worry on her face that I might fall. I can still remember the scent of the clean rag she used to wash my face and hands. I remember sitting on the sofa beside my Uncle Ralph, and hearing the love in his voice when he talked to my Auntie, thinking to myself that's how love is supposed to be.

Mother rocking me at night in her arms because I was sick, wrapped up in one of the old quilts, my head tucked beneath her chin, listening to her voice as she told me a story.

No one's life is perfect. It's not supposed to be. What you learn as you grow up shapes the adult you become. We all endured hardships...but what I remember is the love.

I think that's what it means to grow your soul light...to experience the many ways that humanity shows love. Whether it's from family, or from a total stranger giving you a helping hand...or whether you pulled yourself out of the hell that was your life, and gave birth to the people who will love you most... it's all about love.

Take nothing for granted.

We're only here for a little while.

I see parents in stores having to buy such a huge assortment of things on the 'required school list' for their little children. Certain folders. Certain binders. Different notebooks, pens, pencils, Crayons...glue, boxes of tissue, etc...and they're buying backpacks...and school clothes...and bemoaning the costs and I think back to when I started school.

Mother sent me to school in a clean dress and shoes, none of which were new. I had a yellow number 2 pencil, and a Big Chief tablet with lined paper. I was good to go.

Remember when I bought that potato peeler from Amazon last year? omg...people... I have used the fool out of that thing, and it's still working. Besides the fact that I use it to peel potatoes, I also peeled my pears when I made pear honey. I peeled my apples with it the other day when I made that apple praline bread. If the vegetable is firm (tomatoes wouldn't work) and fairly oblong or round, it'll peel it.

The more years pass, the harder it is for me to grip small things, because of the arthritis in my hands and fingers. Holding on to a paring knife, or a vegetable peeler to peel potatoes was slow and painful going before. This battery-powered peeler is one of the most useful things I've bought in ages.

Today is a new day and another chance to make a difference. I don't know how it will manifest, but before this day is over, I will have been given the opportunity to help someone, even if it's nothing more than a hand up at a curb. Or holding a door open in a store. Or lightening someone's day by sharing a laugh.

You see...there's a catch to this thing about making someone else's day. We won't ever know that our small gesture of humanity is what changed someone's day from bad to good. That's why it's so important to live a life in constant harmony with others, even when you would never live their lifestyle, you still owe the world and the people around you a measure of peace.

I may be having a really frustrating day, but if I take that frustration and rudeness out into the public with me as I do my errands, I am spreading what I feel to everyone else, because they'll see my face and how I behave, and then they are upset because I brought that into their space...and so it spreads.

We wouldn't knowingly share an illness with others. We stay home and heal ourselves before we go back into the world. And yet we take our emotional upsets everywhere we go, spreading it like the most virulent of diseases. That's why it matters to stand in a place of inner peace. Even when you are standing your ground against an injustice, you do it in a place of peace.

❧

It rained again early this morning. A blessing for sure.

Denise came and cleaned my house, so it's lemony fresh.

Someone asked me the other day if I could live my life over again, what would I do different, and I said, "I wouldn't change a thing, because I wouldn't have the family I have now, and everything I learned from that life was a valuable lesson that serves me now."

And besides...who's to say that a different choice would have made me happier in the long run? No one EVER makes a choice knowing it's a bad one. No little kid ever sits around thinking I'm going to be a loser when I grow up. No one ever plans on marrying someone who will make their life a living hell, and no child ever thinks they'll turn into a criminal, or a drug addict, or become homeless. No one thinks about losing the people they love.

But it all happens.

Sometimes because of choices made.

Sometimes because of things out of your control.

It's called life.

The joy of still being alive in the world is that you always have the opportunity to change—even if the only thing you are able to change is how you think—that is enough.

In the midst of grief, one does not give advice on how to move through it. All that is required is love and understanding.

Texas is grieving.

Either donate or pray.

They don't need opinions.

Made Jalapeno poppers yesterday with cornbread and bacon filling. I got the recipe from Facebook some time back, and finally tried it.

I am not a fan of hot, but a lot of my family is, so I took a tiny taste of one, and all I could taste was the freaking jalapeno. Started to just throw the whole lot away, and then thought someone who didn't mind hot should be tasting these, not me. I took them to Kathy's house. Scout tried the first one. I said..."filling's too dry, isn't it?" He's still chewing. Kathy picks up the next one. Her eyebrows go up, and she says, "ummm," and I'm still waiting for a verdict so I say, "Just let me know one way or the other cause I'm tossing that recipe if you don't like it." By now, Scout is on his third popper and Kathy just went in for seconds.

I'm thinking this might be okay after all. I'm still talking because no one else is, and right in the middle of swallowing his third one, Scout says, "Keep the recipe, Grammy. It would be great for appetizers at Thanksgiving." Kathy picked up her third. "Yes, keep it Mama, these are good."

Ha. So it wasn't a clear waste of time after all.

Life is a test. From the moment we arrive, until we take our last breath, we're testing things. That first bite of baby food someone pokes in our mouth may, or may not, be sent back. Test out how it feels to stand upright. Trying out words, learning hot and cold. Everything that is new to us is a test. We're trying out new shoes, new clothes, new relationships, new jobs. Losing loved ones, losing life partners, relocating to a new location...all of it is a test. Am I willing to adjust to what's new, or am I going to sit around and bemoan what I left behind? (you just failed that test if you did that) The point of everything new in life isn't how we reacted, so much as that we tried it, and endured it. We can move on with it, or reject it and set it aside, because it doesn't fit in with the path we are on, but we have to keep moving forward emotionally. Even if you live in the same house your entire life, you are still emotionally being tested every day. It's not WHERE you are physically, that counts. It's what you do emotionally with the tests life puts in front of you. You can't just sit there staring at it until the bell rings, then dump it on the teacher's desk and leave. There aren't timers in life, and the only teacher is God, who gave you free will to make the choices.

So turn in the lesson and keep on moving.

Another day is here.
How are you going to live it?
Reread the last sentence now.
I didn't ask about your troubles.
I didn't ask what hard job you are facing.

I asked... How are you going to live today?
Is this your 'feeling sorry for myself, day?
Is it your "bored day?"
Is it another day of fear and panic?
Have you lost everything to natural disaster?
Are you preparing to say goodbye to someone dear?
Are you now facing a single life, when once there were two?
Each of those things is what might happen TO you, but it's how you react that will help you through it.
Live knowing tomorrow is another day.
Live with thankfulness.
Live knowing change is inevitable.
You can suffer sadness, but it is not infinite.
Live with hope.
Live with persistence.
You cannot be defeated if you continue to get back up.
Live with gratitude.
Live with respect for others.
Live with the knowledge that goodbye is just a word, knowing you can never really lose someone who you still carry in your heart.

I used to soar with eagles until I forgot how to fly.

I ran barefoot over thorns and rocks, racing a storm to shelter.

I danced through a dust devil, and chased the wind blowing across the prairie.

I stood on the tops of mountains.

I have been deep inside the earth.

I have sailed along the Amalfi Coast.

I rocked in a small boat inside a dark grotto off the coast of Italy, certain I could see the walls breathing in and breathing out.

I sat in the back of a pickup truck feeling my heartbeat sync to the drums of my people, breathing the dust stirred by the dancers feet during the festival of Green Corn.

I have watched a night sky turn red from fire as it burned across a prairie.

Seen stars falling from heaven faster than I could count.

I have seen an entire year's worth of work and profit beaten to the ground in seconds by the rapid fire of hail falling from the sky.

I stood beside a child watching her mother's casket being lowered into the ground, and had no answers for where she was going.

I have watched two of the people I loved most in this world taking their last breaths.

I have given birth.

I have given up far more than I could ever replace.

I chased a dream and caught it.

I have gone to battle for others, but will not fight for myself.

I can feel spirits.

I have seen angels.

I do not doubt the healing power of God's grace.

I do not wish to relive one moment of this life.

It was hard enough the first time, and the lessons have been learned.

❧

Starting a new book today. It's not the title I wanted. But I don't ever get that anymore with this publisher, and titles are HUGE for me. I can't even begin the story until that is set.

And I dislike writing synopses, (like an outline only in story form) Same publisher wants 10 double-spaced pages OR LESS, of a 400 page story with all the details, and then when I turn it in for approval, they will sometimes send it back for edits. EDITS on an idea?

That's when I go through the house laughing maniacally, wishing I hadn't quit Diet Dr. Pepper, and then winding down from that fit, to bawling, which is what I do when I am mad. Edit a synopsis? SERIOUSLY? I don't ever look at that synopsis again, and I don't write from it, and my old editor knew that. I don't even know what my new editor looks like, I heard her voice once over the phone, and I've had her for three years.

Every writer I know has a different process in how their own writing proceeds... how they make it work, and as far as I'm concerned, the finished product is all that matters.

Back in the day, I had to fill out a 4 page art fact sheet with detailed notes on characters physical appearances, write more synopses for THAT sheet only - write a scene like the book, but not from the book, that describes something that might look good on the cover, and they want three of those to choose from, and so I did it...and got nothing from the art fact sheet on the final cover...What I get is stuff like - three covers for the next three books that look exactly alike, but with different colored backgrounds, which confuses the heck out of readers. Or I get a heroine on the cover with long, flaming red hair, even though I told them it was black, (reason for change)...a redhead went better with the color of the background. No, that's not a joke. It has happened to me.

And ALL of this stuff is going on behind the scenes that readers don't know about...and then the book comes out, and readers start picking it apart...bad editing...hate the cover...wrong name on the back blurb., missing pages in a book, blah blah blah...and because of self-publishing, the readers NOW ASSUME that's my fault. Not the fault of my editor, my copy editor, the line editor, the art department, or the place where they sent it to be printed.

But I wanted this job, and I am the one who made it happen because I didn't quit, and I wouldn't let defeat stop me from trying again. So I'll start this book with as much optimism as I can muster, and when it's finished, I will have fallen in love with the people and their story, and when it finally goes out to readers, I will suffer the same process all over again, trying not to tell people what I think about their lack of education and grammar, as they write scathing reviews about my new baby.

I was raised hearing my elders say, "kindness is a virtue."

In my world, kindness is a given.

It costs nothing.

It won't hurt you.

And it's free.

In this day and age, that is a bargain people.

Had THE most amazing, healing energy massage this morning.

Delinda at Energy Massage is a master at her craft.

For so long I ignored me and focused on everyone else, but it cost me.

By not taking care of me, I let my spirit be drained. I had not nourished it. I had been feeding my body, but not my soul. So I chose, as a way of taking care of myself, to seek ways to ease my physical pains.

Now I schedule healing massages, or a session of reflexology (both of which help ease, or completely take away pain). They are ways of refilling my well which feeds my soul.

I matter. You matter. We all matter.

We have to take care of us in every way, before we are able to take care of others.

It serves no one to be a martyr, least of all, yourself.

Mistreating or ignoring your own personal needs hurts you worse in the long run. It's the difference between breaking a foot, and stubbing a toe.

Far easier to recover from one than the other.

I bought some okra and squash and a pint of Hagen-Daz ice cream today, hoping the vegetables cancel out the calories and sugar in the ice cream.

Yard mowed again. New mulch looks great in the front yard.

I take no credit for it beyond paying the yard guy to do it.

When tragedy happens, we, as humans, always look for someone to blame. But no matter how young, or how tragic, or how random the passing seems, I believe that when our time is up, we leave. How it happens is that spirit's choice.

It's the ones who are left behind who hurt. We are the ones

grieving the loss, who try to make sense of it. And that's why they need someone to blame. What they should never do is blame themselves.

The truth of that passing is simple. That spirit's work on earth was done.

They come for one reason, and when that is fulfilled, all they want is to go home.

We didn't lose them. They were just here on a job.

When our jobs are finished, we go home, too.

For all the people I've loved and lost, this knowledge comforts me.

I am learning not to repeat the same negative messages to myself each day.

I am learning not to say aloud, that which I do not want to receive, because the Universe is listening.

I am happy.

I am blessed.

I say prayers nightly for peace on earth.

I thank God each night for the blessings I have received.

I thank Him for healing those undergoing medical treatments.

I thank Him for the peace and grace He gives to those in grief.

I thank Him for the light He shines for those who are lost.

It is good to remember that as You are saying your prayers, don't forget to thank God, as well. So many times we ask and ask, but we don't always remember to say thank you.

Thankfulness is light.

Love is light.

God is light.

Everyone is different, as it is supposed to be.

You are loved as you are.

Whether you believe in Him or not does not matter.

You ARE a child of God.

I do not want to be part of a herd, but I am part of the whole earth consciousness.

I am not a clone of someone else's beliefs.
I hold my own truth, and live it without shame or explanation.
I stand in my truth without aggression.
Be the you that you were born to be.
It is the easiest way to walk your path.

※

It's Wednesday, which means it's my day to go let the dogs out at noon at my daughter's house. I will get puppy kisses from Winston, the still baby King Charles Spaniel, and laugh when he lays down to eat, or gets in a barking fit at the reflection he sees in the stainless steel door of the dishwasher, unaware that he's barking at himself. I'll get sweet licks on my toes from Geenie, and TicTac, the mini-Schnauzer, will want me to sit with her because that's what she likes best in the whole world...to snuggle beside one of her humans.

Animals aren't beasts...they're humanity in its most perfect form. Unconditional love, trust, and individual personalities...And all they want is to be loved...

Like us.

Work is going slow on the new book. I have to speed it up. It's due at the end of next month.

Sometimes in life, your heart isn't in what you're doing, but you still have to proceed. You do it because you must...because you said you would, and you know you can, so you do it.

It is so far past the time of believing it is our right to judge.

We have no need for divisiveness.

It has taken one natural disaster after another to show humans how petty they have been in shunning someone who does not think like you do. Everything fades into comparison when the choice is life or death.

We sit down at a table with family to eat a meal. And as the dishes of food are passed around, some take one thing, some take another, and some choose a little bit of all. And we think nothing of it. We laugh because a sister refuses to taste a curry dish. We know one family member doesn't like tomatoes, and another doesn't care for coconut. We choose the food we're going to cook to accommodate those choices. We excuse another for passing up the coleslaw, and don't pay any attention to my son for still not wanting his food to touch on his plate.

That is all taken as a matter of fact. In our hearts and minds, they have every right to choose what they want, and how they want to eat.

And yet...when it comes to choosing faith, or opting for one belief over another, or how we want to look or dress, we disown each other for daring not to follow their herd.

What's wrong with that picture? Do you not understand that people have the right to choose their path, just like they choose their food?

Where did you find the law that says it's your business to interfere? Who told you that it was okay to mistreat those who were different? Why would you think it was acceptable to call others bad names?

You aren't in charge.

It's not your business.

Move along.

One aspect of change is being ready to accept it.

When we were children we took it as a matter of course.

Every year of our lives was devoted to change...getting taller, puberty, advancing from year to year in our education systems, looking for jobs, losing jobs and looking for more jobs.

Marriage, raising families, and the years stretch out before us until, all of a sudden one day you realize the time for changes is shorter than it used to be, and you panic. You begin holding on to the way it is, and then the way it was, until too much has changed to catch up.

The thing is - resisting change doesn't stop it from happening.

The best way to go with the flow is get comfortable and enjoy the ride.

YOU.

In all the world, there is no other YOU.

YOU matter.

YOU are loved by the universe, even if you don't feel it here.

YOU weren't an accident, because God doesn't make mistakes.

YOU have purpose...if not for others, then for you alone.

YOU chose to come here. The souls who agreed to help YOU on this journey are, in this lifetime, your parents and friends...and even the people who have become your enemies. You all know each other in spirit. Here, they are only playing their parts, doing whatever it takes to help you on your path. YOU must remember, we don't come here to play, but to learn.

Despite the rocky path on which you've been walking, and no matter how alone you might feel, YOU are loved.

Lately, as part of my journey I have been focusing on and remembering some of the things from my past that made me happy. Things I remember that felt, in the moment, like the universe and I were in perfect balance. I do that because it makes me feel lighter inside... like the weight of my body almost isn't there...like I can "almost" feel my own soul.

I call my inner being my soul sister, the subconscious me who says "no, no, no, don't do that. Don't say that. Don't go there." You know what I mean. People call it their conscience, but what it really is, is YOUR own soul reminding you of right and wrong, of what's safe and what's not.

So when I think of happy, I think of Christmas morning when I was a child—of Daddy's big booming laugh, of Mother's soft touch on the side of my face as she smoothed away the tangled curls she has yet to brush out of my eyes. In those moments, I had nothing but joy in my heart...no fear...no worry...and all their love.

I think of holding my children for the first time. Looking down into those little faces and wondering...who will you be? Thinking how perfect you are...and that you were mine to love forever.

I think of my Bobby...how his dark eyes twinkled when he was telling some story.

How gentle his touch was.

How big his hugs were.
How much he loved me.
How much he taught me.
Perfect joy.
Perfect partner.
Perfect love.

Just because something is no longer in your life, does not mean it's gone. It's part of what made you who you are today.

As long as you remember, it's always there.

Getting a massage this morning.

This is going to be an amazing day.

Getting my worn out shoulders and back a rest.

They are tired and achy from my typing...and so am I.

But it takes work to get where you need to be, and I know where the finish line is at. I can even see it now. Far closer than it was in January of this year.

Went to an early dinner last night with Kathy and Scout. Ash had to work late. We went to Olive Garden, and then on to Bed, Bath, and Beyond. Kathy needed some new washcloths. My entertainment for the evening was listening to Kathy and her son discussing (arguing) the merits of different colors. Scout wanted red, and then was directed to more muted colors that could be washed together with what she already had. You would not have believed how heated the discussion (argument) raged until decisions were made. Two very strong-willed, red-heads.

They were my after-dinner floor show, very reminiscent of the discussions (arguments) me and my red-headed daughter used to have when she was Scout's age. However, by the time we left, everyone was satisfied...and calm. Yes, the calm did come. Calm is good.

Sending out all kinds of love into the Universe today.

If ever there was a need for peace in our hearts, it's now.

Today is a good day to make that apology you've been putting off.
Today is a good day to let go of old anger.
The past is past. It helped put you in the place you are now, but it does not define you.
If you are unhappy with yourself and the world around you, just shift into a higher gear and don't look back.

☙

Reflexology session again this morning. I can't wait to tell Bob how it's working.

When I got my toenails painted the other day, the bottoms of both my feet were ticklish again. Thanks to Type 2 diabetes, it's been YEARS since I had that much feeling in my feet, which is so important to balance. Hard to stand upright when you can't feel what you're standing on. I can't tell you how many times I've taken nail polish off my toes, only to see a black toenail where I'd hurt it bad enough to cause that, and never felt it. That's diabetic dangerous. Healing without chemicals is my mantra, and the masseuse doing the sessions has given me some feeling back in my feet.

Many things come to us throughout our lives that test our faith... and I don't mean religious faith. I'm referring to our faith in each other.

Accept that humans are fallible—often swayed by vengeful emotion, power, and greed.

Those people are setting up their own karmic disasters. There is no reason to associate with people like that, unless you believe and agree with all they do.

There is no shame in deciding to stop being a follower, and become the leader of your own decisions.

Waiting for someone to throw you a rope, often leaves you stranded and alone.

Find your own way out of the situation you are in.

If you went there on your own, you have the ability to also take yourself out of it.

What are you waiting for?
Not the rope, I hope.

Happy Saturday, y'all.

It's a bit of a gray day here right now, but I'm up, so I guess I'll have to shine a bit brighter today.

I'll be doing a little baking for my family reunion tomorrow.

One blackberry cobbler, in memory of my Daddy who loved his sweets, and in honor of my son, who MIGHT get to come, and for my daughter, who's driving me down there. Niece Crissy is usually the one who goes with me, but she has to work today, and so goes life.

I'll miss whoever isn't there, and hug the ones who are.

Last night I was remembering stuff that used to hurt my feelings, and laughing about it. Being able to let go is one of the best things I've found from growing older. It quickly becomes obvious what matters most, and for me, it's the now, and what lies ahead, not what's behind me.

I know people who hold onto pain like a blanket, who feed on old slights, and who rehash the past, like trying to get rid of too many leftovers...they eat it, and eat it, and eat it, until they've made themselves sick of it. And yet they will cook it again, because they know how.

Yesterday was a huge day of accumulation for me spiritually. Today is already beginning the same way.

It is so because I've opened myself to joy. Not for any specific reason...but for the pure delight of how it makes me feel.

And how do I get into that place, you might ask?

It's easy. I just think of the things in my life that make me happy, and they are constant.

My family.

The greatest joys God gave me were my children, and that includes my sweet niece. I helped raise her from a baby...and she's as much a part of me, as the two children I birthed.

My children have blessed me with the families they are raising...giving me in turn, what I believe most in this world.
That everything in life comes full circle.

※

I picture myself standing on a hillside out in the country, looking East out across the land for as far as my eyes can see, over the trees below, beyond the meadow of yellow flowers, past the broken down fence, to the ranch in the distance where horses run free.

I am waiting for sunrise.

I hold my arms up to the sky, and thank Mother Earth for her beauty. I thank the great I AM for the breath that I breathe. And I stand and I wait, and wait, and then it begins! First with color painting itself over the fading sky of night - then what looks like the beginnings of a halo spreading upward.

I picture the Earth spinning, and the Sun circling, and watch a day being born. Sometimes the sight is painful like birth, and sometimes the sight is nothing short of miraculous, for the beauty of what I see. Today I see beauty and let the miracle of birth fill me.

Then I turn to the South with my prayers, then to the West, then to the North, then back to the East and am washed clean by the God Light... It is time to begin a new day.

※

Right now is a time for introspection.

Listening to other peoples' opinions to make up your own, is NOT making up your own mind.

If you don't know what to think about a subject, then that means you don't know enough to have an opinion. That's when you do your own research, and figure it out for yourself. Gossip and false information are not facts from which to form opinions.

As my Mother used to say, "They came with brains, but I don't think they're using them."

Staying true to yourself is how to get from one day to the next.

Standing in the truth grows light.

Being in a place of constant appreciation grows light.

Even in the dark, all you have to do is look up and see light from the stars above you.

And when clouds roll in at night and you can no longer see them, they're still there. That's when you learn to operate on faith.

Faith that the light you cannot see, and the light within you, is still enough to guide you along your path.

Staying angry makes your soul heavy.

It keeps you in a state of depression.

You want out, but you won't turn loose of your rage,

So you have taken away your own ability to move on.

Some people live an entire adult life in a state of disappointment that their life is turning out a certain way, but if you don't change your thinking, then there is no way to change where you can go.

You can't see past that which you have created for yourself.

We are where we are right now is because of choices we've made in the past, and blaming it on someone else just digs you deeper into the hole you already don't like.

Be the light by which you save yourself.

Everyone has an internal clock that has been set by lifestyle.

Farmers' clocks operate on daylight, and seasons of the year.

Employees' clocks operate by punching in time clocks, or clocks on a wall.

School children mark time by the bell that goes off, signaling for them to come inside from the playground, or the bell that rings when it's time to go to another class.

Babies operate on hunger, distress, or being lonely. Their notification is the most strident for a parent when they hear that shrill shriek of "come get me, feed me, change me, hold me."

Athletes mark time by a game clock and a referee's whistle.

And people like me, who's life revolves around writing one book after another, have deadlines.

Steering from the Backseat

But we're ALL alike in one respect: From the day that we are born, until the day we take our last breaths, we are led by purpose.

Whatever your purpose...whatever calls to you...however you are led...your time on earth is whatever you agreed for it to be...before your spirit arrived with your birth.

But YOU are endless, infinite, timeless.

Never be afraid of this life...because there's no such thing as death.

We don't live here.

We're here and then we're home.

Went to my daughter's school and had lunch with her. I made a ham salad sandwich for her, and a boiled egg sandwich for me. I made a lot of ham salad, and am giving it to her after she gets home today. I am so blessed to be able to do this on occasion. !t is a wonderful break for the both of us. This is my gratitude comment for the day.

Faith isn't always about religion.

It's basically about believing without showing proof.

I have faith in people.

I have faith in you.

Whoever is reading this, I have faith that, no matter how you are being judged by others, you will not let yourself be beaten down.

I believe that, if you want to do better, be different, make changes in your life, that you already know how to do that. You just don't have the faith in yourself to proceed.

So while you're learning to trust yourself, know that I'll be holding a place for you.

I won't let the darkness pull you under.

I am standing in faith for you...holding light for you, so that you can find your own way out.

You don't need to be led.

All you have to do is take one step forward, and don't look back.

Oh my goodness.

Having a moment of heart sad.

I cannot read even two pages of Social Media feed without being overwhelmed by the snark, hate, and diatribe.

I've deleted so many stories.

I'm just trying to find updates on friends, but it's too hateful to even look.

I feel so sorry for all of the people who were born after the internet, and cell phones, and social media had become the norm.

They will NEVER appreciate the sounds of silence.

They will NEVER see the beauty of this world and the people in it, because they're always looking down at digital hate.

It's called programming.

And because I grew up in a different world FIRST, before all of this became the norm, I see the differences and I am saddened, because we lost far more than we gained.

#Iamnotpartoftheherd

Got a call from Little Mama's care facility today. It was from one of her nurses. It seems LM is in a huge snit about her hair. I cannot argue with her dissatisfaction, because it was a mess yesterday, so I assume that is still the case, today. I didn't know I had to direct her hair dresser as to when to cut her hair. She gives her a perm in timely fashion without asking me...so all of a sudden she can't see the obvious about it becoming so long. I had to call and leave a message with staff to tell the stylist who comes tomorrow, to cut her dang hair.

Poor Little Mama. Today that hair is her worst thing ever.

Uplifting message of the day comes from Scout when he stayed over.

"Grammy, I get to be here for Thanksgiving this year!" Yay!!! I said...I'm so excited". It's been years since he got to be here. He's usually with his Dad and family out of state, and is so missed at that time.

So I said...'Mama will for sure have to bring your favorite broccoli-rice with cheese casserole." And then Scout picked up the thread of conversation and unloaded...

"And your turkey and dressing, Grammy. And the Cherry-Cheese Pies...and maybe pecan pie, too. You have to make pecan. And are you going to do two kinds of meats? If there are lots of us...you should do two kinds of meat." And off the wanna-be gourmand went. By the time it was bedtime, my whole Thanksgiving menu had been planned, and he hugged me when he left the room.

It actually brought tears to my eyes.

I can't think of anything better for which to be remembered by your grandchildren, than being the one who makes the best dressing and pies, and gives the best hugs. One of the first things I think of when I think of my Grand, was her food. She made everyone's favorites. It was one of the ways she showed her love.

All I'm doing is following in footsteps of one of the cooking greats... all five feet of her. She would love her great-great grandson SO much because he has red hair... just like the man she married so many years ago. And he would SO have loved her cooking.

❧

My doctor told me Wednesday as I was leaving my annual checkup, to come by the lab to get blood work done at my convenience, and that he would have the paperwork already there.

So...I set my alarm for 8:00 a.m. When it began buzzing, I turned it off, then laid there thinking...don't go...not today...go Monday... And so I dozed for 45 more minutes, then got up and my guilty conscience sent me there anyway.

And what happens when I arrive? No orders. Doctor hasn't finished working up his files. He's not in the office today. Call back Monday and SEE IF IT'S THERE YET.

Snort.

I'm saying to myself all the way out the door..."Yes, soul sister, I know you were trying to tell me, and I didn't understand. Next time just yell. Spiritual subtleties usually escape me.

But did I get mad? Nope. Was I frustrated? For about 30 seconds...and then I laughed all the way out the door, and said to the dark stuff swirling around me just waiting for me to explode in anger "You didn't mess up MY chi... The Sonic is next door to the doctor's building...I'm having egg and cheese croissant breakfast in my car. Don't you wish you could have some?"

Looking for answers as you go through your day and never getting responses?

So here's a question. Is your day repetitive? Do you have the same routine? Do you drive the same route? Do you park in the same place? Do you pray the same way, asking for the same things over and over?

That is about as unproductive you can get, and certain to come to no happy resolution. Like the farmer who loses a cow, and goes down the same path every day looking for her, sees the same break in the fence, and then never goes past that opening to find her.

Step out of the rut. Change your morning routine. Take a different road to work. Make peace with what bothers you. Accept that everyone has a right to what makes THEM happy, and they don't need your approval to do it, just like you don't need anyone else's approval to be the real you.

Once you see your day in a new way, then you are ready to see what else has been waiting for you to find it.

❦

I woke up with a song in my head. It's one we used to sing at church when I was young.

It was, Oh Happy Day. Only I was raised in a Methodist Church, and they sang it like a dirge. I always felt like we should be dancing in the aisles. Guess that was an early sign that I was never going to fit into a box for anyone. Not when God was telling my heart to clap and dance.

I have laundry in the washer, and clothes in the dryer. Denise is cleaning, and I get to have lunch with Crissy today. It is a good day to rejoice. Clean clothes. Clean house. Hugging my girl.

I noticed some people, even women, are offended by the Me Too comments related to recent revelations about women being raped by powerful men who held the women and their livelihoods in their hands. They have been rudely blasting 'their opinions' on Social Media, of how victims should just be quiet, forget it, move on, etc.

So I'm telling you now...it is your divine right to live your life the way you want, but if you're telling men and women to stay silent, then you're part of the problem. That's how this tide of insidious abuse has become so pervasive, and deep-rooted to begin with. Because we all stayed silent. If you're uncomfortable or don't agree. If you can't understand the guts it took to even type it, let alone say it, then the least you can do is not insult the victims with your misplaced judgment. They've already endured enough.

Grace means different things to many people.

Some people say "grace" before a meal.

You can move with grace.

Some people are given a grace period with an insurance policy.

And then there are the times when we would not have survived an event "but for the grace of God."

And I can stand within the Grace of God...which to me means, no matter the reason I am there...the love, forgiveness, and blessing I am being given IS God's grace.

Grace to all of us.

It's never too late to stop a destructive cycle, just back off and stand within the grace of God until you can find your new path.

I slept so hard last night. Dreamed a little, but nothing disturbing...just dreams that signify getting ready... moving... packing.

Blinders were put on teams of horses back in the days before machines to keep them focused on what was in front of them, and nothing more.

They were tethered together so that if one moved they all moved, or they all went down. They obeyed their master's commands, and when he shouted Gee or Haw, and tugged a certain way on the reins, they knew (because they'd been trained) which direction to move. Right or Left.

When they got too old to do the work, their masters sold them to glue factories. Their usefulness was over. Time to train a new horse to take its place.

Does that sound like a good way to live?

No, it doesn't to me, either, and yet that is how people who abuse power view the masses.

They keep them blind to the truth. Focus them on the next new thing in front of them. Keep them tethered together with lies, horror, and religion-based fear while they use them to do their work.

And when they are too old to be of use to them anymore, they make sure there are no health or medical programs available to them, that would keep them cared for and comfortable.

Leaving them without care, shelter, or medicine, IS selling them off to die.

Look beyond the obvious.

Fear blinds us to truth.

I have said it before and I'll say it again.

#Iamnotpartoftheherd.

I keep love alive by using it...sharing it...giving it away.

You want to feel better about yourself?

Then love you for who you are right now...in this moment.

Don't wait until you dye your hair and lose 20 pounds.

Don't wait until your house is clean before you ask people over.

Don't wait until you get new furniture, or paint a room, to open your door to friends.

If they don't already love YOU for WHO you are, not WHAT you have, then those aren't friends., those are acquaintances.

༄

I had to let the dogs out today. Scout had a schedule change at high school. On the way home, I thought I'd try the new taco place that has just opened near my house. I don't mind a little heat in some of my food, so I know to always ask for mild salsa, etc.

Looking for meatless food, I ask for a bean burrito, thought I'd try the potato poppers, and they gave me a little container of queso. I added an un-sweet tea and drove home, put the stuff on a plate, and sat down to eat. Before I add any sauce at all, I taste.

Jalapenos to the max in the bean burrito!

Jalapenos to the max in the queso!

Jalapenos to the max in the potato poppers!

I dug around on the burrito...quit the potato poppers after eating one, trashed the queso after one taste, and drank the tea.

Jalapeno fail.

The reason we don't judge people, is because they are not required to bring their lifestyle up, or lower it down to fit our standards.

You don't criticize someone who has a lot, any more than you judge someone who has nothing.

You're only job on this earth is being a good person, loving others, and staying in a positive space as you walk your path.

Whatever else you choose to add to that life is a personal choice contingent on no one else's opinion.

You are not required to deny your own wishes and dreams just to make other people happy. If they don't love you enough to value you and your happiness, then that is their problem.

Being the best you can be IS what's best for the people you love.

❦

It's cold. Just like the weatherman promised. Jeez Louise... as in winter cold. I have on a sweatshirt and pants, and am taking a blanket with me to reflexology appt. I'll bed down in that chair, cover up, and let Bob, the masseuse, work his magic on my feet.

The cold weather plays havoc with arthritic joints.

BUT. that is not a complaint. This time last year I was in so much pain, and awaiting my hip replacement surgery.

As the saying goes... "I've come a long way, baby."

Every day, everyone seems to be in such a hurry.

There are days when I stop and take a step back from the shuffle and look...I mean, really look...at what we do.

We are ants.

Running, running, scurrying here and there, gathering bits to feed ourselves and family, crawling over others to get what we want, attacking whatever gets in our way...gathering in masses to take what we want and crawl over the bodies to do it.

We are drones.

We are constantly being controlled. By time. By money. By medicines taken at certain times on certain days. We follow rules. We get in cars to move about, then drive like we'll live forever. We are blind to everything except what's in front of us. We live on schedule. Our children are lined up, and move in formation, bussed from one place to another, and pushed daily to succeed, succeed, succeed at all costs. And they respond to the pressures in destructive ways. They are forever changed from who they were meant to be, because they are controlled by someone else's plans.

Then we line up for medicines to calm the chaos we have created in our lives, without knowing what's in it. We eat the food put in front of us without asking what's in it. We follow orders from people who've named themselves our superiors, without knowing why, or to what end we will come.

You should try it sometime... taking a step back and seeing ourselves for what we do and how we do it.

You might easily approve and feel safe within this format.

And you may not.

#Iamnotpartoftheherd

Spirit says trust your instincts.

If it looks wonky, sounds wrong, and you don't know the facts behind it, trust your instincts. They're telling you in every way to say no. To walk away. To don't believe it.

Every day we are spoon-fed lies, sugar-coated lies, or we are being scared into submission, or enraging us to react. Just because you hear it, doesn't mean who's telling it to you is telling you the truth. It may be the truth as they know it, but spreading rumors isn't news.

And news is no longer always truth.

Beneath a sere and sun-bleached sky, a single eagle soared.

Watching the world from up above as a single lion roared.

Across the dry and grass-less plain, a single soul did stand, in what was once a river-bed, that fed a verdant land.

The warnings came, but few took heed, while Earth did shake, and burn, and bleed.

It finally sank and washed away When no one took a stand.

Now all is lost, and ail is gone.

Used up by mortal man.

by Sharon Sala

What happens when you get first choice and then regret your decision?

Do you throw up your hands and quit?

Do you call yourself finished before you've barely begun?

If you do that, then you've just missed the first big lesson life handed you.

Failing and making mistakes are what propels us forward, because if you fail, you're forced to find another way to accomplish what you set out to do.

If you make a mistake, all it means is that way didn't work, so go to plan B.

First lesson in life: Always have a Plan B.

Second lesson: Now you know what NOT to do.

Write it down in your soul book, and keep on truckin'.

INTO THE FIRE

She runs into the fire when others run away, knowing it will burn, knowing it will hurt. But they belong to her.

God-given gifts she swore to protect.

Lives that matter more than her own.

Stronger.

Braver.

Never say die.

Never looks back.

That is a mother's path.

Bearing the pain with the elation of knowing what she grew was God-given.

Some love.

Totally.

Some fail.

Miserably.

Forcing a child from their body like an infection, leaving the child to face fire all alone. And so they do…walking through life with a wound on their heart that will not heal. Abandoned.

Blowing through life like tattered paper in the wind,

Rootless.

Always searching for the one thing they were denied.

Holding the weight of 'unloved' on their backs.

You see trouble.

I see heartbreak.

You see worthless.

I see what could have been.

You see dirt.

I see scars.
You see anger.
I see pain.
God sees them.
God sees you.
God sees me.
Don't judge a life you never lived.
Don't look away in disgust from something you don't understand.
They're not lazy.
They're not wrong.
They're on fire.
Waiting for rain.

by Sharon Sala

I used to hold grudges.

I was an ace at it, too.

I could stay in a place of displeasure for days on end.

I lost sleep over it. I cried buckets over it. I would imagine ways to get revenge.

Had it not been for the laws of man, and my mother's hand on my backside, I would have been a formidable enemy. When you are born a warrior, it's hard not to raise a hand.

Life added even more grudges from more people, until I was afraid to look up for fear of being slapped down.

And all this time, I'm getting older, and beginning to have illness issues. Migraines. High blood pressure. Food disagreeing with me. Panic attacks. Surgeries for one thing, and then for another. I gained weight, and didn't try to lose it, because I felt safe behind that wall of flesh.

I let years pass, and every so often I'd let myself sink into a day of suffering and drag up EVERY DANG SLIGHT I'D EVER SUFFERED.

Don't ask me why. It was, at the time, the only way I knew how to live.

And through all of that, my body was trying to tell me I was my own worst enemy.

Then one day I heard someone talk about forgiveness as being the fastest way back to good health. Forgiving others. Forgiving myself. But I still didn't know how to really do that. I mean REALLY let the grudges go. You know, they'd been with me so long that they were practically part of the family. I know they were certainly a part of me.

Then I heard another person say a few months later how they'd let go of a lot of 'stuff in their life by writing it all down, then releasing each grudge one at a time, by speaking it aloud, and then telling the Universe that memory no longer held meaning for me. So I sat down and wrote, and wrote until had two single-spaced pages of grudges, slights, and broken-heart moments, to give up to God.

And when I was through, I dug a hole, put the papers inside it, then set the paper on fire and watched it burn—imagining as it did, that those grudges no longer existed. That those people no longer held any power over me. And when the paper was nothing but ashes, I covered it over with the dirt I'd dug out, and stomped the top of the dirt with my foot.

Spoken. Burned. Buried. Done.

And that was the first day of the rest of my life.

Oh, that's not to say old memories don't pop back up once in a while, but I stop it before it can hurt, and I say aloud, you're dead and buried to me. Go away.

It's all about being in control of your life.

God gave us free will. That's how we get ourselves into those fixes.

But he also gave us the good sense to get ourselves out.

It just takes some of us longer than others to remember that WE matter.

We are people.

Not doormats.

Just wipe your feet before you come in the house and leave old memories in the dirt where they belong.

Steering from the Backseat

What if...every day...you had to face the world knowing you were going to be harshly judged on your looks and your job? That no matter how hard you worked, and how nice your clothes were, and how pretty or handsome you looked, you would be passing people who said aloud things like,

"Ugh, I just hate that guy. He didn't wash my windows good at the gas station."

"I hate her. Look how her shoulders slump. Look at her shoes! Those are at least two years old."

"She's ugly. He's horrible. I don't like to hear him talk."

"I hate for her to do my hair—to wait on me at a restaurant—to check me out at a grocery store."

"They're all ugly. I don't like them. People are blind if they think that looks nice."

"What's the matter with you? It's obvious they're stupid. I hate his hair. Look at her...her teeth are too big. she looks like a horse."

"His legs are too short for his body. She doesn't have any boobs. Her boobs are huge. He drives a car I wouldn't be caught dead in. He's too broke for me."

"She's nothing but trash. His nose is too big. Ugly. Hate it. Don't like it. You're stupid."

Just reading those words is appalling to me. And yet every phrase on here was taken from other people's posts on social media.

Do you see yourself in any of this? If you think the ugliness in this world is not rubbing off on you, then think again.

Is this really how you want to be?

Does all of this matter so much to you that you are okay with hurting someone else just to get it said?

What happened to us?

When did this become okay?

Did you set your course toward sunshine today, or are you just drifting in a foggy sea?

Just remember, YOU chart your course each day. No matter what is ahead of you…whether it's worrisome, *or* scary, or may become a disappointment, how you receive what's on your path is up to you.

I've seen too much of how ugly this world can be, yet came out of the fray still standing and moving forward.

I don't let negative people get close to me anymore.

They nearly destroyed me.

But I didn't quit.

I know how to start over, and I'm not afraid to do it.

❧

Some people choose to walk in darkness and wallow in what comes with it, crying and wailing at the top of their voices at how they can't catch a break. That life is self-defeating. If you talk about other people the way you talk about yourself, you would start a fight.

If you call yourself a walking disaster, that you hate yourself, you hate your life, you hate your job, you hate your family, no one understands you, no one likes you, no one wants to hang out with you…you never get invited anywhere, and then nothing changes and you wonder why.

Well, I know why. Because you say aloud every day to the Universe that what you're complaining about is really your path. So the Universe loves you so much, that you are given more of it, because that is what you've asked for.

I choose light. I choose to grow it. I make a conscious decision every day to be happy. To look for joy. To laugh. To be kind. To treat myself as I would want others to treat me. I accept me. I appreciate my health. I am grateful for my storytelling gift.

I have way more to be thankful for, than I do to bemoan.

I choose joy.

And because I do, the Universe sees and hears and sends me more, because that is what I ASK FOR.

Happy. Joy. Laughter. Light.

It costs nothing to be kind.

But the cost of living miserable and angry begins and ends with you.

Everything in life is viewed from personal perspective. What I see and feel comes from how I was raised, or the experiences I have had since I was grown. From the things that trigger my anger or my empathy, or that triggers my despair or my fear.

Each of us has this inner guide.

None of them are the same.

It's called being human.

It colors every decision we will make, every job we will take, every person we will love.

So, if you want to be honored for your beliefs, and you believe you are correct and everyone else is out of step, you still aren't on board with the truth.

My truth may never be your truth.

I'm okay with that.

But are you?

That's where divisiveness happens.

Ganging up like criminals, and shunning others who are different is your choice, and certainly your right because of the free will we were given in spirit before we came here.

But the lesson is never about isolating yourself within your tribe.

It's about learning to live among all tribes.

If you can't pass the class this time around, you'll be back, doing it over and over until you get it right.

Isn't it wonderful how there are so many variations of facial features, and skin color, and hair color? And while we usually come with a head, a body, two arms and two legs, the size, proportions, and conformation are never the same, not even identical twins, who are mirror images of the other.

It's the beauty of creation.

It's diversity, and a blessing that we are all attracted to different looks. How boring life would be if we all looked alike and behaved the same.

Little clones, all with the same purpose...following orders.

No thought necessary.

Yes, sir. No, sir. Right now, sir.

I celebrate me...born bald, first hair was snow white, then it began to darken. By the time I was in high school, it was about three shades shy of black, and I was already getting gray hair. I'm going back to where I began...thinning hair, and seriously white again.

I believe in everything in life coming full circle, but not this.

I would laugh, but life always has to have the last one.

Joyful.

Full of joy.

Careful.

Full of care.

Hateful.

Full of hate.

Spiteful.

Full of spite.

There are two ways to walk in this world, but many ways to describe them. They boil down to two identities.

Joy or Anger.

Doubtful.

Full of doubt.

Is this how you receive information throughout your life? Do you lack trust in others?

Prideful.

Full of pride.

Does your pride prevent you from admitting mistakes?

From saying you're sorry?

Careful.

Full of care.

Do you use the word as a word of caution, rather than a person who takes care of others?

It's all in how you see the world.

Is it a place of solace and safety?
Or is your world in a state of constant conflict?
It can be both.
You don't have to hold your heart in constant combat.
There is safety, peace, and love within you.

If you choose to exist within that space.

Had a wonderful day.

Ran errands for Kathy while she was at work. Much fun at Hobby Lobby buying craft stuff. I remember when I got to do that all the time.

First when my kids were young, and then it was for my grandkids when they were young.

I came home tired, but happy.

Made homemade potato soup, hot crusty cornbread, and had some cornbread with molasses for desert.

Made me think of my Grampy. He always had an open jar of sorghum molasses that he bought from someone local. Back when I was a little girl, and even a young woman, people still grew the sorghum cane, harvested it, then cooked off the syrup themselves. Talk about a messy, sticky job, but oh, so good. Not the stuff you buy now that's cut with corn syrup.

Molasses with a tang that ALMOST makes the end of your tongue burn. That's what I grew up eating. I love it, and I taught my son to love it. Molasses on biscuits. Molasses on cornbread or pancakes. Makes the best gingerbread or cookies. Ummmm!

In the long run, you will not be remembered for what you wore, or what you drove, or the grand home to which you aspire.
But you will be remembered for how you lived your life.
With jealousy, anger, and deceit?
Or with joy, generosity, and love?

When you care more for what you have, than what you do, there will come a day when you wonder what you did wrong.

The world goes around while our lives go up, and our lives go down.

Sometimes we're happy to the point of giddy, and other times we are in total despair, or sick to our stomachs in fear of what's happening within our families.

I have been so happy in my life, and I have been in such deep despair that I thought I might die. But I have never been broken.

No one can take that much power away from me, because I won't let that happen.

I deny them.

I defy them.

It's my life...given to ME, and no one else.

Nobody has total dominance over me.

Nobody has total dominance over you.

If they do, then it's because you gave it to them, either by default, or by defeat.

This time in our world is constant chaos.

Don't throw your hands up and wait for God to save you.

God gave you free will.

If you don't fight for yourself and what you believe is right, He's going to assume that is your free will making that choice.

He gave you a brain, too.

Be the warrior for what's right in your life.

Save yourself.

Here I am concentrating daily on holding myself in a place of light, and I had two different light fixtures bite the dust...one in the utility/pantry, and the other in my office.

Yesterday I made a trip to Lowe's and bought two fixtures that are both LED...no bulbs to change ever...with a 24 year life expectancy...and today, they were installed.

I am ecstatic to be able to work at night in my office now, because the old light was never bright enough, and so happy to have light back in the Utility. Doing laundry in the dark is weird...and taking a flashlight to find a can of green beans even weirder. Like when I was a kid and Mother would send me to the cellar for a quart of tomatoes because she was making soup.

I am now bathed in light.

Oh happy day...light washed my troubles away.

Made some Buttery Onion Pretzels (a snack food) yesterday.

It is easy to make, but I drove all over town before I found the kind of pretzels I needed. The ones that Snyder's pretzels makes that come in a box and are really big and hard. (Bavarian style, I think.) You break those up a little (not crumble.) Mother always put some in a plastic bag, then took her little hammer and lightly tapped them until they broke, then tapped the chunks again so that they would usually split in half. The more the white inside is exposed, the more seasoning it will soak up. Then melt a cup and a fourth of butter, stir in a packet of onion soup (dry) and then pour it over the cracked pretzels, and stir until everything is coated really good. Pop it in the oven (250 degrees) for an hour and a half, stirring every 15 to 20 minutes. Then turn it out on paper to cool before storing it.

That is the first signal in our family of Christmas goodies. Mother loved making stuff like this, and spoiled us to many favorites, which I am now responsible for making.

Every day I work at removing another negative word from my vocabulary. I have the word 'hate' defeated. It does not come out of my mouth anymore, and I don't think it in reference to anyone.

Every time I see a homeless person, or someone in obvious need, I quietly ask God to bless them.

And every time I hear a siren, or see an ambulance/fire truck/police car flying past with lights and sirens... I always say..."God bless whoever is in need," aloud.

It may seem silly or over-done to some of you, but you should give it a try sometime. I have found, that no matter what is going on in my personal world, taking myself out of ME to say a quick blessing for another, gives my heart a lighter feel. Almost as if I have unloaded what was bothering me. I think it's like the reminder we all need that we're here for more than personal satisfactions.

Today I celebrate that I am on this earth.

Today, I do not acknowledge anything that does not represent peace, love, or joy. I do not accept "can't."

I can do, and I will.

I do not accept "broke."

I am rich in friends and health.

Steer yourself to where you want to go, even if you're steering from the back seat.

Tell your story the way you want it told.

FAITHFUL

Some people are.
Some people aren't.
The name of GOD defines it.
Waiting.
Knowing.
Trusting.
Honorable.
Joyful.
Peaceful.
Grateful.
Accepting.
Loving.

Forgiving.

Stand in faith that you are on the right path.

Live in faith that you can do what you came here to do. You give up nothing in being faithful.

But what you gain is beyond measure.

⁂

I have finished my Christmas shopping. Everything is wrapped. Stocking Stuffers waiting to stuff into 12 stockings. Yes, I still do stockings for my kids and grandkids because I like to, and because they get so much fun out of digging through the little treasures I find year after year.

Giving for me is from the heart, not from the wallet. I think about each family member personally, remembering what they do, what they like, and if it's practical. Sometimes I'll see one of them using something daily that was in a stocking from two years ago and think...money well spent...and yay me! I picked out the perfect thing.

When I was little, we ALWAYS went to my Grand and Grampy's on Christmas Eve to open presents. Such giggles and excitement, so much shaking of presents, and watching my little Grand sitting in her easy chair, so little her feet don't quite touch the floor, and her belly shaking as she laughed at all the chaos and joy. And when the presents had been opened, and then neatly stacked away to be carried home later, and all of the paper and ribbon taken to the trash to be burned on the next still day, we ate from a table filled with snacks. Hot dips, cold cheese balls, little ham-filled biscuits (homemade...even the ham was home-cured) chips, hot buttered popcorn, fudge, date roll (my mother always made that because it was my Daddy's favorite) Grand's light-as-air divinity with a pecan half pressed into each piece, my Auntie's honey chews. I haven't had those in years. For me, it wasn't just about the food, but the people it represented. Everyone had 'their' special recipes that they shared with all of us.

Looking back, I never thought of a time when those people and those days would be gone. They were my roots.

They held me strong and on a steady path until I was old enough to have good roots of my own.

Roots are an analogy of eternity for me.

My real roots reach far, through other dimensions, and eons and eons of immeasurable time.

I have no fear of anything on earth, because I know I've been this way before, and suffered pain and loss, and experienced much joy. There were hundreds, if not thousands of lifetimes of learning, and in this one, I have learned to be true to myself first. Living in trust of Spirit and trusting the Universe. Knowing that it is my job to set an example, not only for my children and grandchildren, but as I walk through this life.

I tell you all the time to be the light.

But I also know, it is my job to light the wick... it is my path to walk in light so others can follow...

It is the job of all Lightworkers...

To show the way.

Confidence is easy until you face trials or hardships. Staying grounded and not buying into the panic or anger is what saves you. Nothing is solved by uncontrolled emotions.

Take a breath.

Step back.

Let go of what happened, and think only of what has to be done next.

Never give someone money with the expectation of getting it back. If you can't afford to give it, then you can't afford to loan it either. It's like the stock market. If you can't afford to lose the money, never invest.

If ever there was a time when you need to be mindful of your thoughts and your behavior, it is now. The war between light and dark is escalating. You don't have to believe me. Just stay true to what's good and just, and you will stand in the light.

There isn't a way around a mistake. You can't ignore it. You can't go around it. You can't side-step it. If you made it. You own it. It is now up to you to do what is required to correct it. That's called being an adult. You remember adulting? It's what you thought you were smart enough to do. When you were so sure that you were right and everyone else was wrong. So... the only person you hurt is you. That mistake lives on your heart...in your life...on your resume...as part of your history. What a pity. That revenge move didn't quite work out. You didn't hurt anyone but yourself.

Life:

It's full of things to learn.

But if you already took the class, remember the lesson.

❧

A stairwell in a home takes us to bed at night and brings us down to begin our day in the morning. It is nothing more than a short path to get us from one place to another. It never changes. Up. Down. Up. Down.

Like life.

Some people never venture farther than the world into which they were born, and there's nothing wrong with that. Free will. Their choice. Nothing to discuss.

But some people don't like routine. Some people can't settle. They are forever looking for 'their path', but in their search for what they think of as the perfect life, they miss the obvious.

We've all heard the saying, "life isn't about the destination. It's about the journey."

This is true, but this also holds true for the people who never leave home.

A journey isn't just about travel, or always moving from place to place. It's about how you let the people you meet, and the experiences you have, influence YOUR life.

Don't worship and envy lifestyles.

Admire success.

Don't covet excess.

Appreciate enough.

We didn't come here to accumulate things.

We came here to learn greater empathy, more compassion, and understanding.

Understanding that you don't have to run away to find your place in life, and by the same token, your place in life doesn't have to be where you were born. That's just where you landed.

After that, anything is possible.

When you see the end of the road, and the goal you have been working toward is there, it's hard not to start running. But the wisest decision would be to continue at the pace you already set, so you do not stumble or fall, causing a delay in your arrival. Everything happens in its own time, including what happens to you.

This morning I have read way too many posts about people's technology acting weird, turning on without human assistance, turning off the same way. Hearing devices like Siri, and Bixby, etc., that communicate with you in real language, turning on and speaking, but not to you.

And you are confused, wondering why that's happening? What did you expect when you began giving up your autonomy to machines? When you decided you were too busy to change a channel on TV, and you want technology to do it for you? Did you once think about the people behind this technology, and what may or may not have been built into it? Cars that drive us places without touching a wheel. GPS systems that can be adapted to relay our every move. Cell phones that announce our locations at every stop we make. Companies that buy information about what we Google, and then flood us with ads for that very thing...Cameras on us in stores, on streets, at stoplights, in airports, from satellites in space...You think subconscious programming is a joke? You think Big Brother isn't watching and listening?

Surprise. Not a surprise.

So, school has resumed here. It is a new year, and today is, once again, my day to go let the dogs out at noon at my daughter's house. I gave them little doggie toys at Christmas. They were all Peanut characters. Woodstock, Snoopy, etc...

Geenie, their biggest dog, always removes the squeakers, and usually the stuffing, then she happily drags the rag around. Winston just takes his toys apart one thread at a time. I'd given him Woodstock, and Kathy had to give Woodstock a haircut (yellow yarn for his little topknot) so Winston didn't eat it. And TicTac, who has no interest whatsoever in dog toys, just bites hers once, and then jumps in your lap. Dogs are so like people. Quirky individuals with their own sets of likes and dislikes.

In the coming days, stay focused on being positive, it's going to matter.

Wow...

Social Media is pretty hard core this morning.

It's a good thing the Golden Globes award show was televised.

Gave a lot of unhappy people something to complain about.

I'm movin' myself along.

I watched part of it, and nothing stood out to me as controversial, but then I had a couple of phone calls yesterday that gave me something real to think about. One call was yesterday afternoon, and one was last night, and both from Little Mama's care center.

She fell once. They found her sitting up in the floor of someone else's room. Just sitting there.

Then the second call was finding a new bruise on her head.

I hung up from that call and cried.

Didn't give a flying fig about anything after that.

This morning isn't any different.

I have no opinions about anything today except what pertains to me and mine.

Going to have to call a washer repairman, clothes washer...not dish washer. It has to do with moving from cycle to cycle, so some timer is shot somewhere.

Thank you Lord for one more thing, because you know I can handle it.

Denise just left. My house smells like lemon-scented Pine Sol. It is a happy smell for me.

There will be a nap happening here today.

Maybe sooner than later.

My goal on this earth is to leave my children and grandchildren with such loving hearts, that when I die, they do not weep for my passing, but remember to laugh from the memories of what we have shared. Knowing that they will be able to remember me with love, and STILL live full and purpose-filled lives without constantly grieving me. That is how I will know I did my job.

It's cold.

It's raining.

But it's not freezing rain.

Yay!!!!

I dreamed all night about making choices. Choosing drawers that held the right clothes. Opening the right doors. Being in room full of people and sitting in the right chair. Stuff like that, that in real life means nothing of great importance.

But in my dream, it was crucial. And when I finally found everything I was supposed to find, it disappeared and I had to start over. The alarm went off at nine a.m. so I wouldn't oversleep, and I shut it off, turned over and went back to sleep anyway, because I was still making choices, and it wasn't time to stop.

So that's how my brain works.

Don't you wish you were me? OCD in my dreams, but not awake.

Always a tad behind in what I need to have finished, because I will always choose family crisis over personal deadline. Alone. But not alone.

To be completely happy in your life, you need to be just selfish enough to make sure you are okay, before you try to help unravel someone else's problems.

There are as many heartaches in this world as there are joys.

It's how life balances out.

Nobody comes here without purpose.

If you wanted nothing but joy and perfection in your life, you would have stayed where you were—in our spiritual home.

Instead, you packed up your soul self and took a ride.

Some souls can handle being human.

And some can't.

Human is hard.

Human is sad.

Human is scary.

Human is mean.

But finding that perfect balance on earth between your soul and your humanity, is always worth the journey and the pain.

That's why you come, time after time, trying to get it right

⁂

Denise cleaned this morning.

I so wanted to stay in bed, and I could have. It wouldn't have been the first time she cleaned around me, but I had to turn the heat up for her to clean, and I can't sleep with hot air in a room blowing in my face. ack.

So I got up.

Paid bills.

Went to Wal-Mart for the much needed shopping trip.

Came home and cleaned out the refrigerator and the pantry.

Ready to begin work on the synopsis for new Mira title (romantic suspense). I have the synopsis finished, but I need to clean it up and delineate some of the plot more clearly for editor.

Did you know that there are energy flows on this planet that are like moving water? Energy lines crisscross the earth like rivers and streams. And like water, which gets you wet if you walk through it, you can also be somewhat affected by the paths the energy flows take if they are within your space.

This is why it's so important to hold yourself in a place of peace, so that when you do pass through, or find yourself on that energy path, you are not affected, or misled, by how the energy makes you feel.

You know how sometimes we can all be bopping along through a day feeling good about our work and our life, and then one little thing will throw you off? So take that one little thing, and then add in a couple of other little things, and if you decide to buy into all of the drama, before you know it, you are all caught up in something that doesn't even pertain to you. You've let yourself fall into that upset, that dark energy, that feeling that nothing is ever going to all right again, because you weren't focused on your business, and got caught up in business belonging to others.

Young people: Before you existed, we were the youth—the future of what was to be. We danced, we laughed, we loved, we cried. We were here and you were not.

Now you enter into a world that does not suit you...and so you are going about the business of changing it to suit yourselves. You think because age now shows on our faces that we don't know what you're doing? That we don't understand? It is, in fact, you who do not get it.

What you're doing is nothing new. We did then, what you do now. And so it was for thousands of years before. Each generation is SUPPOSED to change. It's called growth.

If a thing does not grow, then it will die.

We don't begrudge your youthful exuberance, or your rush to judgment. Truth is, we have no desire to fan the flames again. We expect your participation. That which you find fascinating and new, is old hat to us. You think you invented protests. You think you invented battles and fashion and social circles. You even think you invented sex, which you should know, is absolutely hysterical to us.

What we want you to know is that we hope you do better than we did, because when we were young, we did better than the generation before. That's how life works. Know your history, or you'll doom the new generation behind you to repeat the past.

A most wonderful day with dear friends.
Had a very affirming session with Leslie Draper today at her new healing center. My friend, Wendy, who is visiting me from Maryland, had one right after I did. Spending time with soul sisters. Priceless.

The time you have to right a wrong is not promised. If you have said or done something you greatly regret, pick up the phone, call or text, and make it right. Do it now.
Trust your instincts.
Don't doubt your soul gifts.
Take what you know and use it in some way to benefit others, as well as yourself. That's called paying it forward.
It is self-defeating to expect more than what you have put in to the process of creation.
It's never about how you look, but how you feel about yourself.
Stop using the word ugly in reference to yourself.
God doesn't make ugly.
Do not take every hiccup, every roadblock, every disappointment as punishment. God is too busy loving all of us to stop and throw darts at our hearts. He isn't the cause, but He is the answer.

A day does not dawn without God's love for you.
Remember that above all else as you get yourself out of bed.
Begin your day with an affirmation, and make it about yourself, not about what you want.
This is the one I say every morning.

"I AM OPEN AND RECEPTIVE TO ALL GOOD."

And then I work hard all day to stay in a positive frame of mind.

I don't want to ruin my affirmation by using negative thoughts all day.

A day does not end without God's love for you.

Trust that as you sleep, your angels will be with you.

Keep your thoughts and your heart in a place of joy and contentment.

Berating others, making fun of them, criticizing them, hating them...changes you.

You, the God-child. The light of His light.

Changes how you enact your purposes.

Puts you in a state of darkness.

Leaves you vulnerable to even more darkness.

Look at yourself in a mirror.

Say to yourself, You are a good person.

Say to yourself, I love you.

Say to yourself, I am grateful for my life.

Say to yourself, I am grateful for the opportunities that come to me each day.

Say to yourself, I am blessed.

Say to yourself, I honor each life on earth as I honor my own.

Say to yourself, Be the answer, not the question.

Twice last week I got emails from Bank of America telling me that my account had been compromised, and to click this link.

A. I don't have an account with Bank of America.

B. Do not respond. Delete. Delete, Delete.

I trust email almost as much as I trust the IRS, lawyers, and cops.

Yes...there are reasons.

No, I'm not talking about them.

I'm still alive. That is enough.

Had a massage this morning. It was the calmest I've felt in weeks. And then it was over.

But aaahhh, was I ever in a state of meditation.

Zen squared.

Took a break this evening to watch Expedition Unknown.

Josh Gates makes me smile.

An Archaeologist with a really great sense of humor, and more than a little bit of ham in his DNA. He does like to play to the cameras.

They were looking for an Irish banshee on the show. She was all over the place there, but JUST out of reach, or disappeared RIGHT before they could get her in a camera shot. Dang banshees. Who knew they were so smart?

The hydraulics that keep the lift gate up on my SUV went out. It dropped on my head at least three times before I figured out it wasn't being blown by the wind. It just won't stay up anymore. Made an appointment to take it in next Friday.

Everyone has times in their lives when things grind to a halt. When all of the stuff you've been doing right suddenly goes all wrong. So...you have two choices. Bemoan the fact that you almost had it all, and spend the rest of your life trying to get it back. Or...reinvent yourself. You can still have the same goals. You'll still be heading for the same destination. But the you who you were, became too big of a burden to hold up. Maintaining an image is, in reality, maintaining someone other than who you really are.

This time around, don't use the same tag line to explain yourself. This time around, don't look at people as competition.

All you have to do is remember that none of you came for the same purpose. And even if you did have similar goals, there is no way that you would all attain them the same way.

The quickest way to fail, is to match your progress against the rate of someone else's path.

There is no secret code to being happy, it is a choice.

No matter your circumstance, you have a choice as to how to accept it.

You can be sad if that your choice.

You can be enraged, if that is your choice. You can be at peace with it.

If you can get to that place in your head and heart where you are not blaming anyone else for your circumstances except yourself, then you have not only fought, but won the battle.

You feel the need to argue that point…I know. You want to shout at me. I didn't choose to be homeless. I didn't choose to get cancer. I didn't choose to lose a child, or my life partner.

But you did.

Before you ever left home…while you were still the bright and shining soul that you are,…your empathy for human suffering led you to make that choice. It is only through experiencing the condition, that we learn the truth depth of what it took to get through it.

And learning is what soul life is all about. In spirit, growth in light and love is our purpose, which is why we agree to return to living another human life, over and over again. On earth we don't remember why we chose to come, (that is part of the lesson) and so we feel abandoned, mistreated, enraged for what we're suffering, lost and broken for what we endured.

Life is a battle, and like any battle, it eventually comes to an end. BUT, when it does, that's when we are reminded of what we chose. We are enlightened, and rejoice in the empathy and depth of love that has grown within us for what it took to endure.

That's what we do. That's who we are.

All of us. There are no walls, there is nothing that separates us there. Read those words again please:

IN SPIRIT, THERE IS NOTHING THAT SEPARATES US.

Today, I wish you joy and peace of mind.

Today, accept your life as holy, because you are filled with the white light of God.

Forget, for a moment, whatever it is you are enduring today, and know that it is nothing more than your vision quest. You are on the path you chose.

You are a warrior for Lightworkers.

You are a good and gentle soul.

Worked until 1:30 a.m. last night/morning.

Slept in a bit, but up and at 'em this morning.

Have to go let the dogs out at Kathy's in about an hour, then back here to work. Book is due on the 31st. I can do it. The trick to meeting a deadline for me is not thinking about it.

I just sit down and write until my mind can't think, and my fingers are hitting the wrong keys. That's when I go to bed. It's what you do when you have to, without bemoaning the reasons, and be grateful that the story is always there. Only once in my life has everything stopped for me.

When Bobby died.

It took almost a year to reset ME.

So being positive is a real thing.

It's how you refill the well within you.

If you spend the day griping, talking about how rough your life is, and being angry about it, you can't recoup.

It's like taking a brand new bucket (which is you) and filling it with water,(energy) then as the day progresses, you use that water/energy for different purposes.

But if you're adding stress and anger to your day, that punches small holes in the bucket (which is the creative and happy you), and you are now losing water/energy faster than you can refill it.

Sleep is how your bucket is refilled each night so that it's ready for you the next day. But if you are so upset and angry about your situation, then nothing is refilled...and you go through each day, starving for water/energy, and realize you have punched so many tiny holes in the bucket that it's no longer useful.

That's when you have to stop and reset you.

Remember God loves you. Remember your angels are with you always so you are never alone.

You are the one in charge of you.

No one else on "earth" has the right to dictate to you the way you live and the choices you make.

If it's happening, it's because you choose to let it.

You don't get a new bucket...but you can find ways to fix the holes.

The Chinese believe that broken china is even more beautiful when it has been repaired...and they use pure gold to seal the break...or the crack. The strange thing about that... the piece of china is now stronger with the patch, than it was when it was new.

The older we get, the stronger we become in spirit, because we have learned what it took to survive. We bear our scars with pride, because we endured, and we prevailed.

You can quit jobs, and marriages, and situations that feel wrong...but don't ever quit on you.

※

I woke up with a song in my head. It's one we used to sing at church. "Oh Happy Day." Only I was raised in a Methodist Church, and they sang it like a dirge. I always felt like we should be dancing in the aisles. Guess that was an early sign that I was never going to fit into a box for anyone...not when God was telling my heart to clap and dance.

I have laundry in the washer, and clothes in the dryer. Denise is cleaning and I get to have lunch with Crissy today. It is a good day to rejoice. Clean clothes. Clean house. Hugging my girl.

I noticed some people, even women, are offended by the Me Too comments, and have made their own statements about women not blasting their business all over Social Media.

So I'm telling you now...it is your divine right to live your life the way you want, but if you're telling men and women who have been sexually abused to stay silent, then you're part of the problem. That's how this tide of insidious abuse has become so pervasive and deep-rooted to begin with. Because we all stayed silent. If you can't understand the guts it took to even type it, let alone say it, then the least you can do is not insult the victims with your misplaced judgment. They've already endured enough.

Grace means different things to many people.
Some people say "grace" before a meal.
You can move with grace.
Some people are given a grace period with an insurance policy.
And then there are the times when we would not have survived an event "but for the grace of God."
Or, I can stand within the Grace of God...which to me means, no matter the reason I am there...the love, forgiveness, and blessing I am being given IS God's grace.
Grace to all of us.
It's never too late to stop a destructive cycle, back off and stand within the grace of God until you can find your new path.
My doctor told me Wednesday as I was leaving my appt to come by the lab to get blood work done at my convenience, and that he would have the paperwork already there.'
So...I set my alarm for 8:00 a.m. When it began buzzing, I turned it off, then laid there thinking...don't go...not today...go Monday... And so I dozed for 45 more minutes, then got up, and my guilty conscience sent me there anyway. LOL.
And what happens when I arrive? No orders. Doctor hasn't finished working up his files. He's also not in the office today. Call back Monday and SEE IF ITS THERE YET, they said.
Snort.
I'm saying to myself all the way out the door..."Yes, soul sister, I know you were trying to tell me not to come, and I didn't understand. Next time just yell. Spiritual subtleties usually escape me.
But did I get mad? Nope. Was I frustrated? For about 30 seconds...and then I laughed all the way out the door, and said to the dark stuff swirling around me just waiting for me to explode in anger, "You didn't mess up MY chi... The Sonic Drive-In is next door to the

doctor's building...I'm having egg and cheese croissant breakfast in my car. Score!

I made my vegetarian version of chili beans for lunch. It's done...just letting all that yummy stuff meld. I usually buy Morning Star meat crumbles...which is something not so good with the texture of tofu, but it soaks up the chili seasonings pretty good and is passable. But I stopped off at Target on the way home and saw another brand beside the Morning Star called Beyond Beef...I thought, what the heck, I'll try it this time. I think I have discovered a new product that actually passes for meat, especially when it's cooked in casseroles or like chili. It tastes so good. I am a happy camper today. Chili beans without the gout pain...woo to the hoo.

Looking for answers as you go through your day, but never getting responses?

So here's a question. Is your day repetitive? Do you have the same routine? Do you drive the same route? Do you park in the same place? Do you pray the same way, asking for the same things over and over? That is about as productive and certain to come to no happy resolution, as the farmer who loses a cow, and goes down the same path every day, sees the same break in the fence, and then never goes past that opening to find her.

Step out of the rut...change your morning routine...take a different road to work...make peace with what bothers you, accept that everyone has a right to what makes THEM happy and they don't need your approval to do it...just like you don't need anyone else's approval to be the real you.

Once you see your day in a new way, then you are ready to see what else has been waiting for you to find it

---

It's cold. Just like the weatherman promised. Jeez Louise... as in winter cold. I have on a sweatshirt and pants and am taking a blanket with me to reflexology appt. LOL I'll bed down in that chair, cover up, and let Bob, my masseuse, work his magic on my feet.

The cold weather plays havoc with arthritic joints.

BUT. that is not a complaint. This time last year I was in so much pain, and awaiting my hip replacement surgery. As the saying goes... "I've come a long way, baby."

Every day, everyone seems to be in such a hurry. There are days when I stop and take a step back from the shuffle and look...I mean, really look...at what we do.

We are ants.

Running, running, scurrying here and there, gathering bits to feed ourselves and family, crawling over others to get what we want, attacking whatever gets in our way...gathering in masses to take what we want, and crawl over the bodies to do it.

We are drones.

We are constantly being controlled. By time. By money. By medicines taken at certain times on certain days. We follow rules. We get in cars to move about, then drive like we'll live forever. We are blind to everything except what's in front of us. We live on schedule. Our children are bused and lined up, moved in formation, from one place to another, and are pushed daily to succeed, succeed, succeed at all costs. Then they respond to the pressures in destructive ways. They are forever changed from who they were meant to be, because they are controlled by someone else's plans.

Next, we line up for medicines to calm the chaos we have created in our lives without knowing what's in it. We eat the food put in front of us without asking what's in it. We follow orders from people who've named themselves our superiors, without knowing why, or to what end we will come.

You should try it sometime... taking a step back and seeing ourselves for what we do and how we do it.

You might easily approve and feel safe within this format.

And you may not.

#notpartoftheherd

Last night I dreamed I was at an award show, like the Oscars. I was invited because they'd made a movie from one of my books, and I'd been CHOSEN to receive an award as the original author, not the writer who wrote the screenplay from it. I was excited until we got there, at which time I overheard the screenwriter making a joke about how they were going to fool me when it was time to present the award, and give me a fake award instead. So I spent the rest of the dream trying to get away from the venue. Finally found my way out and came home.

I am, however, taking that to mean my book, THE CHOSEN, will be made into a movie, because I've been working to manifest this. But the time isn't right yet.

See how easy it is to make yourself happy?

Believe.

I have four women named Leslie within the close circle of my life. A granddaughter, a friend who is also my life coach, my hair stylist, and the woman who was my editor for 25 years. All four of these people are some of the sweetest people I've ever known. I guess Leslie is a favorite name among angels.

When we are young, we run fearlessly wherever our hearts urge us to run.

When we become adults, we learn there are paths on which to walk.

As we age, we search for those paths before we set out, unwilling to chance unexpected delays.

When our work here is done, we need no path to find the way home.

We just follow the light all the way.

Happy, happy day on this cold Sunday morning. Kathy called me laughing at herself...said the batteries were out in her kitchen clock, and she kept working for hours before it dawned on her that it can't be 7:10 a.m. ALL morning.

Now she thinks she's behind. I'm still smiling.

I heard a car door slam in the early morning hours and sat up in bed, looking for a robe because someone would surely be knocking at my door. And then I remembered, I don't live in the country anymore, and the noise likely came from next door.

Oh, how sharp that moment of regret, and then I just laid back down and burrowed back into my warm covers.

Old habits.

New life.

Moving on.

Sometimes when people are unhappy or afraid, they act out by keeping themselves too busy to think. They work overtime. They party every night and every weekend. They overeat. They don't eat. They drink too much. They get in fights with their friends and family so that they don't have to think about what's really wrong.

They are afraid to be quiet.

They don't want to hear their inner voice—their conscience—telling them what they did wrong, and what they should do to fix it.

Sometimes what makes them unhappy isn't anything they did wrong, but they are in a negative place with all the wrong people.

That means, before they can get better, the first thing they need to do is remove themselves from all of that, and they're afraid to take that first step.

There are other people who will choose emotional misery just to stay in a relationship that has all of the bells and whistles, except love.

There's nothing wrong with that, if that is your choice.

But if you need to make everyone around you as miserable as you feel inside, just to be able to exist, then you have become a thief. You are stealing their well-being and peace of mind. You are stealing their joy by walking where you do not belong.

When you are finally ready for change, it will find YOU.

Pay attention.

Answers are always there.

All you have to do is look.

Sunshine is a deceptive bitch.

I looked out the window, saw all that light and the clear, dry roads, and was grateful for no ice.

Then I went out to get the paper, and got a big, slap-in-the-face blast of cold and laughed. "Fooled me again!" I said, as I grabbed the paper and hustled myself back inside.

All is well within my house. The cleansing smudge yesterday morning was enough.

Is all well within your world?

Make a list of things that continue to keep you upset, then begin with the one that bothers you most, and ask yourself, "Why is this still an issue? How long has this been bothering me? Why haven't I done something about it."

Think of it in this way. I let it into my world, so I have the power to show it the door.

Then go down that list one by one. Doesn't matter how long it takes you, but deal with only one issue at a time, and resolve whatever it is. Again...you let it in, you have the power to let it out.

If you have given your power away—if you are letting someone else be in control of your world, then you made the choice to let that happen. Whatever is wrong...make it right or walk away.

Your power.

Your choice.

Your life.

It's time for bed.

Tomorrow, I have three old dental fillings being removed, and three new ones put in their places, plus another tooth to be bonded.

Ack.

Faint.

Thud.

Then I go let the dogs out at Kathy's because Scout has a test around noon when he normally goes home and does it himself, which means I get doggy duty twice this week.

Then after lunch, which I will likely be drinking because of all the dental work, I take myself to Leslie Draper's for my mentoring/counseling session. It may turn out to be 50 minutes of pulling me off the edge of dental hysteria.

Lordy, but I so do not want to go to the dentist. However, I am going to be positive, and say how grateful I am that this can be done, and I mean that. Back when my parents were young, a dentist would have simply pulled the teeth, and moved their patient one step closer to a set of false ones.

Ack again.

Today was a blessed day for me.
I ate lunch with my son.

I began working on copy edits for one manuscript, and when I'm finished with it, will do a final read-through on another one for a different publisher.

To have work is a blessing, always, because that means paychecks.

Take a good look at how far you have spread yourself and your responsibilities.

It may explain your constant exhaustion, confusion, forgetfulness, and distractions.

You aren't losing it.

You have just involved yourself in too many things at once.

Cull some.

Quit some.

Then look at how great what's left turns out, when you have finished them.

It's not how many jobs you finished, but how well you did them, that matters most.

I just finished making heart-shaped Rice Krispy treats for Kathy's class tomorrow. After I cut out the hearts, I dipped them in pink candy melts, and then added small chocolate hearts on top of the big pink hearts. So much fun. I loved making things for my kids classes when they were little, and now because she still teaches littles, which is what she calls her students, I still get to make holiday treats. And YES... I know a lot of schools in other states no longer allow homemade treats, but ours do. Yay us.

Language, and the meaning of words, change from generation to generation. Sometimes for the better. Sometimes because people have nothing else to do.

I gave birth to a red-head. Now people want to call her a ginger. That's a British term that has morphed into our vocabulary over here in the States.

I am not British.

Ginger is not red.

It is a dirty white root.

In my world, she is still a red-head.

When I was a kid, a slider was what you took coming off third base, and then coming into home base on your backside. A slider was also what we called the big hunk of cardboard that we used (poor kids version of a sled) to slide down the back on the pond dam on the snow. The Patio door was the big glass door leading out onto the patio, le gasp. What a logical name for that door, right?

Now most people call that door a slider. Yes it slides, but so do the pocket doors in houses, and they call those pocket doors. And barn doors slide from side to side, but they still call those barn doors. However... glass doors leading out onto patios are now sliders, as are mini-sandwiches on mini-buns. Doors and sandwiches are both sliders? Not in my house.

Change for the sake of change is what it is.

But change for the better has a whole other meaning.

That's what you do when something is wrong, and it needs to be fixed, or updated to still keep functioning.

Change can also mean growth, and growth is good.

Growth is necessary to our purpose.

Change the names of people and things to suit yourself, but when it comes to you, it's what changes INSIDE you that matters most.

Grow knowledge.

Grow understanding.

Grow love.

&

Happy Wednesday.

Yes, it's Valentine's Day, but it's still Wednesday. Another day in the week.

When you first walk into the grocery store where I shop the most, there is a huge wall of flower bouquets for sale. I used to work in a florist shop, so it's very eye-catching, and makes me happy every time I see it. Sometimes I stop and look at the different flowers, only to realize a lot of them have been artificially colored. No biggie. They're still pretty, but nothing like my Grand's flower garden used to look. Lots of people pass that wall without even looking at it, because it's just a wall of something else for sale.

And now...because this day has been ordained as a day to prove you are loved by someone, people will buy those flowers without even looking at them, guilted into spending money to prove they love someone. Don't misunderstand me. There are plenty of people who give from the true love and goodness of their hearts, because they have people they want to honor. The day is marked on the calendar we use as a holiday, where you give gifts of love to your special people. Like my daughter and family did for me.

But my point is... It works fine for those people who have a large circle of friends and family, but for the sweet souls who are walking their path alone on earth, it is a day that affirms their beliefs of how alone they really are. They feel as if this holiday is an in-your-face reminder that no one loves them like that.

But that's not true.

God loves you more than a box of chocolates.

More than a bunch of flowers.

More than a five dollar greeting card.

God's love is infinite, and shining, and that light is inside you.

Like the fingerprints you have that are yours and yours alone.

Like the blood in your body that is part of your DNA.

That God-light is proof of how loved you are.

It is a light we all share.

WE—as in ALL OF US—carry the DNA of God.

Spirit just interrupted my day for this message, so somebody needs to read it.

If your life is in a rut, your choices put you there.

If you are having hardships with relationships or money, your choices put you there.

Now...what are you going to do about that?

Spirit says: Make new choices.

Do NOT go looking for someone else to solve your problems.

If you don't figure out how to get yourself out of the debt you are in, you'll never learn the lesson. You will repeat that mess time and time again in your life, until you die.

Spirit says if you are in a poisonous relationship and want out, find a door.

Spirits says: Your hesitance to change your life IS A CHOICE.

You just let The Universe know that you are fine where you are. You don't need anything.

Because you are staying where you are, you have sent out the signal that you like it.

Do something different. If you always go to the same places, and never meet anyone new...go somewhere else. Change your routine. Unless you're looking for more of the same, I would suggest a bar should not be your first choice. Unless that's what you want. In which case...knock yourself out.

If you dislike your job...learn a new trade while you stay at that job. Go to online school. Go to night school. If you have a skill, open an online business and then advertise.

Don't use what you DON'T have as an excuse. Work with what you've got.

Now...returning to regular programming...

I am on hold.

Not sure why, but I think it has to do with The Shift.

What I do know is this is not the time to make big decisions, so I benched myself for the time being.

Tomorrow is my counseling session with Leslie Draper. I am going to investigate this further. There's always a reason why instinct kicks in, and I have learned to listen.

I sat down today and paid bills.

So grateful to have the money to pay them.

I have lived through some hard times, and learned much.

One specific thing that never changes about those times, is knowing how to be grateful when you come out on the other side of a time of scarcity, and you still have your health, a home, and a car, and a job.

How do you view your life?

Are you constantly measuring your success?

Do you stress out that you aren't where you thought you would be?

Do you measure your career by your age and resume?

Why?

God doesn't measure us by any of that.

He doesn't judge us at all.

You didn't come here to accumulate things.

You have purpose, but it does not require a certain style of home, cars, or clothes.

What it does require is faith that you will always be taken care of.

The ability to rebound.

And to grow empathy for mankind, identify the humanity within all of us, and hold to it, even for those you do not like, or agree with.

And to learn lessons from the roadblocks you encounter as you move through life.

That's your real purpose.

Such a good day.

I had lunch with a friend, and later in the day, an unexpected visitor.

The day is teetering between outright cold, and very chilly. Take your pick.

At any rate, I am loving my seat by the fireplace this afternoon.

Warm feet, and the comfort of my recliner. I mean...that's a whole bunch of blessings and gratitude right here, right?

There is a chance we'll get a little rain this evening through tonight. It is soooooooo needed. We haven't had rain since October of last year. We've been in a burn ban for months, and in a drought, as well. This will be a welcome weather pattern for us.

Already thinking about supper. Why? Because I'm on a very deliberate eating pattern here for a while. You all know I don't go the meat route anymore, but I'm diabetic, and I'd let too many carbs and sugar creep into my diet, just because it was easier to do that than cook. So...on the carb and sugar wagon for now, too, which leaves blessed little to choose from. However...being picky about food does not solve health issues, so I just eat what I can.

Life can be so hard when family goes to war with each other. There isn't anything to say that will make it better. All you can do is not take sides. You own YOUR truth and yours alone. You do NOT buy into what sister said, or brother said. You do NOT go running to another family member to fan the flames, either

Even if both factions are demanding you take a side, all you have to say is, "I love you all. You're my family and I'm not taking sides." And walk away. It's truly that simple.

Once they know you refuse to be part of the drama, it may lead others to do the same.

One thing I know for sure, taking that step absolves you of guilt later, and you will never have to live with regret.

Massage.

Lunch.

Nap.

Because I matter.

It's cold... It's pouring rain...and chance of freezing...

BUT IT'S RAINING. Drought has broken.

First rain we've had in months.

Gratitude abounds.

Crissy and her youngest daughter, Courtney, stayed the night with me last night. Crissy and I started laughing about our first reaction to the buzzer sound on my new dryer that lets you know the load is dry. Scared the crap out of both of us. We laughed until our faces hurt. Diane was surely with us last night. Between her daughter and me, we wrung the last bit of good sense and joy out of the evening. Courtney retired to her bedroom with her phone, and ignored the both of us. Life is good.

We ALL come here wired to accomplish specific goals. Expecting our friends to be on the same wave-length and energy level, is as absurd as expecting all of us to sound alike when we speak.

Have patience.

My Grand used to say, "bear with me, honey," when her steps became slower, and her fingers no longer moved with the speed of light. Mother always said her mother was as quick as a heartbeat, that everything she did, she did fast. Even after my Grand was a grown woman, she could still outrun everyone they knew.

I did not inherit that.

My soul is forever young, but I am having a few 'bear with me' days, too, as per my soul contract.

I did not come here with the purpose of accumulating stuff, and trying to outrun the aging process.

I am safe.

I am happy.

I am enough.

❧

Last night I was bombarded with one dream after another. I couldn't get out of my own head. When we sleep, our subconscious takes over. Mine was a pure busybody last night, and the nap I took today was much needed.

I am not a fan of shopping. I don't much care for travel, and if given a choice, would stay home. I think that's because at night, I am never allowed to rest.

Spirit-walker.

Soul-traveler.

Lessons to learn.

Instructions to receive.

And then I wake and wonder why my eyes burn, and my body feels so heavy…because I've been moving about all night as the light I am. Returning to an earthly body limited by gravity, with a shell that is beginning to suffer burn-out, is a task done with love. I am not ready to quit. My work here is not done.

Emotions can make you sick. They will take root so fast inside your thoughts that you'll never know what happened. One day you were scooting along just fine, living life, being who you are, and you experienced a moment of jealousy...or maybe it was anger...or was it that moment of hate?

And then you took that emotion with you for the rest of the day. It poked at you when you went home, and instead of letting it go, it felt so good to be indignant and pissy, that you took it to bed with you. You even dreamed about the justice you would enact. How you would show "them"...how you would be better, richer, prettier, stronger, more powerful.

And when you got up the next morning, it was the first thing you thought of again...roots were sprouting. It was the beginning of your disease.

You forgot to let it go yesterday, and today it had already found your weakness.

And you know the rest of the story.

Lesson learned: You cannot be hurt by someone else's war, unless you step into their battlefield.

Say a prayer.

Move on.

There are very deep ruts in the path of least resistance.

Is that where you meant to walk?

Did you get there out of fear of the unknown, or were you just too uninspired to step out?

I have often wondered how this world would be now if exploration had never happened. If the people stayed in place where they were born, and never left. Would they have ever evolved?

However, nature took care of that by forcing humanity to follow the food and water. When one source dried up, if they wanted to survive, they had no choice but to move on.

And we're still moving on...following jobs, wanting to be close to other family, searching for a weather-friendly environment...running away...moving toward. It's still all about change.

But these are only physical moves.

There are still plenty of places right where we live, that keep us emotionally tied to unhealthy environments.

It's much harder to get away from something negative when you are surrounded by it.

That's where strength of mind, determination, and a refusal to quit will become your safety net.

Do what feels right.

Not what someone else told you to do.

My alarm went off at 7:30 a.m. Pest service was coming this morning to spray. I rolled over, re-set it for 8:00 and went back to sleep.

Cue loud knocking on my door!

I thought it was next door and squeezed my eyes tighter.

Knocking went from polite to hammer.

Rolled over and looked at the clock.

Yep. You guessed it. 9:00 a.m.

If your eyes are weak enough to need bifocals, never reset your clock in the dark.

Answered the door in my robe and gown.

"Be right in!" he yelled from his truck.

Fastest I've ever dressed in my life.

AANNDD GOOD MORNING TO ALL YOU UP. I'M UP!

Fell asleep last night with the face of Anubis (Ancient Egyptian God) watching me. (If you don't know which one that is, since they had several, it's the one that looks like a dog but is always depicted walking upright). Anubis is a jackal (wild dog). I've always enjoyed documentaries about the pyramids, and the burial sites of the old rulers that they find beneath the sands. Maybe I over did the documentary watching. Or maybe it was just a visitor from another lifetime.

Our lives here weren't meant to be lived in constant perfection and harmony. That's where we came from. Some of us come here to help others. Some of us come here to learn. Some of us are blessed to have a life partner as we work here. Some of us have chosen this time to make the trip alone. But none of us were meant to stay. When we have finished our purpose, no matter how quickly it happens, or if it takes us all the way to old age, when we're done, we go home. There will always be grief at the parting for the ones left behind...but I like to focus on the homecoming of the one that I've lost. For them, it's like going home for Christmas...forever.

I've spent the past two days working and napping. My energy was low and there is a ton of work to do, but I'm grateful for it. I'm almost finished with my editing task. It has been a good change of pace to do this, and it has given me a break from creating, which is how writers tell stories. This time, I had someone else's creation, and all I have been doing is tidying it up a bit. Some of you already know, I LOVE to edit, so this was a good break for me. Even a blessing. I'd say. Through this, I have made a new friend, and that is always a good thing.

Getting my hair done this morning. After that, I'm in for the day.

Yay!! I am, without doubt, a very anti-social being...It comes from being an Empath. It's exhausting to be among a lot of people, feeling the barrage of their energies, and trying not to absorb all of it.

Yesterday when I was with my Little Mama, she was in one of her lucid moments. Real words came out of her mouth as she rubbed the side of her neck and shoulder."It hurts," she said.

I looked. Decided it was likely muscle pain from sleeping with her neck in a crick, or her shoulder out from under the covers, and getting cold in the night. So I ran down one of the aides and asked them to ask the nurse if there was some kind of topical cream we could rub on it. Pretty soon the nurse arrived to check on her. He's about 6'5" and the nicest man ever. Little Mama saw him, recognized him, and told him he was too tall. He just grinned.

He checked her over and said they'd put some menthol cream on it, which was what she needed, and I thanked him. In a few minutes one of the aids approached carrying one of those little plastic cups used to dispense meds to patients, but this one had a little blob of blue gel. The menthol cream had arrived.

Little Mama gave her the stink eye when she saw that blue blob, but I just kept unzipping her jacket a bit so they could reach the place on her neck and shoulder, and we all had a little chuckle when we saw how many tops she had on under the jacket. I counted a shirt and a sweater before I stepped out of the way. It looked like a good time to take my leave, so I was telling her goodbye and waving, and she was waved back with one hand, but the other one was doubled up into a little fist, threatening the girl rubbing her neck, that she was gonna bop her if it hurt. By then there were at least three or four aides around her, teasing with her, and laughing, and helping distract her while they got the topical cream spread on the sore muscle. They were hugging her, and holding onto her so she wouldn't fall, because she was laughing and squealing from the cold gel as I walked away. It was a good sound to leave on.

There are degrees of joy.

Total hysterical laughter.

Shared laughter with a friend.

Smiles that come from the inside out.

And my favorite, the feeling that sits at the back of your soul in quiet appreciation for where you are in the world.

You know that feeling…Like when you've been out in the cold all day, and you see home in the headlights.

It's warmth, safety, and love, all rolled into one.

There isn't enough money, or distance, or luxury:

To satisfy the heartache you feel.

The shame of what you've done.

The despair of what you've lost.

What you carry within you is:
    For you to shed.
    For you to atone.
    For you to forgive.
    For you to heal.

Someone else may have;
    Hurt you, deceived you, cheated you.
    But you are the one holding onto the rage.

You are the one hurting, because:
    It's easier to hurt than to forgive.
    It's easier to be a victim, than to let it go.
    Revenge is as dark as emotion can go.
    It is the purposeful planning of harm.
    It solves nothing—not even the rage you hold.
    All you've done is strike back, inviting a war.

Doctor the wound.
    Let the sore heal.
    Don't pick at the scab.
    Don't hide the scar.
    It is a reminder of what never to do again.

❧

My house smells like lemons. I love Mondays. It's all about Denise and cleaning day, and she just left.
    I AM OPEN AND RECEPTIVE TO ALL GOOD.
    That's the first thing I say to myself every morning.

We have a chance of rain for the next few days. It's sprinkling now, and I am holding the intention for it to happen.

I finished the editing job I was doing for a friend. Completing a task is such a good feeling. Even if it's nothing more than taking the last load of laundry out to be folded, it's a good feeling to finish what you start.

There are so many ways to live a productive and happy life.

People are doing it every day but don't see it, because they aren't looking at what they already have. They're looking at what they still want.

They see a bigger house and say, I want one like that, then go home dissatisfied with the snug, safe home they already have...the home that shelters the family, and provides warmth and comfort. They envy other people's lifestyles and toys.

And so it goes throughout a life unless they wake up.

Too often, it's only after something precious is lost, that we look back and see the value.

We aren't meant to be something we aren't.

We come here for a reason. Our soul remembers, but we forget purpose in a race to gain power, instead.

If you are unhappy with your home, then clean it.

If you are unhappy with your clothes, then fix the hems, and sew the buttons back on.

If you don't like the way your car looks, clean it out and wash it.

And if you're still not happy, then start over, and this time, begin with what's inside you.

Let go of the war within.

Forgive trespasses...both of yourself and of others.

Write down the things that make you unhappy and then burn the list. Let old anger go up with the smoke.

It does not serve you to hold grudges.

Be the stronger person and let it go.

Be the warrior.

But, first fight the battle within.

I was reading the Sunday comics this morning and got to Classic Peanuts, one of my favorites. In the strip, Charlie Brown is standing outside in front of Snoopy's doghouse. Snoopy is sitting on top with a typewriter, writing. Charlie Brown says, "I don't get you, Snoopy. First you were writing a novel, and now you say you're writing a short story. Why did you stop your novel to work on a short story?" And Snoopy says, "Because I only have one sheet of paper." Being a writer, myself, of course I laughed, but I also saw a deeper meaning.

We often jump off into something new before we're ready.

Snoopy wasn't ready because he didn't have enough paper.

And we're often missing 'the paper' we need, as well.

For us, sometimes the missing pieces are that we don't know what we're doing.

Other times, we have the skills, but we're in a place where the skills are not in need...or there are no openings for us to apply.

Sometimes we're judged as being too young, or too old to fill a position. In those cases, we're ready, but they're not. It takes patience, faith, and trust to realize there are times when the Universe is ready to help, but we're so focused on one thing, that we don't see all of the other options.

The bottom line is, if you're willing to stay open to possibilities, you will see the way for you to proceed.

You will have enough 'paper' to begin anew.

And remember, when YOU are ready, the answers will come.

With all that being said, I want to share my favorite verse from the bible.

"Be not forgetful to entertain strangers: for thereby ye may have entertained angels unawares." Hebrews 13:2

❦

In the past two days, Kathy, Scout, and Ash have been over here removing diseased rose bushes for me. There were about 10 in all, and I'm happy they are gone. I'm going to look at Crape Myrtle bushes today or tomorrow. That's what I want to replant. And Kathy has a bunch of Iris bulbs she's going to give me to replant around the garden shed. I say, "I'm going to plant," when in reality it will be Kathy and Ash. She's so excited to have something to plant...even if it's not at her house. Gardening is her joy.

And...they brought me lunch both days, so I've really been given a treat.

Tomorrow is my son's birthday. It's hard to grasp how many years have passed since the day he was born. I was divorced only a couple of months before he was born, and the night before his arrival, it began to snow. By the time daylight came, there was nearly a foot of snow on the ground. My Uncle Ralph drove ahead of us on the dirt roads in his truck to make tracks in the snow, so my family could get me to the hospital. I'd been in labor 15 hours when he was finally born. My sweet little baby. Just me and him against the world.

Life takes you where your choices have led you. Consequences come from every choice you make. I can look back at my life and say with truth, that I wouldn't not change even one day of hard times or grief. Everything was worth the family I have today, and who I am today is because of the choices I made along the way.

I am happy being me.

There are so many people in emotional crisis right now. Jobs are changing, disappearing, or lacking enough pay to live on.

The unhappiness within all of us has as much to do with the turmoil of our country, as it does within the confines of our own personal space.

When you think you are upset with your children, or your spouse, or you are dissatisfied with your place of work, a direct correlation can be made from the lack of trust in leaders and authorities, to the unhappiness that festers within your home.

When there is no rational behavior out there, you have to have roots to bind the behavior within.

This is when you take a big step back and remember that you have to center yourself, before you can bring down the chaos around you. Fix you. The fact that you are calm within chaos brings comfort and sanity to others.

Your demeanor is your compass.

And when you know where you are going, others will follow your lead.

※

It's been raining/drizzling since last night. The gray sky is low and overcast... there are puddles on my walkway, puddles on the back patio, and I've been watching the raindrops hitting the puddles, then spreading out upon the surface in concentric circles all the way to the puddle's edge. It's mesmerizing...like watching waves crashing on the shore...
And why, you might ask, am I so excited about rain?
Because we are still in need.
This is our blessing...
Mercury may be in retrograde,
But, hallelujah., it's raining in Oklahoma!!

I'm thinking about Easter. I'll be making dinner here at the house Sunday morning. At least part of the dinner. Kathy, God love her, is making at least half of it and bringing it with her. She's making everything that requires peeling or chopping, because gripping knives is painful for me right now.

My Grand and Grampy hid Easter eggs all around the yard out on their farm for my mother and her sister when they were little. Then they hid eggs for all of us grandchildren on the same property when we came along. I had the joy of hiding eggs in that very same yard for both of my kids when they were little.

That house and the people in it were the hub of our family, and the center of my world. No matter what we did, or what holiday was happening, it was held at Grand and Grampy's house.

It wasn't until I got older that I realized it wasn't the house that mattered, it was them. They could have been anywhere, and it would have still been home to me.

Years ago, when I was first divorced, I was feeling bad for my kids that I was no longer at home when they would go visit their Daddy.

Then Kathy told me something that soothed every ache in my heart. "Don't feel bad, Mama," she said. "Wherever you are IS home."

And she was right... it's not about the house. It's about the love you have for the people in it.

That old saying..."you can never go home," has never held true for me. I didn't understand the meaning then, and I still don't. I don't go to see where people live. I go to see the people.

So if you think your misery and dissatisfaction in life is based on the fact that you moved away from home...you are looking at life all wrong. You carry home in your heart, just like you do memories. You make a home by appreciating the shelter it gives. You create warmth in that home with love and laughter.

Whether you're sitting on bare floors with the front door open, a dog in your lap. and watching it rain, or you are living in luxury, home is where you lay your head at night, and true happiness comes from within.

Have a happy and blessed Easter.

Blessings to those celebrating Passover, and Have a great Sunday to those who celebrate neither.

In the grand scheme of the Universe, and the unending eons during which we've been a piece of the God-light, today is just a blink in time.

I'm waiting for family to gather later. My brown-sugar glazed ham is in the oven. Two cherry-cheese pies, and a poppy seed cake are in the fridge. I still have the big salad to put together, and when it gets closer to dinner time, bake the rolls, and heat up veggies. Kathy is bringing a hash brown casserole, and a broccoli-rice casserole, and the deviled eggs. I always have to make this cold Jell-O salad for Kathy and Crissy. It's made with a tub of Cool Whip and a box of dry Jell-O powder stirred into the Cool Whip. Add a can of crushed pineapple that's been drained, a cup or so of cottage cheese. and a handful or so of mini-marshmallows, stir and refrigerate until time to eat. I used Lime Jell-O this time so the fluff will be a light mint green. Sometimes

I use orange, sometimes strawberry. It's hardly salad, but they love it, and I love them, so there's that.

Just got a phone call from Scout. He's on his way over, so the arrivals have begun.

Have a blessed day.

Don't put yourself in a place of despair because something isn't going right today. Everything that's happening in this world is old news. As long as people have been on this earth, there has been trouble, and we haven't learned a thing.

We still don't know how to exist without hurting each other.

Today is a day for peace. Make it last.

Enjoy your day, whether it is with family or not, it is YOUR day. Use it as you wish.

I have an eye appointment at 11:00 this morning. Right in the middle of the day. They'll probably dilate my eyes, which means I won't be able to do diddly-squat for hours afterward, because I can't see properly. Ah well, that just means an unplanned nap. There's nothing wrong with that..

I can't get warm this morning. In the old days, a woman my age would have said…Oh, it's my age…my blood is getting thinner and I just can't get warm." I remember all kinds of things like that from when I was a kid, but the truth is…I like to sleep in a cooler house, so it's my fault the house was so dang cold to start with when I got up.

Yesterday was a blessing to me. I was able to help someone, and in return, they helped me. That's how prosperity, (not just money) works.

You give out, and get it back two fold in return, but it's what I get in my own heart that matters most. That feeling of having been of service. Of being able to help without expectation of thanks or anything in return.

To me...just being in the right place at the right time, means I was being used as someone's angel in their time of need.

Did you ever think of it like that? You know how people tell stories of praying for help, and then someone shows up just at the time of greatest need? They were God-sent.

We don't know it at the time. We just think we're driving down one road instead of another, until we find someone in need down that road, and see their need for help. When you see the relief on their face, and hear the emotion in their voice, and realize YOU are the answer to their prayer? That means God sent YOU. That's when you should shed every whine and complaint you'd been holding in your heart for that day. Know that if God trusts you enough to be someone's angel, then you should trust Him enough to know he's also there for you in the same way.

You are never alone.

I don't stress about spring cleaning, because I clean year-round.

I don't stress about dieting for summer because I live within my healthy parameters all the time.

I don't look any better in a swimsuit after I diet, than I did before. Gravity, road-map veins on my legs...my favorites are the blue ones, although the red veins show up better.

I don't worry about how my yard is going to look compared to my neighbor's yard. I was a Smith, not a Jones, so I'm never gonna try to keep up.

I don't wake up in dread.

A new day is always a day of opportunity for me.

I used to let other people get to me all the time. Either my feelings were hurt on a daily basis, or I was so angry it made me cry.

Now I have a way of stopping that feeling before it affects my health.

I imagine my body as a pitcher that holds all of my emotions. I think of that pitcher being full of despair, and anger, of disappointment and rage, of grief and dissatisfaction, of greed and jealousy and hate, and I know if that pitcher gets full, I will have no room for joy. There won't be a place for relief, and there's no way that I'll be able to accept love and forgiveness, because I'm already full of negativity.

So, I refuse to be angry.

I walk away from other people's business.

I don't carry harsh words on my tongue or in my heart.

And I am free.

We aren't meant to live forever.

We set our return home date before we agree to come here.

And when our job is finished here, we go home.

This, despite the people here we have come to love.

This, knowing loved ones will grieve our passing when we're gone. This, because it's how life works.

This place is school.

Home is where we came from.

Never, never, never think of death as the end.

It is but a continuation of the circle of life.

We come here. We go back. We come here. We go back.

And you couldn't lose us if you tried.

Soul connection/ soul family is as real there, as it is here.

We are forever bound by a single thread of God-light.

Be at peace in your hearts.

It's never over.

I don't dwell on the exact date Bobby died, but I remember his birthday. I don't remember the date my sister, Diane, died, or the date my Daddy died, but I remember their birthdays.

I blank out on the days prior to their burials, and I have nothing but bits and pieces in my memory of the day of their funerals. But I remember, oh so well, their presence in my life. All the funny things.

All the times we cried together, but especially the times we laughed together.

I don't mark the day I lost them.

I count all the days I had them.

Denise has come and gone, leaving my house all clean and lemony. She brings love and energy in the door, works so fast, stirring my dust, and straightening up my world. She doesn't just leave a clean house behind her when she's done. She leaves a place of order and solace.

As an Empath who absorbs energy faster than I breathe, I am rarely able to find that state of being within me. But leaving my home in this way is the perfect place for someone like me.

I am grounded by home and love.

I am constantly reminded these days of one of my Grand's sayings. Pretty is, as pretty does.

And in this menopausal environment in which we live…it's easy to find prime examples.

It doesn't matter how succinct your words, or how fine you look, or how wide the smile you are wearing, you can't hide a lie, because it festers, like a sore. You fool no one but a fool by buying your way out of trouble. You can't run far enough away, or bury your secrets deep enough to hide from the eyes of God.

Upon further investigation of my crape myrtle plants this morning, my yellow crape myrtle has a beautiful picture of the yellow bush on the tag, but in tiny print on the back, the name is Red Rocket. LOL I smell a yellow rat. LOLOL I can't imagine why anyone would knowingly falsify a color, but if I were a betting woman, that bush is more likely to bloom red than yellow. Ah well… I don't really care. I wanted Crape Myrtles, and I have them.

I'm off to the kitchen right now. I have a project in the works for later in the week, and today is a practice run. Kathy is coming over later to play with me. We love to get together in the kitchen and bake.

At all times, one family's very happy day, coincides with another family's very sad day, or yet another family is in a time of crisis. It is the way life works.

Never feel guilty for your day of joy, and at the same time, do not look down upon people who are happy, when you are sad or grief-stricken.

These are nothing more than the signs that show us all, how separate the paths are that we walk.

Today I am looking for joy. Everywhere I go, I will be looking for the positive, seeing the humor, finding someone to laugh with, filling the well that is my heart with all things good.

This is how I keep myself in a place of peace. This is how I refrain from slamming people I don't know on Social Media.

This is how I mind my own business.

Today is a day that feels needy to me.

I will be watching for someone I can help, if only in a small way.

If all of us felt this way, and acted accordingly, think what a difference that would make.

Too many people are waiting for someone else to fix the problems they have made for themselves.

I know this, because I lived it.

If your choices put you where you are and you don't like it, then use another one of your own choices and get yourself out...

One day I got enough and said, "No more."

One day I stood up and said, "I will not let you talk to me like that again."

One day I packed up what I could get into my car, and drove away. I started over. From scratch. All I'd left behind were things. You can buy more things. But you can't buy peace of mind. And there isn't enough money in the world to fix a broken heart.

Those things healed on their own as I healed myself.

I found my own power.

I speak my truth.
I walk my own path.
I found the waiting warrior in me.

Today doesn't feel right.

I am going to my massage appointment in a few minutes, but I'm going to smudge my house when I get home, and then stay here.

I can't put my finger on what feels off, but it's like walking on a sloping floor. I keep feeling like one wrong step and I'll slide too far.

I'm sending out love to friends who are grieving...and you know who you are.

There will always be days of strife, and of joy, and of grief in our lives. It's how being alive works. But it doesn't make the sad days any easier for those living with new loss.

Bobby always told me to pay attention, so today I am paying close attention.

I feel The Old Ones close...The Guardians...I feel my Daddy...my Bobby...the warriors in my life who now stand with me in spirit.

They know what I only sense.

The answers for me are to stand in faith and stand strong.

It's that simple. If you know your truth, you know your own strength.

Lessons lived through.

Lessons learned.

Driving down country roads, I often see the remnants of what used to be a gate in the fencing on the side of the road, and beyond that, faint tracks through the high, over-grown weeds. I wonder, as I drive past, where those tracks would lead, and who drove them?

Sometimes I would see what was left of an old rock fireplace, and wonder who used to live out there on that prairie? Was it a young couple, just beginning a marriage? Was it an old farmer, just waiting to join his wife in the little graveyard beneath the blackjacks out behind the house? Was it a house full of life and children? Were they happy there? Did laughter fill the space between four walls, or was it anger...or was it silence and deprivation?

I wonder how long it took that house to die after the last family left?

It held together gladly when there was life beneath its roof, but was the silence and the empty space below it too much after everyone was gone? Did the roof begin to sag in the middle, without people beneath to hold it up? Surely the floors would fall to the elements and the animals, once the echoes of little feet were no longer there.

Storms would come. Was it a storm that blew down the windmill, and eventually took out the thin, glass window panes, leaving the house blind to what was happening? It would have given birds the opportunity to fly in and built nests up in the loft. Did the house care that life of a different sort was using it, and in a haphazard manner?

There would have been no one there to fight the grass fires that always came across the prairie on which it had been built. Did that old house know? Did it 'feel' the heat as its walls caught fire? Is that why there's nothing left but the old rock chimney, and the faint tracks of the road that used to bring its family home?

I see you House.
I see you as you once were.
I see your road.
I don't forget you once existed.
I see my future in your past.
Soon I will be the one with fading tracks.
The one who exists only in people's memories.
And it will be as it's supposed to be.
People die, places crumble into dust.
But the light that was within them lasts forever.

DNA tests are becoming quite the fad these days.

My Little Mama's hobby was genealogy, so she would have been all over this. I've done it. Saw the pie chart with the random numbers pertaining to my bloodline. And that was that. I had a few distant family members I never knew connect briefly with me, while filling in their own family trees...but my curiosity is not at that level...mostly because my mother had already connected those dots...all the way back to the 1500s... by connecting with a cousin she didn't know about who lived in West Germany. All of that branch of the family came from the Alsace-Lorraine area in France. Theo had all of the Shero family records throughout Europe, clear up to when they first ancestors emigrated to the U.S, and she had all of the records from their port of entry records to date. Talk about history. So now I knew who my mother's ancestors were. I already knew my Daddy's side...or at least enough to satisfy me. His maternal grandmother was Cree and his paternal grandmother was Cherokee.

So I knew this...but that was history.

It wasn't now, and those people's lives were lived and done.

I honor those who came before me, but I don't chart my path by looking behind me.

Today. Now. The Present.

This is where I live. This is where my roots are.

This is my focus and what guides my steps.

Be kind in your words and manner.

Speak softly, even if your heart is raging.

Don't give away your power by losing focus.

Trust your instincts.

If you don't want to participate...just say no.

If you walked into a situation, you can walk out of it the same way you came in.

Don't stay in the midst of chaos just to witness the train wreck it becomes.

Negative energy is rootless and viral, and spreads like a disease. It will go with you as easily as it clings to those who carry it with them.

You can't wash it off.

And you can't hide it.

But you can reject it by leaving it behind.

A strange thing happened to me the other day. I blame everything on The Shift, but this was an altered perception of what I was doing, in a way I had never before experienced.

I was in my car, driving on the interstate. I had turned off the radio because I was tired of the noise, and just focused on traffic and getting home when all of a sudden, I felt like I was outside of myself and observing me...

I became aware of how immobile I was behind the wheel...just holding on...and yet I was going fast...so fast. This thing I was sitting in was shooting down the highway like a rocket, and I was just sitting there, being projected forward at a life-threatening speed.

In all my years of driving, it has never occurred to me in that way, that I am my own passenger, sitting inside a speeding bullet that, at any time, could hit a target and kill.

Of course I've always been a cautious driver. And yes, I've even been in wrecks. But this was a whole other realization.

Just sitting on my butt, legs not moving. Arms not moving, and yet I am being propelled forward by what I'm sitting inside.

I decided that it was a piece of soul memory from back when the world was on foot. At any rate, I was shocked by what was happening to me.

The feeling eventually passed, but I haven't forgotten it, or the sensation I had of knowing how close my butt was to the highway, and how fast I was going. Talk about road rash.

Weird, I tell you...just weird as all get out.

The world is always spinning.

Some of us don't pay attention and fall off.

Once in a while, one of us will get angry and jump off.

Every now and then, one of us just quits and wants to get off.

But the prize ring is for the ones of us who make it to the very end of the ride...however long it was meant to be...we hang on.

ON BEING HUMAN—or...the frailties of choice.

For the past few days, I have been saying a new intention daily...and that is, "my body is whole and healthy. My body doesn't hurt. I am strong. I feel wonderful. I am healthy.

I do this because I know WE are energy. And if I say that to myself, if I put enough positive energy into ME... it should affect a change of some kind, even if it's just emotional.

So yesterday was a rough day. I was on the road most of it, and didn't have any good time to stop somewhere and eat my lunch. skipping a meal is a really stupid move when you're diabetic... so lunch was at a Sonic in Shawnee...an order of tater tots and an un-sweet ice tea. And then I ate the last handful of Hershey Drops (chocolate drops about the size of a nickel) from what I'd given Little Mama, and headed home, knowing that was an absolutely horrible meal when you're not supposed to be eating carbs and sugar... but since I can't eat meat without causing yet another kind of pain...my choices suck eggs... Oh...yes, I can eat eggs, but not in my hands...at the Sonic.

So I come home, ran all the errands I had to run here in town, and then go home with two vegetable egg rolls from the cold deli-section of Sprouts, and a single serve container of edamame. And that was my supper at about 6:30 that evening. Followed it up with a bowl of blackberries and cream and called it a night, dreading my blood sugar test this morning.

And then I get up this morning, test my blood sugar, and it's down 30 points from yesterday morning. I stared at it in disbelief. So, I guess a part of my body was listening to me yesterday, because I didn't derail myself at all.

OH...trust me. That kind of day won't happen again. I'll leave the house prepared, like I usually do. But I survived myself.

I'm thanking the positive intentions I am stating daily. And maybe the edamame. Probably the only healthy thing I had that whole day.

We are human, which means we make mistakes.

Some we can recover from, but some we cannot.

Sometimes our choices cause a permanent change in our lives.

And it's when that happens that we must realize we aren't being punished in any way.

It is simply one of the lessons we came to learn.

So we figure out a new way to be and move on.

Souls are pieces of God-light.

Some are new and just learning what it means to be human, and how to manage emotions, and what the consequences of choices become.

Some are veteran souls who have been on this merry-go-round for many lifetimes.

And some souls are so old...so transcended and enlightened, that they aren't here to learn, but to teach.

The younger the souls, the more patience they require from others, as they walk their paths.

When we gather in numbers, there are souls of ALL ages among us...all on their separate journeys, all here for separate reasons...all in different phases of soul consciousness.

And so it is, that we should remember this...and allow each other the kindness of not judging.

Allowing those who wish to speak, the honor of just listening.

It is not necessary to agree. But if they feel a need to be heard, then be the light they need and hear them. They didn't speak trying to persuade you to anything. They simply spoke to be heard.

We all need to be heard. We need understanding. We need kindness.

We aren't supposed to be cattle...all moving in one direction...all listening to the same call for the same reason...to be fed.

We feed the souls of each other by accepting their rights to be different.

I am different from you.

You are different from me.

And yet I honor your presence within my Social Media discourse, and I honor your friendship as you have offered it.

I do not require you to think like me. I don't require you to parrot my beliefs, nor will I speak regarding yours.

And if you recognize something in me that echoes a similar sentiment of your own, it connects us emotionally.

And from the opposite side of the coin, if something I say feels foreign to you, and you aren't comfortable with the thought, all that means is our souls are on different planes of connection.

It's like waving at someone as you pass by their house, without really knowing who they are.

And it's okay.

Rain is coming. Not here yet, but later this evening and into tomorrow. We will enjoy moisture, but we don't need the stormy weather coming with it. However...in the Spring, in Oklahoma, you don't get one without the other.

Bought a couple of big Boston Ferns to put in the pots outside on my patio, and some Pink and green Coleus for the rest of the empty pots. Already planted large marigolds in the front porch pots, and the Gerbera Daisies Kathy gave me to smaller pots on the patio, as well. After this, my job all summer will just be to remember to keep them watered.

Kathy told me she has a new diet tool that's working. It's called Winston In Your Face. Winston being their new King Charles Spaniel puppy.

She can no longer sit down on the sofa and enjoy a snack while she watches TV, because Winston is still learning manners...maybe I should say...still HASN'T learned his manners.

The moment she sits, Winston leaps from the floor into her lap, certain that she's ready to cuddle him. And lord help her if she has food in her hand when she sits. So with her little mini-Schnauzer, TicTac, under one arm, and Winston under the other, there she sits...no snack...

See? Foolproof diet plan.

The irony of this story...Kathy was always a cat girl. She liked dogs, but swore she'd never have one in the house. Now she has three. Last night she sent me pictures of the dogs. All three were in a bed, but none of them were in their own beds.

The tiniest dog had commandeered the biggest bed that belonged to Geene. So Geenie snuck into Winston's kennel, and Winston was on the sofa using little bitty TicTac's bed for a pillow. I can only imagine what a hassle she had moving all three of them back into their beds for the night...just so SHE could go to sleep.

Yesterday, my friend, Leslie Draper, had a premonition that something was wrong with her husband, Scott. (Being psychic really works) She called to ask if he was okay, and he texted back that he was hurt, and getting his head x-rayed. He got hurt on an accident on the job. Got hit in the head with a big piece of steel. Huge gash on his cheekbone near his eye, bad concussion, etc... She will spend the day taking him to follow up doctor appointments. As she said... thank goodness for her 'spidey senses'.

I'm keeping Scott in my prayers today...hoping for good test results from MRI...etc... And praying his pain, nausea, and the dizziness he was experiencing from his injury is lessening.

Scary moment in how quickly life can be altered.

Roads lead to destinations.
Destinations aren't always by design.
One moment you're on the road to one place,
And then life will aim you toward another.
Bemoaning the fork in the road is useless.
You've already approached it and taken a whole new path.
Your job then, is to traverse it as wisely and safely as you can.
And when you reach the end of that road,
You will discover it still led to the same destination.

Lunching with Kathy today, compliments of Panera Bread. I'm picking it up and going to her house. Our lunch guests will be Winston, Geenie, and TicTac, looking at us from afar with wishful glances, and the occasional disgruntled yap.

Home means something different to everyone.

For some, it is a place to show off all that they have accomplished, in whatever way that pleases them.

Others choose a nomadic way of life, and move around constantly, in search of something they can't really name. And then there are people who never venture far from the place they were born, happy in the way of life in which God put them, without a yearning for something more.

For me, it isn't exactly location, but more of what I bring to wherever I live. I choose comfort over quantity, and a place that gives me a sense of safety. And then I take what I have, and do what I do, and find peace in the familiar, and joy in the creating.

I carry home in my heart, so wherever I go, I am always still there.

Life is in a constant state of evolution.

Change isn't always welcome, but it's part of growth.

Learning to abide in a different way during the grief of losing loved ones is the hardest part of being human.

But no one lives forever, and someone is always left behind.

As a survivor, I consider it part of my job is to live the rest of my life to the fullest, with all the joy I can muster, resenting nothing, and appreciating every blessing.

Honoring the time they spent with me.

Not wasting a moment of what I have left.

It is a good day.
Kathy and Ash planted the irises she gave me the other day, while I was in church. And they put up my other bird bath, as well. Happy early Mother's Day to me. I don't know what I'd do without them.

Came home and made some sweet yeast dough, and set it aside to rise to make more Kolaches. That is a Czech sweet roll, light-as-a-feather sweet yeast bread, filled with sweet fruit fillings. Scout's daddy always wants his with apple filling, like apple pie. Those aren't traditional flavors, but who am I to argue with apple filling? And a friend of his wants cream cheese filling in his, so that's my afternoon. I actually enjoy making them, so this is a labor of love for me.

The truth of my life colors every decision I make.
The truth of your life does the same.
We see the world from the perspective of how we were raised, and from our life experiences since.
This is why people who are prone to panic, get angry when they meet someone who thinks and believes differently from them.
They are coming from a viewpoint of fear.
Fear because they don't understand.
Fear because they feel threatened by something different.
Fear because of being judged by their peers for accepting a person different from them into their friend circle.
Fear comes at a high price.
You may miss knowing the greatest people.
It could slow down the life journey you are on, because you saw someone new as a threat, instead of an opportunity. And you will, most certainly, stagnate your energy, because fear-based energy is negative.
That keeps your view of the world very, very small.
It would serve you well to open both your heart and your mind to new possibilities.
This earth is changing.
It requires broader vision and less conflict to navigate.
God let us come here.
But His plan was never to segregate, never to administer judgment,

and never to lay down your rules for others. When you turn away people because they are different, as my pastor reminded us this morning, you have gone against the one thing He asked of all of us.

"Love One Another, as I love you."

You know when you're talking to someone, and you can tell by the look on their face, and the fact that their mouth is already halfway open, that they aren't hearing YOU, but waiting to insert their frustration/anger/bad attitude/agenda into it next, despite the fact that it has absolutely NOTHING to do with what you were saying?

That is conversation as it stands today.

Every day something will happen that throws us off balance. Sometimes in a good way. Sometimes not. But it's up to us to reset our own attitude. It's no one else's responsibility for how you behave, how you react, what you say. It's yours.

So despite whatever happened, your job is not to let is spread. You do not take your bad self through the day, hurting others, spreading ill will, and leaving a very negative impression of yourself for them to think about when you are gone. Just because you finally get over it and move on, doesn't change the fact that you have forever changed how people will think of you.

It was a night of frustrating dreams. Another one of those dreams where I'm going from room to room, building to building, trying to get where I'm supposed to be, and I can't get there. It's just an analogy for being unsettled, which I am at this time. But today is a new day and I shall swim rivers and climb mountains. (Those are metaphors for accomplishing things and recognizing new opportunities)

If you are willing and able, it's never too late, and you're never too old to do something new.

The worst thing you can do to yourself is assume that you can't, or fear that you will fail. When you believe that of yourself, you make it true.

The Universe is like a great big mirror.

Everything that you give out in the way of energy is what comes back to you.

If you berate and complain and send out negative energy, that is what will encompass your life.

Light can pierce darkness, but how will it find you if you don't believe you can see it?

Picture yourself standing on the highest mountain top, and everything you see around you is shining and beautiful, and so bright it hurts your eyes. You want to be part of that, but instead you find yourself stranded on this mountaintop because someone told you that was where you go to find happiness. You didn't trust yourself. You trusted someone else's word and now you discover that they lied. Joy and peace are not found where you live.

They can't be bought by the money you own. You can't bully anyone into giving it to you.

So now you say, I've reached the pinnacle of success on this earth and yet joy and peace are not here. What is it I'm missing? What else do I need to do—to have—to be happy?

You still have the Universe—the mirror to your true self, remember?

It's waiting for you to say thank you.

It's waiting for you to be happy for the breath you take, and not the money in your pocket. It's waiting for you to be grateful and kind.

The Universe is waiting for your light.

Once you have light, you can always find your way.

You give out, that which you want to receive.

༄

I got up at 8:00 a.m. without setting an alarm and I didn't need to be up early. I feel good, even if it is another cold windy day outside.

I hugged the center post in the hallway as I came through the house to turn up the thermostat. I said Good Morning, house...thank you for taking such good care of me. I also told her that she's beautiful, and I am so happy to be here.

It never hurts to praise that which gives you solace, whether it's a person, place, or thing. You're still giving joy and praise into the Universe, and that's always a good thing, because it's what you'll get back. The Universe is your mirror. Always remember that. You are the reflection of yourself. If you don't like what you see in that mirror, change you, and it will reflect your progress.

I have friends who grieve the age on their faces.

I don't mind the wrinkles, the creases on my face that are there from the lifetime of a million smiles. I don't mind the wrinkles at the corners of my eyes. They remind me of squinting into the sun to watch my son play baseball when he was little, and sitting at the swimming pool down in the park watching my children learn to swim. They are part of my journey as a woman, and as a mother. I earned them. I don't want them Botoxed away.

The only thing I don't want to see on my face are frown lines.

They are the scars—the memories—of what put them there.

And they are reminders to step away sooner when I see my life spinning out of control.

My hands look like my Mother's hands now. Spots from the sun, wrinkled from a lifetime of work, and the knuckles slightly swollen from the arthritis that runs in our family. But they are also a part of who I am, and I make no apologies for myself?

Why would I want to apologize for how I look?

Own your truth.

You're certainly not going to hide it, so wear it proudly.

There is nothing sadder than a person who lives in the past, while wasting today, and unable to see tomorrow.

Scout spent all yesterday afternoon and last night with me. Within an hour of his arrival, he'd eaten the lunch I bought him from Raisin'

Cane (fried chicken place), set up TWO different gaming stations, one in my game room, and one on the dining room table. One on a television, and one on a laptop. He settles into the extra office chair from my office, puts on his headphones and proceeds to entertain himself.

He moved from room to room all during the afternoon. I could hear him talking to his friend Michael on his headset, so the same event was obviously going on at Michael's house. I called a halt about five, and told him I was about to make him some dinner. He came into the kitchen and built his own BLT while I reheated vegetable soup. And then he was at it again, about eight-thirty, he roamed through the kitchen for some cheese and crackers, and a refill on his ice tea. I went to bed at eleven-thirty. He was in the game room. Told him I was going to bed and the security system was armed, which means no opening outside doors or windows.

I have no idea when he went to bed, but it doesn't matter because today is a national holiday and there's no school. He is sleeping in and it makes me smile. I don't know how many teenage boys still like to spend the night with a grandparent, but I am grateful I'm still on his list.

Achieving personal success:
Being kind.
Being empathetic to others.
Willing to concede for the sake of peace in a family.
Knowing when to fight for what is right.
Grateful for what you have.
Happy to be alive.
Appreciating who you are.
Sacrificing your comfort to shelter another.
Seeing people without judging them in any way.
Remembering we all began at the same place.
Accepting your flaws as part of who you are without taking your dissatisfaction about them out on others. Being truthful.
Rejoicing for someone else's success without coveting their gain.

Being open to better understanding.

Saying to a loved one what is in your heart, is better than regretting after they are gone that it was never said.

Staying quietly humble. The gesture is lost if you brag to other people of your deeds.

And knowing love is enough.

It's been a busy morning.

Not sure my laptop is fixed after all. Turned it on yesterday afternoon, and it began getting hot again. I turned it off and am going to take it back and get the fan replaced, but that's for another day. I'll still have my PC, and I wrote a whole lot of books on one, before I ever bought a laptop. I can still do what I have to do.

Talked to Kathy a while ago. She was making Ash an apple pie.

She's like me. Baking was always what we did when we were bothered, or anxious about anything. It is a very calming task for me and I miss doing it, too. But, I'm not going to bake in my house right now because I'm still off sweets and carbs.

Everyone has strife in their life, some more than others.

And everyone has the option to choose how they deal with that strife.

If you choose to be angry and resentful at what's happening to you, that is certainly your right, as well.

Or, you can choose to carry the burden with a grateful heart.

Everyone lives in the same world, but it's how we look at it that makes the difference. Some see the burden in their lives and others see the blessings.

That, too, is your choice to make.

For every baby born without anyone willing to love them.

For every child who's grown up without family.
For every adult who walks their path alone.
For anyone, anywhere, who grieves a life believing they were never loved, you are forgetting The One who loved you first.
Every soul consists of energy formed from light and love.
God is love. And you are of God.
Walk with knowing in your heart that you matter most to the One most high. You are never lost. You are never alone. He is always with you, no matter what you're doing, or where you are.
You don't believe?
You don't understand?
God will never lose track of you. He can't lose track of you.
You are tied to the Source by an infinitesimal thread of His light. Despite what you are enduring here, it matters only that you learn from it before you go home, back to the light and love from which you were created.
Hold this in your heart, when you are yearning to be held in someone's arms.

&

If there is a SKIP button to life, please forward me the link to find it, because I don't want to do today. I want to go back to bed and wake up in tomorrow.

I am so struggling. There isn't a happy place today.

The weight of life is very heavy and I'm tired.

But... if I was a loner...without a person to love or care for, I believe the weight of a solitary life would be heavier.

Ah... the conundrum of being human.

At least it won't always be the case. Returning home looks ever more inviting.

If you are still young, you wouldn't understand. And if you're afraid of death, you won't understand. But the older one gets, the less tolerance they have for panic, whining, and bullshit. The less painful it is to give up a friend, because you know you're that much closer to seeing them again.

Living life without regret is a beautiful thing.

Live for the love of being able to take a breath.

Live for the gratitude of friends and family.

Accepting this life isn't meant to be forever, and the fear of the unknown disappears.

You can't fight time, no matter how many nips and tucks, and Botox filled needles you use. Hiding the age on a body is a rejection of all you have accomplished. If you value only your youth, you have missed the importance of living. To appreciate it all, you have to live it all, accepting the aging process as the last important thing you will do.

Not everyone gets to age.

Consider it your blessing, not a curse.

We all came from the same place, and we will all return to the same place. There is no separation with God. Every soul, in every body of a different color and a different religion comes from Him. He created the Universe and in His heart and mind, there is no separation. That is all man-made.

There is much we don't understand, and the ability to take things on faith is part of our lesson.

Don't shout out to God for help for every facet of your life. In doing that, you are demonstrating your lack of faith in Him. Trust that He already knows and hears your quiet prayers. The rest of life is meant for us to figure out on our own. He gave us free will and a brain to make decisions on our own. And whatever happens in that life, He's not going to judge you as having failed. It is just a lesson. And if it didn't turnout as you hoped, maybe you were wishing for one thing, but your lesson was to learn something else.

These beliefs are what holds me steady, even when the burden falls heavy on my shoulders.

This part of my life is just another lesson. I don't have to like it, but I do have to live it.

Life is all about hills and valleys.

Sometimes the slope of a hill is steeper than another, but when you finally reach the top, the joy of knowing you got there is special.

The valleys are for the good times, the calms in our lives, and those are gifts, preparing us for the next hill to climb.

Keep your eyes on the path and watch out for landslides.

Once in a while, life will knock that mountain right out from under you, but remember you still have God. He's got your back.

A blip:

When the Universe is telling you that you are on the right path in life, by showing you several random things that have a connection:

I had one today.

I was listening to an oldie station on the radio while I was driving to OKC this morning, and an old song came on from the Sandford-Townsend Band. Smoke From a Distant Fire. So I'm belting out the song as I drive down Pennsylvania Avenue...

"Your eyes have a mist from the smoke of a distant fire," And to my right, I see a big sign at a strip mall. SMOKE was the name of the business, and then I'm following a car with a bumper sticker that said No Smoking.

I smiled. I'd gotten my blip. I was still smiling when I parked at the restaurant and walked in. Looked down, and saw a bright shiny penny on a dark carpet, and smiled even wider. Bobby came to lunch.

It was the beginning of the best time I've had in ages.

Busy morning.

Met Kathy at VIP NAILS where we both got a pedicure.

While we were getting pedicures, Kathy shared a funny picture she'd taken from her classroom. She had handed out a paper to each one of the students with one question on it. They were to answer it, and then draw a picture of what they'd said. So the question was: If you were president, what would you do?

One little girl wrote, "Glue chocolate to everyone."
The pictures were so cute. Fat stick figures...with little brown squares all over them.
I'm voting for her.

I went by Wal-Mart on my way home, and as I walked toward the store, I saw a large folding table being manned by little Girl Scouts and their mothers. They were selling those yummy cookies. I don't buy them anymore, but I always stop and give a donation, because Girl Scouts use that money to send boxes of cookies to the Armed Forces.

But as fate would have it, just as I walked up, one of the mothers looked at me, got all red in the face, then asked if I was Sharon Sala. I said yes. Ah... the power of being a published author for many years, and the joys of Social Media. But because of that, I met the sweetest young woman who said she read my books, and was also one of my Facebook friends!!. We had to hug a bit, and take pictures together.

A task can be overwhelming if you look at it as a whole.

Like the books I write. Looking at the blank screen of page one, and knowing I have to put the story in my head onto that, and have it make sense so that my reader can see it too. A little intimidating, unless you lose the big picture, and focus on the now. One step, one keystroke at a time, day by day, and it will be done. That's how you live your life, one day at a time.

Got my hair done this morning.

Getting my new laptop back this afternoon. Tech guy worked on it here yesterday until Microsoft locked him out. My fault...couldn't find my password. So he took it home...and then Microsoft sent me a message that someone was messing with my account. I laughed. Yes, that would have been poor tech guy trying to set me up. However, he took it home to work on, I got that message and forwarded it to him, and off he went. Hey...I can write books, and I can cook, but I can't tech. Okay? I don't have the desire to learn, either, it just isn't my thing.

I'll know by tonight what I think about the new Word program. Instructions are like a foreign language to me. I have to SEE it done. I have to do it myself with someone showing me how, and then I'm good to go. It's just how I learn. Probably why I hated word problems in math when I was a kid.

You know... "If a train is moving at 50 mph and it's 30 miles to the next station, how long will it take them to get there?" My answer: "A hen and five chicks, because it's Monday."

Still dreaming. Still traveling in my dreams. Still lost.

I have changed. I don't know exactly how, but I'm seeing stuff in my dreams I never saw before, and experiencing things I didn't know existed.. Maybe it's just my willingness to be.

I am, therefore I know.

Even if my conscious self does not remember, I accept that my past memories will guide me. That kind of faith.

To be completely one with yourself is to be open to accepting a new truth. We didn't come here as a fully baked cookie, so to speak. We have been evolving, changing, growing, learning, aging, ever since we took our first breath in this life. Therefore, it should be simple to understand that nothing is set in stone, and that every day presents a new thing to see or to learn.

Living a life of constant disbelief and fear, is like looking at the world through a peephole in the door.

Alrighty then.

Watching Tree House Masters during lunch.

Lady hires Pete Nelson, the builder to put a tree house on her property. Her budget is $80,000 dollars. She's also JUST purchased land with an old two story house on it, and is planning to renovate it for a writer's retreat. So she's building a tree house, while she renovates the big house, because she's going to write a novel.

Snort.

I could save her some money, because if she can't write in the middle of life and dirty dishes, with the phone ringing and someone needing help, she's just playing at being a writer.

Like anything in life, you don't need the clothes and the drama of the setting to live it, you just take a deep breath and wade in.

Some people spend life in flight—looking up, pushing forward, unhappy they are not

flying highest, while others soar through the beauty of life, elated they are the wind beneath.

߶

Today is not sunny. The wind is beyond brisk, and doing all it can to bring in the next storm front. Storms predicted tomorrow, as in Spring thunderstorms with strong winds, the possibility of hail and more. It's hard to enjoy Spring in Oklahoma when all it means are storms which, more often than not, produce tornadoes. Whatever Universe. I am ready for you.

The positive side of life involves belief.

It's the law of attraction.

What you envision in your life, and hold as your truth, becomes your reality.

When you trust the process you see the result.

But it's not a joke. It's not a 'slide the quarter in the slot, and get the gum' easy. It's a way of life.

You live in a positive manner, without judgment, believing with all your heart that which you need, you will receive.

Seeing yourself and your life in a positive manner and trusting that where you are at this moment, is where you are supposed to be.

We are given free will.

So for every choice we make, there is an action and then a reaction.

Think of it like this.

If you lash out in anger, you've said your piece, but you've also sent negativity into the Universe, and the person who receives that negativity also reacts, usually in a similar manner, and that's how turmoil always begins. And that becomes the world in which you live. You have put a wall of anger up between you and happiness. You didn't mean to, but you did it by words and actions.

But, if you do the reverse. If your words are meant as helpful or kind—if you refuse to react to a negative force, then that force has nowhere to go. You have diffused it.

When you live with a joyful heart, all of that beautiful energy surrounds you, and others with similar energy are drawn to you, until the power of positive living manifests in a myriad of ways, bringing good and all that comes with it to you.

Life is never about being the one who dies with the most toys.

It's supposed to be about living that life with peace and joy.

A Delete, and a public reminder to myself not to let anyone know I care about others, and have an empathetic heart.

The first Hunger Games movie I saw, I came home and told my family this is happening now in our country, and they laughed. No one is laughing anymore. The old divide and conquer is working like a well-oiled machine. They don't even have to lie anymore to make people angry. Their truth comes out every time they open their mouths.

I remove myself from the turmoil.

I will not take part in bitter debates.

I do not have to accept the status quo.

I am my own person.

You can't make me hate, and I won't buy into your ugly world.

Not my people.

Not my tribe.

Today was the last day for early voters in my county so I went to vote. I already chose the elevator instead of stairs, to get up to the 2nd floor of the voting precinct. Two young men also held a door for me, so I have accepted my elder status. BUT... if today is any example, I have officially moved into the dotty stage.

As I signed in to vote, the lady pointed, more or less up in the air, not in any one direction, and said, "Go down to the other end and get your ballot."

I did not know she meant the other end of three tables lined up end to end. So I wandered off,(in the wrong direction) and was redirected to the gray-haired man at the far end of the fourth banquet table who was grinning at me, and holding my ballot. I said, "Thank you so much. What are you...about sixty?" He nodded. I rolled my eyes. "Just wait," I said. He was still grinning when I went to a voting booth and made my mark, as they say, then ran the ballot through the scanner and left.

I kept picturing how I must have looked. Blue pants and shirt, brown shoes and a black leather jacket (yeah, I was style personified) dragging my purse, and wandering through the mazes of little cardboard booths set up. I laughed all the way home.

Ate a late lunch, and am eating a combo of fruits as I write this. Going to work on the manuscript all afternoon, unless I feel the need to nap...like right now.

Sometimes I say that my time is not my own, but that's not true, and I need to stop saying it like that. My time IS my time. Obviously I am choosing the ways I use it or I wouldn't be here, doing what I'm doing.

We can't blame what's happening to me on someone else.

The only way to get away from a distasteful situation is to take yourself out of it. Whatever is happening in my life is a direct result of prior choices that I made. All of it...right down to the bad back I have from choosing to get in a car with my first husband and go to a drag race instead of church, then getting in a bad wreck, to my bad knees from choosing to overeat, to financial issues for choosing to help everyone else before myself. My choices. My life.

I choose to own it, and then as Dr. Phil said the other day, I choose to shut the hell up about it.

The older I get, the more fragmented I feel, which is diametrically opposed to what I yearn for. A part of me wishes for the freedom to do what a butterfly does before it is born. The Empath in me wants to roll myself up, crawl into a safe and comfortable place, and just be there until it's time for me to fly away.

I've already lived the struggles my children and grandchildren face, and yet I understand the wisdom I have gathered could help them if need be, and so I stand on the strength of God to keep me steadfast.

I do not want to be a part of sadness anymore, and yet it still weighs heavy on my shoulders because my path and Little Mama has taken me there.

Life is different for all of us. Some will struggle until they take their last breath. Some will go through an entire lifetime with few troubles, and only fleeting sadness. It depends upon the depth your soul is willing to go to experience life lessons.

Today is a beautiful day, so I look for the positives. I remember when I was still excited about a new season. Spring would be a time of new growth and rebirth. It's on the way again, but I have no desire to till ground or plant seed. I don't want to plant flowers I will later have to water. I just want to coast. I have earned the right to coast. But my lessons are not over.

And so I will do what life demands, be what I am called to be, and fight the good fight for my Little Mama, because she can't. I will do it for my sister, who left us far too young. I will do it for my Bobby, because he would do it for me.

Life isn't about building castles.

It's about keeping the walls high enough so that when the troubles engulf you, you won't drown.

Thunderstorms are almost on top of me, so have a wonderful

Tuesday and stay safe. I will be riding out some wind and rain, but so far nothing else predicted. I woke up not feeling too great, so I'll be inside today. No big deal but I think just a bit tired. I'll be better with some rest.

The best days are the ones where I curl up beneath the covers, and listen to the rain blowing against my windows. I think it's a soul memory from the times when shelter was one of the most important needs a person had. So I have food and shelter, and the means to be warm. I am loved, and I know the Universe is with me every step that I take.

It is enough.

We are all held hostage by the technology we now use. If they change support protocol, we can gripe, but they don't care. We have the freedom to drop one company and go with another, only to find out later they're doing the same thing. Cell phones are great until they're broken, or you have no service. Computers are great until they fry. Business is done quicker online UNTIL you and 50 million other users are hacked. Identities are stolen so much easier. Lies spread so much faster. People are so gullible to what they read online, that they never bother to see if it's true. Anonymous confrontation and harassment is commonplace. There is no real safe place to be anymore, or safe way to communicate by today's standards. People don't solve their own problems. They either get online and ask everyone to pray them out of trouble, or donate money to get them out of trouble. More family fights take place on Social Media, in front of thousands of strangers than I can count, and I understand why. Because you're not being heard at home.

I fully believe that my one sincere prayer to God, is as mighty as 500 hundred from people who don't really mean it. It just makes them feel self-righteous to be in constant prayer. And that's fine is it's your thing.

Me? I just want to finish my walk in kindness.

Just because the rule of thumb for our current world is racial prejudice, constant anger, and judgment against each other, doesn't mean it has to rub off on me.

I am not one of the crowd. I don't play 'follow the gang leader'. I don't have to agree with my friends if I don't want to, and they don't have to agree with me to stay my friend. Not from my viewpoint. I can't speak for them.

Part of how we view the world and the people in it, can be linked directly to how we were raised. But why continue that lifestyle when it means continual chaos?

Why do you think you always have to fight?

Why do you receive every new idea with anger and disparagement?

Are you THAT afraid of change?

Do you REALLY want to be the person who hates?

Who taught you to look at a world so narrow?

Who beat the joy out of you at such a young age that by the time you were an adult, all you could think about was fighting back?

Is that how you want your children to live?

Being held hostage to their emotions by what you taught them to be?

Today could be the first day of a new way of life.

Today could be the day you let go of the old hurts, and the old ways, and step out into a new way of life.

It all starts with a smile and a thank you to a stranger.

After that it becomes contagious.

Hold fast to truth.

Not what you want to be the truth.

Not how you want to perceive the reality before you.

Just the truth.

Even if you hate it.

Even if it is in complete opposition to how you've been raised.

The truth.

It can be manipulated.
It can be lied about.
It can be ignored.
But it will never change.
Truth.
Belittling it won't make it go away.
Humiliating those who live by it, won't stop them from living it.
Being angry that it is not yours is a waste of time.
It costs nothing.
It's free for all to hear. To see.
Yes, God gave us free will,
But He also left truth as our guidepost, to help us when we've lost our way.
You are either willing to accept it or you're not.
But if you are struggling in every aspect of your life,
The truth will set you free.

The simplicity of life is often overlooked.
We make it difficult by wanting. Often never satisfied with what we have, and always wanting more.
Many people are in need. They don't want, they need, and often desperately.
And that's where the simplicity comes in.
Those that have, and those that don't.
Somewhere in that statement, another word comes into play.
Share.
It's a simple act. If you have too much. If you have more than you need. If you have more than you will ever use, then why don't you just share?
If you can't bring yourself to give it away, think of it as sharing.
That's what you do with someone you love. You share.
So is that what's missing? Is that the reason you look away when you see someone in need?

You don't love them, so you don't care that they are hungry, homeless and in pain?

God doesn't have rules for loving us.

We should not have rules for loving our fellowman.

Either we care that they are in need and act accordingly.

Or we don't.

It's that simple.

There are guideposts to life at every crossroad. Sometimes they are hard to read, in which case you on have to stop, look, and listen, to find the way.

The day is gray and windy. Low clouds move across the sky as if they're on wheels, leading in a storm front that is supposed to be our first taste of tornado weather tomorrow afternoon. We'll see. I've listened to the weather reports all winter waiting for snow that didn't come. Freeze that didn't happen. Rain that missed me time and again. So, I'm waiting until tomorrow afternoon, at which point I will go outside, face the wind, and look for a green cast to the clouds. Then I will close my eyes.

The energy will either make the hair stand up on the back of my neck, or it won't. I'll watch the weather reports and I will be ready if the need arises to take shelter.

I'm still dreaming of being in charge of people who can't make a decision on their own. It's a weird dream.

In the dream I just want to be left alone to do my own thing, but realize the responsibility of making choices falls to me. When I woke up, I was in the midst of trying to get them to eat. They didn't know how to feed themselves, and were dying from starvation. Like I said, weird dream, frustrating, a kind of frightening dream.

God gave you all the tools you will ever need to live this life. He didn't promise it would be easy. He didn't promise it would be safe. You chose to come with his blessing. So when you get stuck in a negative cycle, pick a tool, (reason, decision-making, compassion, etc.) get yourself out, and move on.

***

I've been writing a new synopsis for one of my editors. The story is already in my head so having to smoosh it down to a few short pages, just for them to have the story 'in a nutshell' makes me crazy. But I suppose it's only fair, since their part of this process, besides copy edits, and line edits, etc., is writing back cover copy, and creating a cover for my story, and to do that, they have to know what it's about. Writers go through such detailed hard work just so a book, #mybaby, you may or may not buy, winds up on a bookshelf, or for sale in an online bookstore, etc. After the purchases are made, there will be public reviews, allowing total strangers to tell other people how pretty or how ugly your baby is.

Anyway, wanted to tell you, from my perspective, how special new stories are to me. As I write, I am creating a new family/new world, and new people who will become alive to readers, just as they are alive to me. I think back over the 115 plus books I've written, and I can't always remember the titles, (I never could remember titles even when I was just a reader) but I always remember the people, and their stories of survival and redemption.

Someone once asked me why I wrote dark stories. It sort of took me aback. I'd never thought of them in that way. To me, they were just stories about life. It made me realize how different some people's lives are from others. From childhood, I remember fun, but it always came at a cost. I guess I write about life as I see it, I write about survivors, because I am one.

Whatever it is that makes you taunt the weak, and laugh when other people are crying, is broken. You carry no light. Without light you lose your way. Fix it and get back on your path. You have many things to do before you sleep.

***

Are outward appearances important to you? Do you worry about what other people think of how you look? Do you stress about neatness, and cleanliness, and need everything around you to be in perfect order? Do you care for everyone but yourself?

Well, chill out people and slow down, because I have news for you.

If you do not tend to yourself first, then everything else becomes the sham, the wall behind which you hide the perfect truth of you.

Never hold yourself up to anyone else's life.

You can't be them, but you can be you.

The older you get, the more you can look back, and see what choices you made that shaped who you are today... maybe twice divorced, to trying to eat yourself into an early grave from grief. Those last two were some of my choices. But when I began to lose me, when I realized that I was not living, but existing for the care and comfort of others, that I made a hard choice and changed me.

God isn't going to change you. He gave you free will. So asking God to change you is simply giving away the rest of you. If you aren't going to make the effort to get yourself out of the life you and only you have created, then you have wasted what He already gave you.

We come to this place already full of the most perfect love—God's love. And then as we grow, we are inundated with all that is around us... We experience what our parents put us through, and as we grow older, those experiences are part of what shapes who we are. So when you're older and now in charge of your own choices, you have only yourself to blame if they don't work out. You cannot spend your entire life being miserable, and using what someone else said or did, as the reason you are too emotionally crippled to get out. If you don't like what's happening around you, pack your shit and get the hell out. I did.

Wasn't easy. Suffered fall-out from family and friends like you wouldn't believe.

Lived through it.

Got over it.

Happier.

Bada-bing.

Love is universal, it has no color, no denomination, no rules or regulations, and it's free. How much love have you have given out into the Universe?

You receive a thousand-fold that which you have already given away, and the beginning to making that happen is to first accept and love the person you already are.

I just read hurtful words on an old friend's post and such is life.

I've been shot at. I've been stalked. I've been broken in so many pieces I didn't think I would ever get up.

I know what she's going through.

I'm sorry that it took her to this place of anger, and even sorrier she took it out on me, because I think one day she will regret it. It was so not like her. But if that's all she's got, then I have it made.

Life lesson for today.

Let it go.

So, yesterday while half of the state was enjoying a pretty day, the other half was wrapped in tornadoes. It was eerie. Looking out a window I could see clear blue sky to the east and a few white puffy clouds. To the west and south, huge billowing clouds were gathering so high they looked like mountains. And within all that, the gathering stew that created tornadoes. Some were big. Some weren't. They didn't hit any cities, although me and mine escaped by the grace of God.

Two people died.

Some rural farmers and ranchers lost homes, outbuildings, etc.

For them, it was a disastrous day.

Today, families are grieving the loss of their loved ones, and planning the funerals.

It is the kind of thing that puts life into perspective for me.

It's a reminder to never take anything for granted.

I have a busy day ahead of me and I have a book to write.

It's supposed to get into the high 80s and low 90s across the state. The hottest day of Spring.

Because I was reminded yesterday how fragile life can be, I plan to celebrate life today in every way that is special to me.

I will laugh.

I will hug my loved ones.

I will pay it forward.

I will do an act of random kindness.

I will be grateful.

I will be thankful.

I will be humble in the eyes of the Lord.

***

I guess this is my 'being tested' week.

I'm heart-weary.

We used to know people without needing to qualify their religion and political leanings.

Sick of it.

What's the matter with everyone?

Like I didn't know your family was always Republican or Democrat?

Like that freaking mattered before?

Like I didn't know some of you were racist?

Like I didn't know you love your church and God?

Why does that suddenly have to be shoved down everyone's throat?

I loved you as a friend then.

It's getting difficult to even find you through the dissidence you project.

I still think of you as my friend, But it's becoming obvious you no longer return the feelings.

So, well and good.

Life often puts us at crossroads, so this appears to be happening.

Do us both a favor.

If you suddenly so dislike me for my personal views, then take your self on down the road you're walking, because that's not my path, and it never will be.

I don't do hate.
I don't criticize.
I don't judge.
I don't fight.
Life is all about evolution.
If we're not learning and growing, we failed.
We came here as light.
We're supposed to grow it, not put it out.

Getting a massage this morning.
Back is so messed up. Sitting too long at a computer can do that.
Maybe by the time she's finished with me I'll be able to focus enough to tell you a Bobby story.

Clock Watchers:
Waiting to go to lunch.
Waiting for your work day to end.
Waiting for an important phone call.
Waiting for good news or bad.
Waiting for your life to change.
Waiting for answers.
Waiting in line.
Waiting for doors to open.
Waiting for a miracle.
Life becomes shorter while you're waiting for it to happen.

Yesterday I did that goofy Before and After app on FB. I just realized this morning when I sat down at the computer and it popped up, that the Before picture was taken just after Bobby died, and after my Mother had come to live with me, because her Dementia was getting worse. No wonder I didn't smile. The after was taken 15 years later, and it's affirmation for anyone who cares to know that, no matter how hard or how long something lasts, you can survive sad things and find a way to be happy.

Today is the last day of school here.
I'm sure every teacher in the city is past ready for this day, as are the students. Wishing all of them a peaceful exit today. LOL.
I got a healing yesterday evening. Won't talk about the how and why, but for now I am walking without pain, and sitting without pain, and I am forever grateful for the respite from that misery. Blessings to the healers in this world, for their gifts come straight from God.

The strongest power within us is belief.
    You can do whatever it is you need to do if you believe in yourself.
    The most important power is trust.
    It is the way we move forward, believing it can be done.
    The swiftest way to happiness is acceptance.
    Being grateful for what you have and where you are.

My back feels great.
But my right hip will not bear weight.
One thing is obviously not connected to the other.
Waiting for clinic to open.
Messages from Facebook friends, and reading posts from people I know from home. So much sadness over the weekend. My heart hurts for your loss. My prayers are with you. No explanations for why loss occurs. Nothing can explain away grief. Even when we see loss coming, even when we think we are prepared, but when it happens, we are not.
As I age, I have learned many things, none of which ever prepared

me for the sudden absence of someone who was part of my life. Memories are poor substitutes for the miracle that was a life.

There are years ahead in which you can be strong.

Today you grieve. Grief is a valid part of loss. Today you wail. Acknowledge it as readily as you acknowledged your love. Hold it close. Feel the emptiness within you. If you do not acknowledge the hole in your life, how will you recognize the need to refill your sense of self?

PICK ONE OF THESE AS YOUR DAILY MANTRA:

Just because someone does not like me doesn't mean I don't matter.

What someone else thinks of me is inconsequential to my path.

I am responsible for myself.

I, and I alone, own my words and deeds.

Blame is a weakness of the spirit.

Faithfulness is a virtue.

Love is divinity for humans.

SO YOU HAVE CHOSEN, NOW LIVE IT.

One time someone was mean to me and I cried.

One time someone I loved died and I cried.

One time life wasn't fair to me and I cried.

One time I needed help, and no one was there for me and I cried.

One time I didn't get the break I needed, and I cried.

But that was then, and this is now, and I am not the sum total of my sad days.

Stop blaming today on yesterday.

If your life sucks now, what are you doing to change that?

Stop blaming others for what you don't have.

It's your life.

Fix it.

Last night I dreamed of making choices.
My choices existed of things with all their parts, and things missing parts. Instead of choosing something that worked, and going about my business, I kept trying to fix what was broken.

Sometimes that isn't possible.

Sometimes things break and cannot be fixed, and yet we can't let them go. We dwell on what was...how it used to be...why we want it back...how much we needed that broken thing, and completely miss what is in front of us.

I am, by nature, a fixer. I want people happy in their lives, and when they're not, my first instinct is to fix it.

One of the most difficult things I've ever had to learn, and I'm still working on it, is to let people get themselves out of the mess they are in. Why? Because they have to figure out how to solve their own problems. The choices they made put them there. They will never learn to make better choices, if someone continues to bail them out of trouble every time their choices set them back.

I never let people know I had problems. I didn't want anyone to know I was struggling. I didn't want someone pointing at me and saying 'she did something wrong'. That comes from having a mother who made me do something over and over until I got it right. Sometimes to the point that by the time I finished, I not only didn't like it anymore, I didn't want it. You know? Made me think twice about everything I did, which isn't always a good thing. Made me doubt myself. It started out as reluctance to fail, which turned into fear.

Fear of failure isn't real fear...as in life and death fear. Part of it has to do with disappointment. Part of it has to do with what failure will cost, and it's not always measured in money.

So here's the deal. When faced with choices, make one.

If it's not what you thought it would be, make another choice. Don't dwell.

When you need to be assertive, do it.

You lead with your chin and keep moving.

Even when sad things happen, you have to believe that you will survive it. Even when you don't want to face it, hard decisions and sad days are part of life lessons.

Make today what you need it to be.

Be in control, not adrift.

If you feel like you're getting too far from shore, then paddle, damn it.

Sharing a Meme that ridicules, belittles, criticizes, shames...and then making it okay by saying..."I'm sorry, but this is funny." Really?

So here's how you tell if it's really funny.

In your mind, substitute the person you admire and love most in the whole world, as the person who is the butt of the joke, and then say that to yourself again.

Are you still laughing?

I'm not. Not even if it's someone I don't particularly like.

We're not in the schoolyard any more.

Better things to do.

I woke in the night to a rumble of thunder and a little lightning. I went back to sleep and woke to more of the same. It's a gray rainy morning. Certainly not the 90 plus degrees of yesterday. So this is the weather that begins my day.

Bed is made, awaiting the noon time, and company I am expecting. My hip is still pretty sore from surgery, but manageable. I made myself laugh last night getting ready for bed. After the near-fall, my skin looked like the last passed-over peach in the produce bin. It was, and still is, marked all over with bruises, some large, and some small. Right before I went to lie down, I rubbed some stuff over my hip and right leg. I smelled like my Grampy and his Ben-Gay. At my age, I now empathize with why he always smelled like camphor and menthol at bedtime. The life of a hard-working farmer probably gave him many aches and pains.

Dear Grampy, Sorry I ever teased you about 'your perfume'.

Family has nothing to do with bloodline.

They are the people of your tribe, to whom you have given love and trust.

Off to write some more.

Just wanted to say good morning first.

I've already greeted my house (as I do every morning when I come out of the bedroom) and I wanted to greet my Social Media friends as well.

Even though I now live alone, I still have a happy home. It is my sanctuary, my happy place, and my shelter. It is the gathering place for those I love, and the keeper of my worldly belongings.

She (my house is a girl, but FYI I think all houses are female...like ships) is my friend because I cry on her shoulder, laugh with her, eat with her, work with her, and I even sleep with her. Oh...the scandal!! LOL.

If you don't know your house, you should get to know her better.

Her roof and her walls shelter you. Shine her up once in a while, and just so you know, like any female, she likes to smell good, but she's not particular. If you're out of scented candles., baking chocolate chip cookies will make her just as happy.

So, I just went into the kitchen and proceeded to get all of the stuff out to make my morning protein shake. I'm doing Plexus Protein shakes, these days. Nothing remarkable about that. I do it every day, right?

BUT my balance sucks because of my back and hip, and as I made this darling little pirouette from the fridge to the bar, to pour almond milk in my smoothie, my elbow hit the bar above the ice dispenser where water comes out, and promptly filled my hip pocket with water, which then soaked my right hip (where all the pain has been), ran down the back of my leg, and filled my shoe...AND it did all of that before I knew where the heck it was coming from, or had the good sense to move.

Lord love a duck...and ducks love water, but not ice water.

It was definitely an eye-opening experience.

I went to change clothes.

And then I mopped.

I'm pretty sure an LG refrigerator isn't the same thing as a baptism by a preacher, but if my right hip is suddenly healed from all that, I might be spending my Sundays in front of the fridge, waiting for the word of God to come flying out with the ice chips.

Fantasy is a little like hope. You are in a world that's not quite real, but you so want it to be. They both lighten the heart, and give credence to the possibility of a better life.

Did you know that every time you come through a crisis with the understanding of how it happened, and what you willingly sacrificed to get through it, that you grew your light?

Every crisis we avert.

Every crisis we experience.

Every crisis that puts us on our knees...

When you find the strength to stand up again,

Is when you know that it is over.

Those are life lessons...

It's why we're here.

꽃

You know on FB how everyone is always posting a Meme about once in a hundred years, or a life time, or years ago...like a solar eclipse, which won't happen again for 103 years... or posting about an approaching comet... won't happen again in your lifetime...so then you go crawl out of bed, set outside in the dark with the mosquitoes, and watch it go by.

I always think... that's a cool thing to do if you are a sky watcher. Since my full belief that I came from there is so strong, I've never been one for getting out of bed to go look at my old neighborhood, you know?

However... there is a date we can ALL celebrate. A date that is

NEVER going to happen again, and that's TODAY. Now that's something to get out of bed for!!

That's something to celebrate.

I sure don't want to miss today.

I mean., right at this moment it's all a mystery, and I LOVE mysteries.

I also love surprises and this day could be full of them.

Adios to June, ya'll.

Don't freakin' waste the day.

Walk like you own your space.

Not like you're sneaking through it.

What a day. Woke up tired. Went to get my hair done, picked up lunch at City Bites with my grandson, Scout, and came home to eat it.

As we're driving home, he looks over at me and says, "Grammy, you have on a pretty blouse." I smiled. "Thank you, honey." He nodded.

It had a lot of color and design, so what he said didn't surprise me. That's how he does graphic art, swirls, lines, shapes within shapes...with lots of color. It's kind of cool to see how someone like him views the world. He's spending part of the afternoon with me. I'll be writing and he'll be gaming, and that will certainly keep Earth balanced on its axis,

Blessings abound.

Stop and say thank you for yours.

Even if you don't know it yet, it's already in place, waiting for you to find it.

Sleep.

I remember that.

Something to look forward to.

Today it is time to begin a new story.

I don't much like to do that. I think it's because I am, by nature, a shy person—a natural introvert who has been forced to participate in life. So when I begin a new story, it almost feels like I'm pushing myself into the lives of people I haven't met. I "know" their story, because it was given to me in a dream, but I don't know them. That will come as the pages grow.

But you can't move forward until you begin the next part of your journey, and that requires taking that first step, so today is my first step into my next romantic suspense, A RACE AGAINST TIME. We shall see how this story goes.

Most of my life I have followed my heart instead of my head. I can't live life any other way and be me. But It has its own set of problems. Yesterday I took a conscious choice to end the problems. I kept thinking, If I came this way, then there was a reason, so yesterday—I gave up worrying about defeat.

It served no purpose. The energy I expounded worrying never changed one outcome. I was reminded that, if I no longer see failure as an option, then it doesn't exist in my world.

I already knew that we came with free will. But why I didn't associate that with my life in this way, I'll never know. It should have been obvious, right? If I have free choices in my life, then why am I choosing to even consider failure? That's doubt. It did not belong with me. I am someone who accepts my purpose and the reasons for it, and they are very clear. So today is my first day without doubt. I am. I will be. And so it is.

Looking back, I am certain I learned truth by watching those around me. Until they are old enough to see truth for themselves, children are mirrors of their environment. My mother was so busy looking out for what was wrong, that she never taught me how to look for what was already right. My daddy was the one in our family who was always the first to laugh. I might have gained more insight from him as my formative years were happening, but he was so busy fighting his own demons, that after a time, laughter was a rare commodity in his life, as well.

And I think understanding this also comes from hard lessons already learned.

We readily change clothes or shoes without question. Changing the way you live your life is equally simple. Do it because you can.

Because you are part of the Great Source which is the Universe, remember it is also a part of you. Light, Love, Compassion.

With you always.

Even if you shun it.

Even if you ignore it.

Even if you don't believe.

It is there.

Today has been about putting things right within my world, and I don't mean just things that were broken.

I mean things that were not right.

Connections to people that were toxic.

Stepping away from the urge to speak in the middle of an argument.

Calming my heart.

Cleansing my house.

Finishing things that had been left undone.

Just got a call from Little Mama's care center.

She broke her glasses...again.

They found an extra pair of glasses in their lost and found, and she said she can see just fine now, so I told them I wasn't going to get the broken glasses fixed then, because they weren't hers anyway. She hasn't had her own glasses in a year and a half, and only God knows where they are. So she's wearing another pair that work, and that's that.

I can't take her to get new glasses anyway, because she could never get through an eye exam. The directions and the questions make no sense to her anymore. She doesn't know how to answer, and just makes stuff up, or tells people I'm mean, to draw attention away from her failure to answer properly. I roll my eyes.

People have NO idea of the scope of debilitation that comes with Dementia, and I have NO way to fix it for her. So she's wearing someone else's glasses, and often wears someone else's clothes, and I had to let go of trying to control that long ago. She's fed and loved, she's clean and medicated. She has a new pair of glasses and for a while, all is well.

I have to let go of all that. I have to.

I want to bake something so bad. It's what calms me. It's what takes away my sadness. Something about the act of feeding people. It's a task as old as time. Sustenance for survival. On the days I feel like I'm over my head with responsibilities, making food is my emotional survival tactic, and eating it is my emotional trigger to burying what I cannot fix. I can't win for losing here.

When you think you can't go another day without losing your mind, change your habits.

Change your morning routine.

Change the food you usually eat for breakfast,

Change your hair style,

Change the route you drive to work.

Change your attitude toward people by saying hello to someone at your job you don't really like.

You want change?

First you have to change yourself.

Finally time to breathe.

Had to help get Scout off to his Boy Scout camping trip. Everyone else was at work, to his Mama's chagrin. She hates missing out on the mama things in life...but these days everyone has to work full time. Grammy is still working, too, but I am my own boss, so I called a halt, and went to the rescue. All I did was bring him breakfast, laugh with him, and wave goodbye. But it made Mama happy, and Scout happy, and Grammy was pretty happy too.

Funny side-note. Scout's dog, Geenie, was sad and pouting. She knew he was going on a trip. I guess all the packing, and his camping backpack being out for at least a day was her warning. Scout told me she wouldn't sleep with him last night, and he was hurt. My heart hurt for both of them, and when I got there this morning, Geenie wouldn't even get up from her bed to come say hi to me. She just laid there with the sad eyes. When Scout sat down and tried to get her to come to him...she got up and came to me instead... I could just feel her little heart saying..."please make him stay. I don't want my boy to leave me."

By then Scout was bothered, too. I don't think he was all that keen on the trip to begin with, and this made it worse. He went to the kitchen, came back with a piece of cheese and sat down, which made me laugh. Geenie came to him, ate bites of cheese, and then laid at his feet, and let him pat her belly. When Kathy was young, she used to sneak the pre-wrapped pieces of cheese just like that, then go outside where she and her dog, Charlie, would eat cheese. I only knew it when I'd find the empty wrappers under her bed. LOL So I saw a moment in time—like mother, like son.

I went outside to get the morning paper, and walked straight into a single spider web, strung from the house to a shrub. I felt it break across my forehead and wiped it off, then when I bent over to pick up the paper, the spider I hadn't seen either, came scampering down my arm.

I carefully brushed her off, and she ran away down the drive. But it made me remember my spider dream. I had to honor the real spider, as I had the one in my dream.

Inside, my house is my world, and I will not be as gentle with dismissal of any insects, but outside is her world, and I accidentally intruded by breaking her web.

We parted company in peace.

Laugh first.
    Cry if you must.

Step back from rage.

Hold love close.

Disavow jealousy.

Grieve with open arms so that when the time comes, you will be ready to let go.

Crossroads.

The moments when you have a choice to make.

We come to these often, sometimes daily.

Some are small, almost insignificant, and others seem huge.

But looking back, you will realize that even the smallest of decisions you make are sending you in a specific direction. Like knowing a clerk gave you back too much money, and keeping it anyway.

In that moment you have told yourself it is okay to steal, because at the end of the day, you took money she will have to replace out of her own pocket, and you didn't care.

Do you choose with your heart, or with your head?

Do you think of only yourself...or how your actions may impact others?

No one call tell you how to behave.

If you are an adult, you already know.

Sometimes I wake up in the night with my legs aching, and wonder where I've been.

How many thousands of light years did I travel before I came back to this body?

How many beautiful sights did I see?

Am I all young and strong again when my spirit walks, or am I the bright and shining light that burns within me now, darting among the heavens like a shooting star?

Did I burn out in space?

Is that why I come back to my body in pain?

Some people dream of traveling to countries here on earth...of seeing the old world cities and the beautiful lands.

I dream of what's above me...of where I came from, and where I long to return.

This earth is sick now. There is a darkness upon it. I don't know for sure how it's all going to play out, but I hope I'm long gone when it all falls apart. The higher something sits upon a pedestal, the farther it has to fall. When you hold yourself above all others, thinking you and your ways matter more than others, you have set yourself too high. Our Source...which man calls God... is held in the highest of esteem. And God does not recognize wealth, power, and human bickering as worthy of note. He only sees us as the souls we are. What a disappointment it must be when a soul returns to the Source darker than when it left. We came to grow our light, not use it to spread hate and discord, in the name of power and greed.

Take one day to set aside personal grievances and just be happy.

It might feel so good that you'll want to do it again.

Plans today?

Fry okra. Cook purple hull peas, fry squash, slice tomatoes. Eat it. Write.

My dreams were so frustrating last night. I kept dreaming of a time way back in history. I was in the middle of a war, but as a spy. I knew something and needed to get across a border to tell my people, but knew I'd get shot as the enemy, so I let myself get captured, taken back across into the territory where I needed to go, and finally got someone to help me. Message was delivered. Some big disaster was averted. And then I woke up. Really?

That sounded so Hollywood I didn't even believe myself when I woke up. Not movie worthy. Not book worthy. Certainly not up to my dream levels.

I think all this negativity in the world is screwing with my zen.

My heart is heavy. My soul is tired. I am too full of other people's sadness. I need to go sit outside for a while, and be one with the world, instead of listening to what's happening to it.

Nothing that is happening on earth is new.

Cities have fallen. Cultures have disappeared. Wars have come and gone leaving whole civilizations in ruins for ages and ages.

We're just witnessing some of the same thing, and I suspect doing some of the same things others did when it was happening to them. Praying to their gods. Preparing for battles. Sacrificing humanity in the name of power and greed.

Rome was once considered the most powerful city of its time. It was the hub of commerce and culture. And it fell. We visit the ruins now as tourist attractions, talking about the architecture while taking pictures in front of crumbling ruins, dripping melting gelato upon the ancient streets, and complaining about the prices.

What will this place be in a thousand years?

Probably something like that.

I should be buried with a plaque that says, WE DID NOT LOVE ONE ANOTHER, so if they happen to dig up what's left of my bones, I want them to know we saw it coming, but were so busy worrying about THEM and US that we didn't have the guts to stop it.

For anyone who thinks no one cares.

For anyone who thinks they're bearing a burden or an illness alone.

For anyone who is too private to share their medical issues.

For anyone who hasn't been able to turn loose of the grief of losing a loved one.

For anyone who's lost and hasn't been able to find their way back.

Know that I pray for you.

Every night I ask God for healing and strength for those undergoing medical treatments.

Every night I ask God for peace of heart and grace for those still grieving the loss of loved ones.

Every night I ask God to shine His light to help the lost find their way.

Every night I do this, no matter whether you have requested prayer or not, no matter whether I know you or not, no matter how long it's been since you lost your way.

Every night.

For you.

Lord love a duck.

Every day things happen that are in direct opposition to what you wanted.

Knowing that, you now have two options:

Remember you are not God, and do not have, nor were you supposed to have, the power to change that. Or focus on the fact that you have approximately ten hours of daylight to make yourself happy doing something else, at least four hours or so of moonlight to make someone you love happy, and the rest of the time to rest before you start all over.

I know which one I would pick.

Put a smile on your face people.

It's the quickest way to put joy in your heart.

My back is out.

I wish to hell it would come back, snort.

Sarcasm does not become you, my Mother would have said, but it hurts enough when I take a deep breath that I have to decide whether to laugh or cry.

The ache is what's left of a wreck that should have killed me. I was nineteen years old when the car I was in went off the road and rolled five times. I woke up paralyzed from the neck down, thought that I would spend the rest of my life that way, and then five hours later, I was on an x-ray table in Midwest City Hospital when my toes began to tingle. Slowly, all the feeling came back in my body. I will gladly bear the pain, rather than what it might have been.

At least I don't have much to do today. Pick Scout up after school, and take him home after we run an errand for Kathy. And Scout's doing all the lifting.

The hardest part about the death of a loved one, is being left behind. I have several friends who are grieving the recent passing of someone they love, and struggling to find foothold and a new way to get through the rest of their own lives.

I know the pain. I am so sorry. Today I send you peace and grace.

Found a notation I'd made to myself to use these phrases in a book one day that has a small child in it.

They are words my granddaughters used when they were little.

"I like cottontail sauce." (cocktail)

"I want to eat at Ella Chico's house." (El Chico—local Mex. rest.)

"Daddy, Daddy, Daddy, make pantycakes for breakfast, please."

The last one needs no explanation.

I have to put those in a book one day.

You can walk the same path from day to day, never changing your routine or any aspect of your life and if that's your choice, then it is fine. Just remember, after a while a path highly traveled without repair grows rough and deep, and you are soon traveling in ruts that grow deeper and deeper with each passing year. When they become so deep that you can no longer see over the sides, is when you forget there is life beyond the circle that is yours.

This life is a gift.

God gave you the world in which to live and play.

It did not come with monotony.

You created that on your own.

Obviously, I wasn't supposed to go to bed and hide from this day.

My phone has rung all morning.

So I'm busy, and life is good regardless of the detours, and nothing more to say about me, except that you bless me with your love and prayers.

One toe dipped into the waters I did not want to talk about, but the pressure to address this won't go away until I do...so here we go.

There are so many hard things going on daily in people's lives, and there are so many good things that are going on in others' lives.

It doesn't mean anything except that you are on a downswing, learning curve, and they are on an upswing, like a vacation from turmoil, if you will.

Neither instance lasts forever. unless it is permitted to abide.

If you accept all of your hardship as hopeless, and you look for no way to better your circumstance or get yourself out, then you have chosen it, and you are continuing to draw negative energy into your life by inaction, for it to be any other way.

But if you are determined to better the place that you are in, it will happen, because optimism, laughter, good deeds, and good days, draws good energy to you.

Now. Knowing this, and knowing that you should be tending to your business, and yours alone, and you still can't keep your opinions and judgmental and challenging behaviors to yourself, and continue to hurt others with words and actions, you are negating ANYTHING positive that might have been coming to you.

SO.

Anger is not meant to be shared.

Coveting what others have is a learned behavior. Unlearn it.

When you show up at someone's house unannounced, and then they open the door to let you in, do you greet them with a slap?

Do you shout at them and spit in their face? Do you denigrate everything they stand for?

Then why are you there? You weren't invited.

THIS is exactly how your behavior appears when you drop in on someone else's Social Media site, attack their status, berate the friends with whom they are already visiting, and challenge everything that THEY believe just because you can.

I would hope your Mama raised you better.

If she did not, now is the time to correct yourself.

It's hot… no, it's muggy. That means hot and steamy. Temp is only 86 degrees right now but it feels like a 120 degrees, sauna-grade.

(that is my pun for the day. sorry, it's only Monday. I'm not at my best)

Nearly noon. Leftovers today. Scalloped potatoes, fried eggplant, tomatoes, coleslaw, corn-squash mix… all bits and pieces of other meals. So, it's eat it today, or throw it out tomorrow.

I lost my sister, Diane, 31 years ago this week.

The summer of '85 was a hard time in our family.

Daddy died in June. Diane died in August.

It wasn't the first deaths of loved ones though, and it hasn't been the last.

I've lived a whole other lifetime since.

Not being sad. Just remembering how special they were to all of us.

And so it goes.

Why, when you already know that something you've tried didn't work, do you do it again?

That was your lesson. A do-not-repeat lesson.

So now what are you doing?

Repeating it.

Really?

At this exact moment people are taking their last breaths, while babies have just taken their first.

People just got fired, and others just got hired.

Bad news just came to a family, while glad news came to others.

Homes are lost, and others built.

Somewhere a war is lost, as another begins.

Disease is not a punishment.

Death is never well-deserved.

That is the extent of human existence.

We were given free will for this time that we are here.

That means we were never meant to make the same choices.

Stop fighting about the details.

Do not assume anything. You are walking in your shoes only.

You weren't sent here to be anyone's judge and jury.

That's left up to God.

I think I saw an angel yesterday.

No, not the kind you're thinking of.

I'm talking about one that is sent to test humanity.

I was in the car, and he was crossing the street in front of me at a light, and the moment I saw him I was struck by the tragedy of his appearance. No, he wasn't scarred or in a wheelchair, or anything obvious.

At first glance, one would just assume he was a vagrant.

He had on a pair of over-sized flannel pajama bottoms, and even though it was 98 degrees when I saw him, he had a black long-sleeve sweatshirt with the hood pulled over his head. I could barely see his face within the depths, but the sunken eyes and drawn expression were telling. As he walked, the wind blew those loose flannel pants against his body, and it was then you could see how thin he was. Like the pictures I saw when I was little, of the people being released from the Nazi concentration camps. That's what he looked like. The only feeling I got from him was despair.

I kept getting the question...'why am I still here?'

He broke my heart.

I wondered if he had ever been loved, or if he had family somewhere who didn't know where he was? If they were as sick at heart of losing him as he felt to be lost?

And then the moment was gone. He was across the street and walking north, and the light changed I was driving west, and then he disappeared.

I felt as if I'd just been tested and failed.

I saw him in his pain and did nothing.

The longer I drove, the more I thought. Maybe I wasn't supposed to give him a handout.

Maybe my test was not to sneer. Not to judge. Not to be disgusted by his condition. Maybe my test was just to say a prayer for him, which I did.

Every day we are faced with something or someone that makes us uncomfortable. Most times people look away, or comment in disgust.

We should never become comfortable with suffering, because when that happens, the next thing we do is ignore it.

We must remember always..."There but for the grace of God go I."

Had an electrician come out to change the bulbs in my living room light. It's a pretty fixture, but the dang thing is hanging from a 10 foot ceiling, and not even Scout could reach it. My step ladder wasn't tall enough. So the guy who came was at least 6'4" or taller with very long arms and legs. He climbed halfway up a really tall step ladder and changed them out in about a minute. Problem solved.

Did you know that you don't have to have a reason to be happy? You don't have to presents, or something special going on in your life. You can 'choose' to be, just because it's easier to walk through this world without anger, or dissatisfaction, or jealousy. You can have sad or bad things going on in your life, and feel threatened or overwhelmed, but if all of it is out of your control, let go of your need to fix it. Say a prayer for peace in your heart, add a prayer for healing, and then move through your day with grace and a smile. You draw to you that which you expect to happen. If you expect to be disappointed or sad, you will most likely be that because you 'told' the universe it's what you expect.

Life isn't about how much you can collect, but about what you can learn. The idea is not to repeat the same mistakes.

&

Going to have lunch with Kathy during her lunch period at school. It's gonna be Plain Jane baked potatoes from Jason's Deli today. And a Mama hug and kiss. Everyone needs a hug and a kiss.

I was thinking of the family dynamic this morning. It's so quiet in my house now, but I remember when it wasn't. And I remember how it was when I was growing up. Usually, one child in the family is the leader, one is the peacemaker, and one is either a rebel, or the baby, and keeps that role throughout their years at home. Even though there may, or may not be other children involved, these three dynamics are part of the whole. Their roles have little to do with age.

I was the oldest, and yet my younger sister was the leader, and the most vocal. I think my role would have been best described as the observer. It wasn't until I got older that I became the peacemaker/referee. There was a third child, our little brother, but he died the same day he was born, so there's no way to know what his role would have been.

In my son's family, his oldest child was definitely the leader but she was 4 1/2 years older than the next child. His second child was definitely the quiet one, like I was. She was the observer. She would sit and watch everyone talking and playing, without attempting to join in. It was almost as if she hadn't made up her mind as to whether they were worth her time. It was a funny thing to see from a baby not three years old. She has since become the one most assertive—it's like she's finally seen enough of the world to know what needs to be said and done now. Their youngest took on the role of baby of the family with all the rebel she had in her, and is finally growing into the young lady she is today.

My daughter only has one child, my grandson, Scout - the very Old Soul in our family.

One day when he was three, it was a hot summer day, his Mama was exhausted, and I picked him up and was taking him for ice cream. He was sitting in the seat beside me, already so tall for his age, his little hand patting the seat beside him in a happy, absent way, when he looked up at me and said, "Gwammy, isn't this a pwetty day?" I smiled. "Yes, it sure is, honey." He nodded, then looked up through the windshield toward the sky and said. "Just like the day, Jesus died." I nearly fell out of the car. I knew, without being told, that he was remembering another lifetime a long, long time ago. Being only three years from heaven, he hadn't yet forgotten his soul life. It was the day I also understood why he was so quiet, and such an individual being at such a young age. He was young in that body, but his soul was ancient. He's a teenager now, and walks through the world his way, without care for what the crowd is doing. He has no problem being in the company of adults, and says what he needs to say. I can't wait to see what he becomes in this life as he grows up.

My niece Crissy has three girls, and I don't know the dynamics of their family at home, but when I see them, the middle one is usually the leader, the oldest is already firmly set on a path she wants, and the youngest is the social butterfly-talker—the never-met-a-stranger-kind of kid.

I'm explaining all this to illustrate a point.

It doesn't matter what role you play, but you have to be your authentic self.

You should own who you are without apology. The world needs all of ua for balance. The leaders, the peacemakers, the ones with social skills, and the observers too. The quiet people, the silent people, the ones who have stepped out of the rat race that has become our lives. We all matter. We are the perfect recipe for the human race. Now all we have to do is act on it.

Many times the hardships we endure in this life are a direct result of our past one. We either lived a life outside of the boundaries of kindness and understanding, or we failed to understand the lesson, and so this life has been dedicated to learning what we failed at the time before.

When people ask "why me?", it would be so helpful if we could remember that we chose these lessons before we came, but we don't. We don't remember, because it would change our reactions to what we have been given to endure. Our strength of mind, our courage, and perseverance in spite of what seem like insurmountable odds, are the tools we are given when we are born. Some people throw up their hands and quit, then go through life without growth. Others bear down and get through it. But it's not JUST getting through it that matters. It's what you've learned once it's over that counts. Did it make you stronger, or did it make you more angry to have had to endure it?

Life is up to us. Always.

I only recently moved, and I'm finally going to get the new roof on my house. The previous owner has to pay for it, because it was from a hail storm that happened while they still owned it, and they denied the existence, and sold it as it was. I think they hoped it would pass without notice, but it's hard to miss the fact that nearly every house in this huge housing addition has had a roof replaced this year from the same storm. He has delayed and delayed compliance for months now. I moved in in May. It is nearly November. Such disappointing behavior from a man who is a preacher, but then maybe I expected too much. Daily I see proof of the fallibility of people who should have known and done better.

So today I am taking a deep breath, stepping out of everyone else's circus, and minding my own.

Be the kite in flight.

Not the mound on the ground.

Lift your head and see the world around you for what it is, not what you want it to be, and then adjust accordingly.

Yesterday I heard someone say "the leaves are dying".

I looked at the vibrant orange and red leaves still locked to their branches like an old lady's Easter bonnet pinned tight to her head, and I frowned. They didn't look dead to me. They were waving in the wind with a "here I am, look, look" feel. They did not represent any part of what I think of as coming to an end. Instead, this is their time of glory. And so it is so with people, we just don't always see it.

When I was young I saw gray hair and thought old.

And then I turned thirty, and saw myself with a full head of gray hair, and thought, no, hair color is not the signal of growing old.

When I was young, I thought people who walked with canes, or sat in wheelchairs were old.

And then I turned thirty and saw people of all sizes and ages, in different states of infirmity and thought, no, being unable to stand and walk on your own is not the signal for growing old.

When I was young, I thought people who couldn't remember things were old. And then I turned thirty and realized there were lots of things I could no longer remember as perfectly as I did before, but I wasn't old.

What I know now is that age is a state of mind, not a marker of time.

What I know now is that there is no such thing as death, only a move from one dimension to another.

What I know now is that we are constantly evolving, and life is forever.

In my mind, I will be like that tree with the glorious leaves, living in the moment, shining from the grace and love that is in my heart, waving at all of you, saying 'Here I am, see my smile. See the love shining through?"

I will never die, but one day I will move past you.

It will simply be a season coming to an end, getting ready for the next.

It is the never-ending circle of life.

Fear nothing, because you never walk alone.

Once I tried to be hypnotized because I needed the experience for a book I was writing. (STORM WARNING— under my pen name, Dinah McCall)

The man was a noted family counselor in our state, who also worked with the OSBI and police helping witnesses recall what they saw during crimes in progress. He had degrees all over the wall in his office. I made an appointment and when I arrived, told him why I was there, and what I needed from him in the way of information. He was delightful and happy to oblige.

He spent an entire hour trying to put me under. As hard as I tried, my subconscious would not relinquish the control. When he told me to focus on something at the top of a flight of stairs, I couldn't even see the freaking stairs. He tried every technique he knew, and was sweating, embarrassed, and apologetic, when it was over. I told him it was okay, and I did get the technical information I needed, but there was no personal experience to go with it.

So I will be a person who cannot be hypnotized.

This morning, I downloaded a meditation and listened to the beautiful voice instructing me how to be calm...

I cannot visualize what I'm being asked to see/do.

I can't see the river. I can't see it flowing right to left. I can't see my exhaled breaths turning into leaves and floating away. I can't focus like that. It's maddening, the only way I truly focus and be outside of myself, is when I'm writing.

So, I will not be a person who meditates either.

I will be a person who sleeps and dreams.

I will be a person who writes what she sees in her head.

I will be the maddening one percent of the world who does not follow direction. Not cannot, but will not.

I suspect it has something to do with my journey here.

I suspect it's because my heart, and my subconscious already knows the paths and secrets, and shows me the way when I need help.

I believe it's a fail-safe I was given before I came here.

Don't know why, but I'm sure it's necessary.

I Don't question the Maker.

He doesn't make mistakes.

🙢

So everybody's scared of more refugees, even though they were who populated this country, after they made refugees of the Native Americans, to whom this land first belonged.

I was scared the first time I had sex.

I was scared to have a baby.

I was scared when I told my second husband I wanted a divorce.

I was scared starting over at the age of 52.

I was scared when I had to have surgery eight different times in my life.

I was scared when a tornado blew down everything around us but our house.

I was scared when my son got tick fever, and then took so long to get well.

I was scared when my son got a staph infection and nearly died.

I was scared the night someone tried to murder my daughter.

I was scared when Timothy McVeigh blew up the Murrah Building in OKC.

I was scared on 9/11.

I was scared the first night I spent alone after my Bobby died.

I was scared when my mother started losing her mind, and I was the only one left to care for her.

I was scared when there wasn't enough money to live and pay taxes.

I was scared when I thought my daughter was going to wind up in a wheelchair because of so many issues with her back.

I was scared to start over—again—at the age of 72.

I was scared every time, and I got through it, and then I got over it.

Life is about facing fear, not maligning and terrorizing the people suffering it.

How dare you?

🙢

I never shop on Black Friday. Swore I wasn't going to, and then realized I needed to. I was stunned at how little traffic there was downtown, parking lots were hardly full at Wal-Mart and other shops. I didn't go as far as the Mall, which was surely busy, but who knows?

Called Kathy to see if she was free, and we wound up having soup together at Panera Bread. I'm home. Finished cleaning, and put all of the good dishes away from Thanksgiving dinner. Now it's me again.

Not a lot I wish to discuss today. Holding some things close to my heart. It always happens after a family gathering. No matter how fun the day was, and how many came, when they all finally leave and I'm in the house on my own again, I think of the ones who are no longer with us. I think it's because I handle their things. Use their dishes, the antique pie servers, the gravy boat that was a gift from my sister, the things from before. I put all of that away this morning and as hard as I try not to dwell, it makes me feel like I've put them away, too, even though they are always in my heart.

So, I'm going to go write. I can get lost in that world and turn loose of this one for a while.

Heard a conversation in a ladies room at Wal-Mart this morning. I felt so sorry for the woman telling her friend about a phone call from one of her grown children. I could tell how it had hurt her. The pain in her voice was evident. It seems one of her daughters had called, given her mother lists from all of her family as to what they wanted for Christmas, and then somehow had belittled what she'd gotten them last year, and expected her to buy from the list she was giving her.

That's not what Christmas is about. That's what buyers and sellers have done to the day. How horrible would that make you feel? So many people live from paycheck to paycheck, and the ones that don't live on credit cards. The woman's friend was aggravated on her behalf, and told her what she should do was not get them a thing. I didn't know her. But on Christmas I will think of her, and hope they do not hurt her again.

A gift should be received in the manner in which it was chosen, and when one is chosen from love, it is exactly what you need, whether you know it or not.

Had the best laugh with two total strangers today at Wal-Mart.

I'm sort of in the middle of the aisle looking on shelves, and an elderly couple came up behind me. I pushed my basket one way to get out of their way, and they accidentally pushed theirs the same way. I giggled, and then pushed it the other way to get out of their way, and they'd done the same thing again. I looked at the funny expressions on their faces, and burst out laughing. They started laughing too. I said, "If you'll give me a second, I'll just park my basket out of the way, and get in yours and ride with you. Looks like we're going the same way." They laughed again, and told a funny story about how fast brain cells die when your hair turns gray.

I said, "I'll tell you how bad I've become...I can drive down Main street here (It's mostly one-way in the old part of town) looking for a store. I see the store, realize I'm on the wrong side of the street, and traffic is too bad to try and get over, so I'll go around the block and wind up doing the same thing again. I am directionally challenged."

The old man turned and looked at his wife, pointed at her with a grin on his face, and she threw up her hands and said, "Okay...fine... I just did that but it wasn't all my fault!".

We laughed and laughed. I was still smiling when I left the store, and I didn't even know their names. There is so much joy to be had during any given day if you'll give yourself up to it, and be willing to laugh at yourself.

Ate a cup of tomato basil soup and a couple of pieces of Bruschetta (fresh tomato, mozzarella, pine nuts, and a drizzle of fig jam with balsamic vinegar on a toasted baguette) at La Baguette today. It is a bistro/French pastry shop with so amazing things to eat, or to buy and take home. Sometimes you just need to step out of your rut, and do something solely for yourself. I don't mind eating alone, although company would have been fun, but if you wait for the perfect moment, you miss the best parts of life. Spur-of-the-moment is how I roll.

Today I saw a young man staggering from one side of the sidewalk to another, with a small bag of food clutched against his chest. His face was red from the cold, his hands were filthy, and I could see every jerky breath he took, by the intermittent puffs of condensation in front of his face. I felt his fear. I felt his pain. And I know he's lost. Maybe not from a specific address, but from himself. He has lost his way in the world, and isn't strong enough to go look for the path. I said a prayer, and cried for a couple of blocks, because when you are that lost, only God can find you.

Pay attention to what children are telling you, for they still see the face of God.
  Places to be, things to do this morning.
  Something to remember.
  That which we cannot change, we do not take as our burden.
  Pray as you are led, and move on. Do not let someone else's sorrow light YOUR path.
  I say this as an Empath, because the most toxic thing about this gift, is bringing sadness and darkness into your world because you feel it.
  Last night I tried to watch a little television because I feel the need to stay current with the world in which I live, but finally gave up. The world is an ugly place right now. I won't turn away from it. I am not in hiding from it. But I refuse to let it move me off my path.
  I am here for a purpose, and it does not include hiding from the world because of someone else's actions. I wanted to hide away with my daughter, when a stranger broke in when she was spending the night with a friend, and tried to murder her years ago. But the truth of that was soon revealed. She not only saved herself, but her girlfriend she was staying the night with. Her safety later, depended upon how she perceived the world, not specifically where she was in it. She had to heal from the emotional trauma as best she could, and learn to live with how it had changed her.
  The bottom line is that there is no perfect place, If I want to get away from what's bad, all I have to do is live the best life I can, and it

will keep me in the light. Even if darkness finds me, the light I shine on it will be stronger, because I have faith that whatever happens to me, I am right where I was supposed to be. Either it will be another lesson, or God has come to take me home. I cannot control my fate, any more than I can turn back time. My destination was set before I came here, and I am guided by that destiny, no matter which paths I take to get there.

Don't be afraid.

It's just how life works.

❧

I slept more soundly last night than I have in years. Thank you, Leslie Draper. From what I read on your post this morning, I'd say you gave up way too much energy yesterday working healing for others. You are a blessing in this world. I have put off my trip to see my Little Mama though. Not feeling like making that long trip today.

I have come to understand that what I say, and how I react, manifests what I receive. I have to be thoughtful not to project panic onto an event that hasn't even happened. (I can thank my Little Mama for this ingrained behavior.)

I have to curb my knee-jerk reactions to news I don't like.

Instead of panic, I have learned to envision the answer. I see it, believe it, and know there will be a way to correct or get through it.

You might say this is ridiculous. You might think that is wishful thinking, and too simplistic to the world in which we live.

But that's just it. The world in which we live is complicated because we've made it so, with other people's rules and guidelines.

Truth doesn't seem to matter anymore if it's cloaked in sensationalism.

Instead of straightforward, we have convoluted everything, and then like mindless robots, react to the lies by hurting each other.

You are unique. There is no other person in the world like you. So how do you think fitting YOU into someone else's template is supposed to work?

We all follow the laws of the land, but we do not have to be alike in any other way. Celebrate diversity. Be the one who dares to be different, and celebrate your differences. I promise you, what you think is necessary and beautiful, is something I wouldn't be caught dead wearing, or looking like. I like it on you. But I won't like it on me. And that's how it's supposed to be. Different. Not alike.

I value people, not things. I cherish the simple life. I do not long for adventures. I am no longer the explorer. Those were my choices for many, many lifetimes... learning, learning, learning. I am how I am now, because of all I've been. I've seen it, lived it, done it. When you are an old soul, all you need—all you crave - is peace and quiet. And when that mindset is disturbed, I struggle to find my way back, and I resent what I have to deal with in this world, because I have dealt with it so many times before.

I have no more patience for inept. I have no patience for stupid. I abhor lies. I lose respect for people who pass them on, in an effort to sway others to how they want them to think and react. It is juvenile behavior.

How you behave, and how you think, and what you say, is exactly what you draw to you. If you foresee failure, it's yours. If you bemoan the bad luck in your life, and say you never seem to catch a break, then that will be your truth, because with every negative word that comes out of your mouth, you have set that into the universe as your reality.

I reject that. I will not step into that mindset.
Believe what you need.
See it in your hands.
Know it is already yours.
Have faith.

Going shopping with my Kathy girl after a while. We'll lunch and piddle around a bit. No big events, just spending a little time together. It's good for what ails us, and refuels our souls. That's what spending time with loved ones does for you. It's not just the blood connection, it's the love/soul connection.

Once again I slept deeply, I dreamed, but nothing weird. Just the usual stuff that's always in my head. Bought some Karo syrup yesterday to make peanut brittle, a tradition for the coming Christmas holidays. I try to send some homemade candy along with the gift I send to my literary agent every year. I've lost track of the days, but she may already be celebrating the Jewish holiday, our religious differences never matters to either of us, I get her a gift, and she gets me one, and we love and appreciate each other. She's been my agent for twenty-seven years. Only one I've ever had. One day she may retire, but I'll still be writing.

No retirement anywhere on the horizon for this ex-farmer's wife. I gave all that up for peace of mind.

Sent a text to Scout last night asking him about a certain t-shirt he would like for Christmas. He had already told his Mama it would be a good present, if anyone wanted to know. He makes me laugh. He funnels all the pertinent suggestion info about presents to his mama, who shares it with the family. So the text I sent him, involved specific color, long or short sleeve, and size.

So I said in the text...Mama says you want white.
Reply: yup.
Mama said short sleeve. You want short-sleeve in the winter?
Reply: yup.
Okay, I said, but is this size correct? And I type it in.
Reply: yup.
Was he being rude? No. He was multitasking. Playing XBox with his stepbrother, and having a text conversation with me at the same time. More power to him.

I sure couldn't do all that. He cracks me up.

Yesterday I was thinking about children who've grown up without a mother. It was something I saw my niece, Crissy, had posted that put me in her shoes. It made me think about all of the milestones those children meet, without their mother helping them understand, and cheering them on. And then when they are grown, all of the times they needed someone to remind them they're okay. Someone to hug them when life gets hard. Someone they could call for advice. Someone who loved them regardless, unlike in-laws, and other relatives who don't think in that context, or don't care about how isolated those people are. My heart has been sad for Crissy ever since I saw the post. I was in and out of her life after my sister, Diane, died as much as they would let me. Mother and I both were. But she missed so much, and needed so much, and didn't have the option to reach out for help, because she was so little when it happened (five years old), that she didn't know she could.

By the time she got old enough to know, she was already a hardened survivor. She had to learn everything alone. And that's still happening. And she's only one of millions. Forgive me Crissy, for using you as an example today, but I personally think you rock. You are the best mother, and the best person ever, and you have so earned the right to be proud of everything you do, because in spite of all we tried to help you do, you figured it out all alone.

It's never about the tragedy itself. It's always about the lesson.
Did it break you, or did it make you stronger?
Did it change your perception of survivors?
People who suffer most, are usually the first to help others, because they remember the pain.
The old saying, 'you can never go home' isn't true.
Home is where the heart is.
Home is you returning to the source.
Home is forever you.

꼬

We have all mentioned at one time or another, about being frustrated with daily posts on Social Media about inflammable subjects. I have spoken more than once about how hateful people can be on here, and we are all taken aback now and then at what someone says to us, or says to someone else.

But it occurred to me this morning that there is actually a positive aspect to witnessing the hate and prejudice. The anonymity of Social Media has allowed them to take off their sunglasses, remove the masks they hid behind, and remove the blinders we all wore regarding them. Familiarity blinded us to many things, not the least of which were dark and angry hearts. This has actually performed an unexpected service, in that we have been shown the true feelings, and buried prejudices of people we thought we knew.

It was a hard lesson to learn. A shocking revelation for me many times over, but it has also cleared a path for me to know those aren't the people I need in my life—not in person, and not even in a virtual world.

Social Media has shown us who passes on the lies, and who preaches hate, and who judges the world by appearance and wealth, and the color of our skin, by the things they share, and the words they use when they give an opinion.

I think I will have a whole different outlook about Social Media from now on.

It may be a venue for fun and communication, but it has also pulled an entire group of people onto a public stage. It is no longer possible to hide how you really feel from the rest of the world.

So... think about that the next time you have a knee-jerk reaction to something that is intrinsic prejudice, and you click Like because you think it's funny.

What you don't realize is that "it's only funny to others like you."

As my mother would have said, "Your petticoat is showing."

You have revealed your true self to the world.

My nightly visitor arrived on time last night.

My Bobby.

Always, just as I have gone to bed. Always waiting until I have closed my eyes. And then in my darkened bedroom, he makes the face of my phone light up. It's like a search light in a darkened corner. So, while I don't get the words from my visitor, I DO get the message. "I am here," he's saying. That's when I smile. "Thank you for letting me know you have arrived," I say, and the moment I respond, the light goes off.

Mostly, communication with Spirit is just about paying attention.

Denise is here scurrying around sweeping the dust off my ceiling fans, and off the high places in my house. She is going to have to mop up red glitter from everywhere in the kitchen though. I tried but failed miserably to get it all. It was on a tube of wrapping paper I bought. Scout opened it to use on one of the Christmas presents he was wrapping, and when he did, he started shouting "Oh no! no freakin' way!" I come running, and see this look of horror on his face. "What's wrong?" I asked. He points. "Glitter! It's everywhere!"

Well, it wasn't really everywhere, but it WAS on him, which was, I guess, everywhere that mattered to him. I laughed. As soon as he finished wrapping he had to go change his shirt. So. Lesson to Grammy. Scout does NOT do glitter.

I made fudge last night. I will make peanut brittle multiple times today.

And I will nap. Multiple times if I want to. Because I can.

I used to look at people who succeeded in life, as people who kept getting the lucky breaks. I thought hard work and sacrifice would 'make things' happen for me, and then wondered why it never did. It never dawned on me that I had already told the Universe I was going to fail by bad-mouthing myself, saying I never win anything, saying I'm afraid it won't happen, predicting my failure long before I ever gave something new a try. And because I did that, it was exactly what happened. Life gives you what you believe you deserve.

Having a poor me, woe as me, never get a break, belief system is what puts you in that rut, and unless you change how you look at life, and what you expect of yourself, what you know you can do, then you will live and die in that same mind-set. It wasn't until I took that leap of faith, and moved me out of what was hurting me, and onto a path of freedom, that things began to change. Even now, I have still had struggles to believe I am capable of whatever I think I can do, but I'm getting there. What I do know is that I am here, and while I draw breath in this place, I manifest my own success.

Nothing is forever except the light within you.

※

Up until 1:30 a.m. editing. Had to quit and go to bed. Back up at 8:30 a.m. to finish. I just hit Send on the manuscript. It is now in the hands of my Sourcebooks editor.

I want to sleep until tomorrow, but I can't. Going to a party at Little Mama's care center .It's from 4 to 6 p.m. After dark, and right when all the residents will likely be going into Sundowning mode, which makes them angry or disruptive, and also an hour drive home in heavy traffic. Sure wish they'd had it earlier in the day.

Kathy and I are going from here. Crissy and her girls will meet us there.

It will all be good and I will be glad I went.

When you begin to feel as if life is too much, you just yell Stop the Presses, and give some of it back.

Savor where you are at that moment, and close your eyes.

Remember the peace of slower days and simpler lives.

It's not gone.

You just buried it in too much.

※

Scout spent the night with me.

I'm taking him Christmas shopping for his family this morning.

It's a tradition with us that's been ongoing since he was a little guy.

Best part about all of it? Other than getting to spend time with him, of course.

Seeing the thoughtfulness he puts into each gift.

He starts out already knowing what he wants for them.

No grabbing the first thing he sees to get it over with.

He 'sees' them in the gift.

I've said it before, and I'll say it again until the day I die.

My grandson is a very, very old soul.

So we will shop a bit, and have lunch together, and I will listen when he talks, because he is like me, not much of a talker. If he has something to say, it is usually worth hearing.

My children, Chris, Kathy, and Crissy, are the beats of my heart.

Their children are the jewels God put in my crown.

Living a steadfast life is how we're meant to be.

It isn't necessary to be the hero all the time.

A structure cannot stand tall for the pinnacle to be noticed, without the strong but simple building blocks that bear the weight of all.

Scanning through Social Media for the first time in two days, and seeing so many

Christmas posts in varying degrees of joy or sadness.

Lots of beautiful family pictures.

Lots of posts about people doing 'their' own thing on this day.

Lots of posts about personal time spent with just a loved one, or some alone.

Lots of posts about people in grief.

And some wonderful posts about people getting engaged, or welcoming new babies into their lives.

And as I read them, laughing at their comments, or tearing up for the sadness I felt in the words, I realized there was a pattern repeating itself over and over.

It's called the circle of life.

At any time, somewhere in the world, someone has died, someone has just been born. Someone is rejoicing. Someone is grieving.

It has been happening in this fashion since the beginning of us.

And so it will continue as long as we exist.

In an odd and comforting way, it makes sense to understand that nothing lasts forever. Happiness will change, but in that same circle, grief gives way to peace.

It is a thing to hold onto if you're grieving. Know that this is what's now in your life, but there are better things to come, because nothing ever stays in place.

The earth revolves.

The planets are in orbit.

The day turns to night and back again.

We are born and we die.

Everything revolves...because that's how we evolve.

We grow up, and we grow old. Circle. Circle. Circle.

Grab the ring and hold on.

While we're here, it is a memorable ride.

It sleeted all night. The wind was strong. I prayed the tall pine tree in my neighbor's back yard would not fall on my house. Snow never made it to my side of town. Just the freezing rain and sleet. I still have power, which means I have heat and lights. So grateful.

Everyone is reminiscing about the events of the past year, but I've already lived those days. I am looking forward.

I don't make New Year's resolutions, because I never kept them, so why set myself up for an emotional failure? I will choose each day to set my course, allowing for what is happening around me. Like a ship that sets sail on deep, dark treacherous waters, I will begin each day with the faith that I will also float above the fray.

A thought occurred to me this morning that I have already set firmly in my mind and heart. I will no longer see disheveled appearances and unkempt bodies.

I will look at the faces, and see them as part of the whole that is our humanity.

I will look for the sorrows and disappointments that took them down.

I will not take another's anger as leveled at me, but know they are railing at the world around them, and I just happened to step onto their path.

I will look for the child in the man, instead of what the man has become.

I will remind myself daily to thank God for my life, instead of praying to him constantly to fix it.

I will not ask for more, when I already have enough.

I accept that I manifest what comes to me.

I know I have the power within me to live for the highest good.

I do not mistake my gentle heart for weakness.

I have faith that God is with me.

I know of angels.

They walk beside me every day.

They are the whisper in my ear warning me to step away.

That sense of self-preservation that tells me to run when I see nothing of which to fear.

The things you call strokes of luck that you missed being in a wreck, are the angels keeping us safe.

During the heartbreak we suffer when we lose someone we loved, or the devastation of having to start over in life when all has been lost, it is the angels who hold us up, and hold us close.

They are God's voice of reason.

They are all God's love.

They give us strength and faith all the days of our lives.

This is the road map of a life.

🙢

This is a blanket Happy New Year to all of my Social Media friends. Please don't feel like you need to respond. I just wanted to get it posted. I already know what a great bunch of people you are, because I already blocked and deleted the radicals and the nuts. (that's a joke) I love you and you know it.

If we've never met, then take in the knowledge that someone you don't 'really know' thinks you rock.

And if we're friends, then you already know how much I value your friendship.

And if we are kin, well, despite what you may or may not think of me, you're freakin' stuck with me anyway cause blood's thicker than water.

I'm lifting a Diet Dr. Pepper at midnight to all of us.

It snowed in the night and is still snowing a bit.

I got out to pick up a package at the post office, and a prescription at the pharmacy, and now I am home. Sending prayers to those in need.

Sending strength to those who are faltering in body or in faith.

Sending hope to those who feel trapped.

Sending faith to those who feel they are all alone.

I've said this so many times, but it is on my heart to say it again today, because someone is so very afraid.

So here's your truth—even if you don't know it—even if you don't believe it:

You bring to you, that which you manifest.

If you are spending your days in fear of something, you are leaving yourself open to it becoming your truth. Always think of each aspect of your life as a positive. Even when it's not at that moment, thank the Universe for your healing and blessings.

Picture yourself standing in an open doorway with a smile on your face, waving at health and blessings to welcome them in, as you would a dear friend or beloved family member.

If you can accept that you will have the strength for whatever life has in store for you, you will move through life without fear.

Fear is your enemy for everything, but when you are sick, it will defeat you. It will slow healing, and sometimes stops it.

It's like going to a doctor, needing the skill and medicine he has to make you better, but you're too afraid to go in the door, so you bemoan your situation without being able to do anything about it. Fear has held you hostage.

I have been afraid many times, and what I've learned in through all those years was that my fear did not help me through any of it. It just made it worse.

It's all about attitude. No matter what, hold up your head, put a smile on your face, and open that door. Let the Universe into your life. Know that a greater power exists within you, but you have to acknowledge it to set it free.

Last night was unsettling. I knew it would be despite all of my intentions not to go to bed with a heavy heart. As an Empath, it's almost impossible for me to put hurt aside. I'm not good at blocking, so I'm usually just washed away with all of it. My sleep was intermittent. I tossed and turned, and had to concentrate so hard not to relive that visit with Little Mama yesterday. One more day to get through with it still haunting. I gave up trying to make sense of her continuing hold onto a life of 98 years, existing without cognizance, with nothing but pain from constant falls and a continuing mantra that she wants to go home.

I just live through it and keep going.

People keep saying how lucky I am that I can still see her, and talk to her, and hug her. It isn't lucky. It is a bitter trial we are both living through. I can't talk to her like they think. She's nearly deaf, so I yell, and she pretends to hear, but I can tell she doesn't. When I hug her, those tiny arms snake around my neck, and she is whispering in my ear the whole time, 'take me home, will you take me home?" That isn't joy. That is our hell on earth, because I can't take her where she wants to go.

People who have loved ones with this same horrible disease understand. But trust me, this is not something to be happy about, or rejoice that they are still lost and suffering. So... that was yesterday and this is today. And life goes on until it stops. I will have a positive attitude today until something knocks me off my happy chair, and then I will have myself a great big fit first, because that's what my people do... and then pull myself together and pretend I'm all Zen, until it becomes my truth.

Intention is worth half the battle.

Going to begin another Chapter today. I finished the one I was working on last night. Going to see the movie, Revenant, starring Leonardo DeCaprio, with Kathy and family Saturday afternoon. I'm so excited to see that. I loved the old movie out of Hollywood that was also this story. That movie was Jeremiah Johnson, starring Robert Redford. This movie is exactly the kind of movie I like to see. I'm not much of a fan of contemporary movies where people are in a city, and they just move from one scene to another talking and talking, or in and out of bed and talking some more. Kind of hurts my eyes to sit through all that. Isn't it funny how different we all are? Kathy has always loved any movies that have anything to do with the Mafia. I think I teased her once by telling her that her guardian angel must look like Joe Pesci.

Weather is changing here. The three straight days of high 50s are gone. Cold front came in...chances of rain and snow, or just snow through Monday. But it is winter, so it's to be expected.

Some people make choices every day. What to eat. What to wear. Where to park. How to respond to questions. Whether or not to respond to degrading and belittling comments, racists or gender-style insults.

Other people blast through a day without thought, ripping through lives like a bullet ripping through flesh, without care for who, or how many they hurt.

I used to wonder what made people like that tick? What happens to someone that makes them like that? Then I realized that wounded people are like wounded animals. They strike out at any who come too close, because they already know they are weakened by what hurt them...(in a human's case, by the spiritual or emotional wounds) and that they are simply protecting themselves from further hurt by keeping everyone away. Basically moving them out of their paths... because life has already taught THEM that people cannot be trusted.

It is something to think about the next time you encounter someone in that state of mind. Maybe say a quiet prayer for them, and move on without taking whatever they said or did to heart.

Maybe, if you can, see them as the wounded, bleeding child who nobody rescued.

Secrets abound. There is a mystery afoot!

Ha.

I always wanted to say that... that something was afoot. I didn't always know what it meant, but when I got older I figured it out. I don't think it's an American term. Sounds British. I think Americans would say something like, "what the hell's going on?"

Whatever. I still have new things stirring, so it is a good thing.

It's odd how our culture has this need to divide people up and put them in different niches. Blue collar—white collar. The arts, which include actors—artists—writers, and all of the subsets that go with this. Career minded—day laborers. Common—rare. And then they separate us even more by calling certain careers/jobs as being creative, and then others as skilled. Like one comes from the soul, and the other from learning.

It makes me crazy because everything is from the soul, and we all learn, and we all create. From turning a messed up landscape into a sight most pleasing to the eyes, to designing and making an elaborate cake, or a designer dress. From taking old clothes and turning them into quilts that not only keep us warm, but hold the memories of the people who wore them.

All day, every day, creation is at work. Some things are coming down, and it will take creative thinking to build them back up. Some peoples' lives hinge on the creative thinking of a surgeon faced with a an ill patient, and a disease he cannot diagnose.

We look at things around us and laugh at the accidental happenings that turn out to be fortuitous. But nothing happens by accident. The Universe knew it was coming. We were the only ones who didn't see it coming. We had forgotten this was part of our path. We are wondering what in God's name made us think this would ever be a good learning experience?

The next time you admire and long for a work of art to hang on your wall, while you look down on the man who unclogs your sink, or long for money and fame, when you are already at the height of personal joy, you need to rethink your priorities. You need to take a step back and look at where you are and what you're asking.

It might already be there.

❧

I made a choice today to do one thing at a time.

I decided I'm less stressed when a thing is finished, rather than two or three things working at once, but nothing is done. So, I made Kathy's cookies. Then I made the vegetable soup. Then I loaded up the food and ran an errand, then had lunch with her. Came home and cleaned up the kitchen. Have to pick Scout up after school, and take him home. Then I'm coming home and working on my book. I will finish one chapter today. I have many things that need to be done, but since I can't complete them today, then they will wait on my mood. I want to take a nap, but there is no time in THIS day to do that, because of picking up my boy, so I'll go to bed earlier tonight.

Found a penny from Bobby when I was running my errands. I picked it up with a smile and dropped it in my purse. "Hey baby. I'm glad you are riding shotgun today," I said, and off we went.

Nothing is promised. Nothing is for certain.

So don't get all upset because something didn't go your way.

All it means is something better for YOU is coming at another time. The Universe always has your best interests at heart, but not always in your timeline. Expecting things to go your way because you think you are deserving, or when you believe you are entitled, or when you demand that YOUR needs be met...just slides you down the chute to where the darkness dwells. Selfishness, lies, even white lies are negatives, and anything negative is without light. Stay positive, even when it's a disappointment.

Understand you haven't been forgotten.

It's all about the timing.

❧

Using someone else's success as a reason for your failure is a cop-out.

Expecting to fail before you ever start, is exactly what will happen. Everything we do is a choice.

You cannot continue to blame others for your lack of education, your lack of skill, your inability to create, your refusal to try something new, on anyone but yourself. Why? Because for every excuse you throw out, someone will point out a success story of another who began life in far worse conditions than you, and despite all odds, succeeded. Why? Because they wanted out bad enough to do something about it.

I have a sweet FB friend who is on that road. She's in a miserable situation, and you know what she's doing? Going back to school online. No, she doesn't have the money, but she can get student loans, and while it would appear she doesn't have the time because she already has a job, she's going to make time. Because she wants a change. My hat's off to her.

I was in a similar situation in my life once. Married with no money of my own. Working hard every day as a farmer's wife, working in the field alongside my husband, planting a huge garden, and putting up food by canning and freezing to keep down grocery costs, making my own clothes and some of theirs, doing everything I knew how to get along, and no matter how hard I worked, it wasn't enough. I was never enough. Nothing I did mattered. Everything we owned was in HIS name. The house, the land, the cars, the machinery. If he could have, he would have listed me as property when he filed taxes. I felt like a shadow, and his presence blocked out the sun upon me until I was invisible. And then one day I snapped. And I sat down and began writing a book and the rest is history.

I know people who have walked away from lucrative jobs because they were miserable. They chose a life with less money just for the privilege of living it joyfully.

Every one of us came with a gift. It's up to you, whether you use it as part of your livelihood, or whether it's something that's just a part of you. But there is always a way to change your life, or change your lifestyle. You just have to take that leap of faith to do it.

Yes, it's scary to leap when you don't know what's beneath you. And yes, you can make that choice to stay. Some live with the 'better the devil you know, than the one you don't' belief.

Yes, bad health can keep you from doing what you want or need. But in those instances, you still have a choice as to how you deal with it. We all have the friends who go through horrific cancer treatments with what I can only call, a miraculous outlook. They have made a choice not to bring everyone else down around them, through their huge hearts and faithful spirits. We have also known people who hated God the moment they were diagnosed, and died cursing him. It's all about choices. No matter where we are, or the condition in which we find ourselves, we have choices as to how we face them.

My sister, Diane, was an amazing woman, and I'm going to leave you with a line from her own work ethic.

"I may die poor, and I may die sick, but I will be at work somewhere when it happens."

Yes, she died. But she never quit fighting the good fight.

In the generations to come, people will look back on this time, and use it as a teaching point, as one of those pivotal moments in history where we could have changed things, and didn't.

If nothing changes for the better, we will be blamed for ignoring the last chance to impact climate change.

We will be blamed for squabbling instead of problem-solving.

We will be blamed for the political unrest.

This will be the era humanity let the power-mongers win.

They will chide us for trying to pray our way out of problems.

We will be derided for being the herd of sheep who thought it would be a good idea to be led by a wolf.

They will call us violent, ignorant people who had centuries and centuries of evolution and civilization to get it right, and in the end we were still fighting about weapons when we died.

What a heritage we will be leaving behind.

All of the technology and advancement that was around us, and the things we valued over all were money and power.

I'm doing what I can to foster mercy and grace—to seek to surround myself with others who cherish health and happiness above all else.

The thing about being human is this... we will destroy ourselves far faster than anyone else can do it for us.

Welcome diversity.

Accept that we are all God's children.

Some of us are good. Some of us are bad.

You do not dismiss an entire race of people just because of zealots, any more than you would throw away an entire week's worth of food, if you found a bug in the grocery sack.

We are all born naked and helpless, and no matter what causes our deaths, the end result is still the same.

It's what you do between Alpha and Omega that marks your presence and your passing.

Make it count.

§

I used to lie on my back out in the back yard with my sister, Diane, and watch the clouds changing shapes before our eyes. The first one of us to get tired of the game was usually Diane. She wasn't as prone to daydreams as I was, but I could never, in a million years, imagined the path my life would take me.

So today is my grateful day.

Grateful that I survived the bad times.

Grateful that I learned how to set aside the sad times.

Grateful that life has given me perspective...a much clearer perspective than seeing shapes in clouds.

Perspective on the human behavior:

Being a stickler for proper language, and loudly pointing out about people missing punctuation, are ways some people use to reassure themselves. It has less to do with judging the other person's intelligence, and more to do with proving something to yourself. That you know better, do better, live better, than the way you were raised.

God bless all of you who learned how to step out of a denigrating way of life.

Constantly changing your looks, your hair, your style, the decor of your home, even constantly changing the dishes you eat from, doesn't have anything to do with wanting to be a fashion maven. It's from a childhood lived in shame and trauma. It's about wanting to be seen by the people you love that you ARE pretty, that you DO matter, and that you will not disappoint them again. God bless all of you. It wasn't you who was at fault. It was the fault of the people who broke you. But you don't have to stay in the mindset.

Hating every day of your life, resenting everyone around you, and failing to believe there is hope, falls on the shoulders of the people who brought you into this world. You were not nurtured. They fed you, but they did not show you love.

Maybe they didn't know how, but as an adult, you should now see the cycle in which you're caught, and if you want to live life in a different way, then change what you're doing. God has always loved you. Find your joy. It's in all of us...somewhere.

Being afraid of looking old doesn't mean you're really afraid of losing you looks. You're not getting a face lift because you hate your wrinkles. You aren't getting a boob job because your breasts went south, and you hate your looks. You are afraid to die. You don't believe there is another plane of existence. You think this is it...once you die, it's over.

But that's not so. This place...Earth...is just a trip you're on. One of these days you're going to get enough of the traveling, and WANT to go home. And when you do, you will be welcomed back with open arms, and you'll laugh from the joy, and be stunned by how silly you were to have forgotten that you came from The Light, and all of this will be nothing more than a fond memory.

Perspective comes with age, and life-experience.

But yours.

Not someone else's.

Believe your truth.

Believe that you are beautiful now, and that you matter now, and it doesn't matter what you have or where you live, you are loved.

Life moves too fast now.

We live in a greedy country, and often live unhappy lives because we think we haven't measured up. But measured up to what?

Who's rule of thumb are you living by?

We're missing everything that would renew us.

We cram something into every minute of our waking days, just so we can reassure ourselves that we are busy, and making the most of our lives, and accomplishing great things and working, working, working, to make the most money, and live in the biggest house, with the biggest mortgage, which makes us work harder, and spend even less time than before, with the people who are supposed to matter most.

What in the world are we trying to prove?

That being richer makes us more important?

That having a title after our name gives more credence to our existence?

Yes, if you're rich, you can buy a bigger, fancier tombstone when you die and yes, if you have educated yourself to the point of ridiculous just so you can hang more degrees on a wall... like the sign that says the one who dies with the most toys wins.

But when you die, you die.

What are you doing while you're still here to refill the well that is your soul?

What kind of a legacy will you leave behind, if the people who are supposed to love you don't even know what makes you laugh? What kind of a life lesson are you teaching your children, if all they can remember of their childhood is that you were never there.

It's easy to marry.

It's easy to make babies.

But family isn't about the number of people bearing your last name.

What you have created…you owe allegiance to, whether it be a multi-million dollar company, or the people you call your family.

Take a step back and look at who you are, where you're at, an what matters most.

If your priorities are screwed up, unscrew them.'

Wake up with joy.

Appreciate what you have.

The best part of life is free.

Denise is here cleaning…Have I mentioned how much I love Monday mornings? My home is going to smell SOOOOOO good…home again, home again, jiggity jig. Talking about the delightful sides of life today.

Today is my granddaughter Logan's 21st birthday. She is one of the joys in my world. This afternoon I must make cherry kolaches for her. Never a birthday cake. Just kolaches. At least it will be fun. I love to bake. My youngest granddaughter, Leslie, is the cook in that family, and I am happily passing on all the cooking knowledge to her that she wants. Chelsea, the oldest, was the first grandchild I had, and one of the first things we did together in the kitchen was making kolaches. My son, Chris, who is their daddy, likes several flavors of fillings, but cherry is his favorite as well.

A lost art:

Sending thank you notes. I am guilty of this, too. Too often I just write a thank you via email or messaging. My Grand would frown. It was not how I was raised.

She used to sit down at the kitchen table every morning after breakfast was over and the kitchen cleaned up, and write letters. She'd get the small pad of lined paper and a good ballpoint, or sometimes just a pencil, and write just as if she was talking. I wasn't much more than eight or nine, but I knew to be quiet at that time. I knew when she was telling of something serious, because her eyebrows would knit...and I knew when she was relating a funny story, because she would unknowingly be smiling as she wrote. When she was finished she would put a stamp on each one, and send me to the mailbox at the end of the driveway, to put them in the box "for the carrier" as she would say, always reminding me to put up the flag before I came back. A sweet memory from my childhood...such simple delights.

Nothing lasts forever except shoes and purses you don't like.

When I was little, my sister Diane and I would get tired playing and flop down in the grass to rest. She laid on her belly watching ants in the grass and ladybugs crawling and the dragonflies darting above her head.

I laid on my back watching clouds, making up vignettes of great daring, and remember the times when I could still fly in my sleep. I don't remember when those dreams stopped, but I once could soar above the treetops, and take off from mountain peaks to fly home before sunrise. Dreamwalkers are real. I am one.

Family coming to visit, and me hearing laughter from all over the house is my joy.

In the Bible there is a verse. 'Joy cometh in the morning'.

I await joy from any time of the day, and welcome the light and energy that kind of emotion brings.

When you look in the mirror, and see nothing but disappointment in your eyes, and age on your face, you are missing the most important fact of all.

It's not where life has taken you, but that you are still here to tell the tale.

I have this overwhelming urge to weep.

Which always means to me, someone is suffering today. It's part of my life.

Don't anyone tell me what's wrong. I don't want to know what's happening.

It is enough that it's making me sad.

Just know that I am also now praying for you.

Praying for your burden to be lifted—for you to find your own way out of the pain.

Pain flows through me, but does not settle.

I am a sieve, and not a kettle.

Going to get my hair done in a bit.

That, and keeping my nails done, are my only luxuries. I don't need anything. I don't want anything.

Some people live in a world of their own making, innocent of everything going on around them. They are the fragile souls. The delicate beings who cannot cope with the ugliness of what is around them, and so they create what they need within a world of their own making. Some people call them stupid. Some people refer to them as airheads or flighty. Some people don't understand that it isn't a choice for them to be that way. It is a necessity, or they would surely die from what they see and hear.

Understanding that we can all be ourselves, and still be accepted and loved is a wish, even a goal to work toward, but it has yet to become a fact of our world.

You! All you people who have been voted into office...you do not sit higher than me. You are not worth more than me. I do not hold you in higher esteem because you have a title before or after your name. You are not someone I look up to. I pay your salary. You represent ME...

DO YOUR JOB.

That is all.

❧

Awake again every three hours last night, up and down. Up and down. I wake up tired and decided to sleep in this morning, and stayed in bed (mostly) until 10:00 a.m.

I've been up an hour and ready to start what's left of this day.

Something I talked about with my Bobby and the angels last night.

I tell them every night I am so tired of hurting...and then I add...I also know many people hurt worse, and have hurt far longer than me, some of them most of their lives, and I pray for them nightly. But last night I also told them there is something I have come understand.

I can empathize and pray for, and weep for the pain and sadness of others, and still regret what's happening to me. I don't have to put myself on some sliding scale of misery, before I am allowed to suffer my own.

I don't accept that their truth diminishes mine. I am allowed to be sad, and frustrated, and feel like this misery will never end, because this is my truth.

We each have a life to live, but to do it well, we must acknowledge everything we go through with understanding and sympathy for ourselves, as well as ourselves.

Humanity is fallible.

When we are doing our best, it is all we can do.

I don't want to be some long-suffering old lady who has decided her next step in aging is to begin ticking off what hurts.

The last thing that went through my mind before I fell asleep was, This too shall pass.

One of my Grand's favorite songs to play on the piano in church was, Living on the Promises. I can still hear my Auntie Lorraine, singing the verses. I remember the words just like I remember all of my life. There were good times, and there were hard times.

This is one of my hard times, and this too shall pass.

No matter how many miles I might walk in someone else's shoes, I will never fully understand what makes them tick, because that is not my job. My job is to do my thing. Mind my business. Not the business of everyone else.

Good Sunday morning to all of you.

This morning is amazing. It feels like fall.

It's in the 50s right now. I can hardly believe it. Highs will be in the mid-80s today.

The perfect weather!

Prayers still going up for everyone in fire danger in California, and all those still coping with the 1000 year flood in Louisiana. Both of these events brought catastrophic losses for people. My heart goes out to all of you.

I said aloud to the shadows as I began to wake this morning.

You can hide in the darkness with your pain and your diseases.

You can hurt me and mine until I take my last breath,

But you will never be evil enough, or dark enough, to cover my light.

Amen.

And that is my prayer for all of you today.

Hold the faith.

When it feels like all has been taken from you, hold the faith.

When you hurt to the point of screaming, hold the faith.

When you cannot see a light anywhere in the darkness—look inward and hold the faith.

Fought a hard battle last night and lost miserably.

The Bed—winner.

My Sleep--loser.

So tired. Cried. Felt Bobby's hands on my back and legs. Cried some more.

It rained in the night. A much needed blessing.

It's daylight and college football game day.

Entertainment while I write.

Experience comes from living life.

Wisdom comes from learning what not to repeat.

Understanding comes from listening.

Empathy comes from the heart.

Strange how some people rationalize their behavior.

A woman sees a man drop a five dollar bill as he's walking out of a store.

But she grabs it and puts it in her pocket, instead of running to catch him and return it.

Same woman then turns around two days later is out shopping, and loses a credit card, or maybe a phone, and carries on about how dishonest people are, and how they will steal you blind.

What's strange?

She doesn't see the correlation between what she did, and what happened to her later.

Karma.

Live and learn.

Time flies with childhood, painting memories of fleeting laughter, sticky kisses, baby hands pulling at the legs of your pants begging to be picked up.

Shrieks of disapproval as only a baby can make.

The engaging, addicting sound of their laughter as you repeatedly make a fool of yourself, just to hear it again and again.

Celebrating their milestones as they learn to hold a spoon, or drink from a cup.

Stories read as eyes grow heavy.

Rocking them against your breast, as their eyes finally close in sleep.

The satisfaction and relief of getting them safely through one more day of childhood.

Knowing you would die for them without thinking about it.

Praying that choice never comes to pass.

Never wanting to give up the journey, and yet knowing the day will come when they won't need you anymore.

That's when you know you got it right.

Last night I dreamed I was a kid again, living out on the farm south of my Grand and Grampy's house. Everyone in the area always called our farm the old Dukes place. In my dream I was standing at the back fence separating the yard from the barn lots. In the distance I could see my Daddy walking out in the pasture, calling the cows up to milk. Once he got them started home I could hear him whistling "Red Sails in the Sunset," an old country song. My Daddy could whistle any song...he had a good voice, too. I could see him so clearly in my dream... those long legs and broad shoulders...his black, shiny hair. I don't know why I was waiting for him. But I was so happy in that moment... And then I woke up.

So I had that moment back in time with Daddy...and me being able to see him, but not talk to him is our truth. The distance between us now is a whole other dimension.

I am blessed to have learned at an early age not to be critical, or judge others, in any way. Part of it came from being the child of an alcoholic. I knew my Daddy as a whole, complicated person. Others only saw him as the drunk and judged him. There are always two sides to a story, and two sides to people, as well. The public side you see...and the truth of who they really are.

Never set someone on a pedestal.

It's too easy to fall off.

Kathy is coming to get me as soon as VIP Nails opens up today, and take me to get my nails done. Lord love a duck, they are so long it's been difficult to type. I haven't gone on my own because there's no room for my walker, (awaiting a hip replacement) and I don't know if I can manage with just the cane. This way I can use my cane and hang onto her.

I will be so happy when all of this is behind me.

BUT... I have already seen and understood the reason for this lesson.

I am being taught another level of empathy. This is a hard and painful way to live...and yet I know people who have never lived any other way.

That isn't just strength of character...this takes you down to the bone in patience, pain level, and learning how to move through a mobile world, in an immobile way. Learning how to live beyond what your physical body won't allow you to do.

My hat is off to all of you who have found your groove within physical limitations and endless pain.

I have never been one to look for rainbows, or take too much stock in happy ever-after, even though I write about them daily. Maybe that's why writing romance fits me. I want to live in a happy-ever-after world, and so I do it in my stories.

It's not that I'm not a romantic... because I am.

I love to the last fiber in my soul, and I do not let death separate me from the ones I love.

It's not even about me thinking I should be practical.

I see the rainbow. I see its beauty. But I don't search for them. I'm just grateful when one appears.

It's more about me finding the safe path.

I can't stay on a path if I'm always looking up.

But I can stay focused if I'm always looking ahead.

Live in the now with good heart and gratitude, but with an eye on tomorrow being a better day.

For some children, when you are young, time and distance are just words. The future means nothing to you because you are so busy living in the moment trying to survive what life is dragging you through, that you don't want to know what happens next. You don't want to think about seventy more years of what's happening now. You aren't living...you are fighting to exist.

The burden of being responsible is often thrust upon the shoulders of the eldest child... or the oldest daughter, when there's an absentee parent or two.

What hopes they may have had for a better life are sacrificed for the sake of the others, and no one understands except someone who's living a similar life.

By the time the babies are grown and gone, the caregiver is so tired and broken, that changing a way of life is not only too far out of their reach, but they're too tired to care.

They accept that they have missed their chance.

Some become bitter. Others have come to terms with the sacrifice, and take pride in the small steps of success their younger siblings make.

What no one else knows... what cannot be seen beneath garage sale clothing, and graying hair pulled back in a skin-tight ponytail, or a head balding way too soon, is the valiant and heroic heart beating in that chest. You see and judge them based on what they look like, where they live, and what they drive. If they are afoot, you often don't see them at all.

But God sees them... He knows them well. They are the old souls... the earth-bound angels who willingly came to serve, knowing full well what a burden this earth-life would be.

Think about that the next time you see someone in that position.

Think about the pure heart beating...faith never wavering...sacrificing over and over until their work here is done. Just because you judge them by the human rule of thumb... the lack of education...no high school or college degree, living in poverty in some rundown house they'll never own, know that they did not fail at life.

They did exactly what they came here to do.
They succeeded beyond a measure you will never understand.
Next time you see someone like that, pay attention.
Hold a door for them.
Please and thank you to them.
Honor their life and recognize it matters as much as yours.
See them for the true angels they are.

Lemmings.
Little rodent-like animals who move in swarms...who follow one leader of their pack blindly...even straight off a cliff to their death.
They exist in the animal world.
Never thought I would see it in this world.
All I have to say about us now is...think for yourself.
Don't read something, and then flare up like a hot spot in a forest fire.
Just because everything ugly that you read fits the drama going on inside your head, still doesn't mean it's true. It only means you chose to be a lemming.
I quit following orders the day I divorced my second husband.
I stopped investing myself in the lies of other people.
I don't do drama.
Don't bring it to me.
I'll delete you again and again, and block without prejudice.
Don't push me toward your herd.
I am not a lemming.

❧

Somewhere between deep sleep and twilight sleep, I saw the Universe at war. It was in darkness everywhere, and the angels and demons were fighting blindly, seeing what was before them only when the Universe lit up by blinding flashes of lightning, from a storm cloud so vast there was no beginning and no end.
My heart was pounding when I woke.

I won't discuss this.

It scared me.

I cannot speak aloud what this felt like inside me.

Do good works today.

Grow your light.

Let it shine.

Don't let what's bad in your life outweigh in your heart what is good.

The day you give someone else control of your choices, is the beginning of the end of that relationship.

You may think it's sweet when he tells you to quit your job, and that he can take care of you.

You may believe your life has just been made perfect because you are so loved.

But the day will come when you realize he's separated you, not just from your friends and family, but the outside world in general.

Beware of the man with a big smile and a firm grip.

He wears two faces.

It doesn't matter how much makeup you wear, or how much money you spend on clothes and hair, you cannot hide the truth of who you are for long.

If you want to look pretty for the world, you must first fit your deeds to the task.

Life becomes complicated for two reasons.

One is because we find ourselves facing an unexpected situation not of our making, like a natural disaster, or poor health, or some kind of accident.

The other time is because we didn't do what we should have when it was time to do it.

Procrastination: It is the bane of my existence. I suppose I tell myself I work better under pressure...that I need a deadline to produce...but the truth is, I put it off because I don't want to do it.

I've been this way all my life, and even after I get the issue resolved, and give myself a good talking-to about doing better next time, I don't.

I don't know why I'm like this. I don't know why I repeat it either. I grew up hearing "no one is perfect except God."

I am certainly an example of that saying.

But, on this beautiful Sunday morning, with a full day of tax papers ahead of me, and a book to finish, there's my procrastination issue of the moment. I have more than enough to do. And because I put it off, I now have a third thing to make it all harder. It hurts to sit down, and it hurts to stand up, so I'm adding some pain to my panic.

No more than I deserve for getting to this place... again.

Ah well, I will persevere and prevail. That was my Grampy's motto. Persevere and prevail. Only I have to add one more P word to make it fit me.

Procrastinate, Persevere. Prevail.

Might have to put that on my tombstone.

So, time to quit yapping and get busy.

I'm trying to un-complicate my day.

I read so many posts on Social Media that reflect sadness, trouble, worry, frustration, and even fear. As aggravating as it is with the trolls. and the radicals who walk around waiting for someone to set their hair on fire so they can react, it has become apparent that it is the only sounding board a lot of people have.

Here, you can talk about what's on your heart. You can admit you're scared. You can admit someone hurt your feelings. You can talk about the loss of a job, or the loss of a loved one and know you will be heard.

That simple act of listening is becoming a lost art.

People don't sit down and talk to each other anymore. They might sit down together, but they spend more time on their phones than they do with each other.

There is a sense of justice in being heard.

It is our right to speak up for ourselves.
When loved ones won't hear you.
When friends don't want to hear you.
So who's left? The people who are just like you...that's who's left.

And so we gather here on Social Media, and sometimes we fuss, and sometimes we step back from something that became more than we need it to be.

But for the most part... we have become a touchstone.

So today—from me to you—I hear you today.

I pray for you today.

I cry with you today.

I celebrate with you today.

I feel your rage from injustice.

I honor the pain of your loss.

I pray for you to find peace and grace.

I beg of you to lay down your anger and walk away—today.

Today you are heard.

§

When I was young, the only world I knew was my little family, my church, and school. When I grew older, the world grew larger, more exciting and at the same time, scary. As time passed, the world was no longer exciting to me. It had become a trap, and scarier by the day. When I finally found the exit door, the world had no boundaries. But what I had learned by that time was, that all I wanted was peace and safety. The world no longer held a magic for me. It was just a place for others like me.

Some were young, some were trapped, some just looking for a way out. Some ran when they got free. Some couldn't take the freedom and destroyed themselves.

But there is a simple truth for the runners to know.

What you're looking for isn't out there...it's in you.

It doesn't matter where you are, or what you're doing, or how well, or how badly your living conditions are. What matters is how you make peace with yourself. Reminding yourself that nothing ever stays the same. Life will take care of that for you, no matter how hard you try to hold on. Perfection is a myth.

So now I am standing in the winter of my life with no knowledge of how long it will last. What I have come to accept is that it no longer matters. I have made peace with myself. I don't want more. I just want enough. I don't need someone else's opinion of me to matter. I have learned to love myself.

The world has become small to me again. I don't want to know what's on the other side of the mountain. What is important to me now is what I had all along. My family, my friends, and my faith. All this living, and worrying, and the passing years of life and joy, and sorrow and loss, and what I had been searching for was already there.

Inside me.

❧

Going to get my hair done this morning. There's still a bit of a drizzle going on this morning, and promises to linger today.

I need something to pep me up today... like Bobby and his infernal bottle of hot sauce. That might do it. I always carried a mini-bottle of Tabasco Sauce in my purse for that man, so that when we went out to eat, he didn't have to panic if they didn't have any.

It was the first thing I wrote on any grocery list, and the first thing I put on the table before a meal. A small thing to keep a big man happy, and God knows he did the same for me. I don't know how many times he came home from town with something for me from the Sonic Drive-in. Usually a fruit smoothie, or a large Diet Dr. Pepper. It was a very touching thing to me, after two husbands who only thought of themselves.

So... now that I've written this... I do feel better. He could make anything better with a hug, and one of his secondhand kisses. That's what I teasingly called them, because I knew he kissed the horses first. That accusation always made him laugh, and he never denied it.

Everyone is going somewhere...every day we travel, even if it's only from room to room inside our home. Even those who are bed-fast travel in their dreams. Every new thing we experience is a lesson. How we take that lesson and use it to enrich our lives, is on us.

I have been thinking about this ever since pain took me to using a walker. One day I will be free of it again, but I think of those who have lived an entire life with some form of physical handicap, and it has given me a whole new appreciation for their physical stamina, their strength of heart, and the courage they exhibit, as they adapt their body and their skills to a world built without the infirm in mind.

I will never look at them the same way again. Pity is not a word that applies. They are the true road warriors...living their lives on wheels.

Went to bed at 2:00 a.m. Up twice and got up to stay at 6:45 a.m.

There are no words for how utterly exhausted I am.

It promises a rainy day in part of the state today and tomorrow. Hoping we get some of it here.

Finished chapter one of new book yesterday. I would tell you the title but I have yet to hear a firm okay from publisher on that front, so I have to wait and see. Onward and upward.

Mother Earth is angry. The earthquake we had last night was just a warning. They told us at first 5.3, then later lowered it to a 5. But the geological stations they have set up here in Oklahoma to register the quakes had numbers all over the place, depending on where they were. News reported on the late news last night that one of the stations registered a 6.7. But he said they take all of the numbers, average them out and then that's the official count.

If our world had been created in such a way that the Earth's weather patterns and geological events always reflected the behavior of the planet's inhabitants, we would already have killed ourselves.

Man is destroying eco-systems for greed. Rain forests cut down, waterways fouled by chemicals and man. Destroying what is above, for what's below. Beneath the earth's crust and below the seas is a whole other world, and whatever happens down there is always manifested by some disaster to us.

I sat outside one day and closed my eyes, wondering if I could hear what Mother Earth is surely doing—calling out to us, begging us to stop before it was too late to reverse the damage being done. But all I could hear were cars and sirens, planes flying overhead, and the madness of too many people living too close together.

I do not thrive in this environment, yet here I must be. This place will be where my journey ends. At least I have known better places, quieter places, places that renew broken hearts, and weary souls. And that is life. Nothing ever stays the same. It's not supposed to.

I would urge you to stay quiet within yourself today. Try not to react to the growing madness, by using patience and grace to conduct yourself and your words.

Woke up near 7:00 a.m. I looked at the clock and went back to bed. Woke up 3 hours later and now I'm up

With regard to the story I'm writing - First someone poisoned the food on set (actress) meant for her, and someone else ate it. Then the private elevator to her penthouse just crashed, but for a twist of fate, she would have been in it, and when her apartment building becomes filled with smoke from the fire the bomb started, she's rescued from the roof. I think someone wants her dead, right? Enter the bodyguard...what in the world happens next? One last hint. The rest of the story takes place somewhere other than Hollywood. Oh...and I just got word that my title was accepted. It's LIFE OF LIES.

It's a cold gray day here, this Sunday.

Scout is on his way home. He spent Thanksgiving with his Dad and family in South Carolina. I miss him being in and out, so I can only imagine how much his Mama has been missing him.

People are always complaining about talking to people they can't understand, and accents difficult to interpret, and laying hateful claims that this is America, and to learn the language. So here's the scoop people, When I grew up, America was proudly known as The Melting Pot...with many people here of many ethnic backgrounds.

All the gains we've made toward human rights was a heartfelt celebration. Nothing has changed but some people's hearts, but they are not allowed to speak for the whole.

No one else speaks for me.

Jesus asked all who suffered to come unto him.

God says pray to me and I will hear.

God sees us all the same and hears us all the same.

God is love.

In the midst of great changes, that which lives in darkness, crawls out from under the rocks beneath which they have been hiding.

When it rains, worms come up from beneath the ground to air it out.

Snakes are flushed out of the holes in which they live. Scorpions come out. People who have been in hiding, begin revealing themselves a few at a time, testing the new atmosphere to see where they may, or may not fit in.

When they announce their arrival, and no one shoos them away, or denounces them, more come, and then more, until the atmosphere of what was here is gone, and the atmosphere of what stayed behind becomes the new normal.

The freedom of being able to show their true selves takes on new and frightening implications.

But it didn't happen overnight and they didn't do it alone, it was simply a side-effect of the permission they'd been given.

Some saw daylight and mistook it for God's light.

All you have to remember is that water always finds its true level, and nothing lasts forever.

Some people are watchers. They observe without interfering, making their own decisions without anybody's input and moving on, but they know. They were given the gift of discernment...to see beyond the obvious...to hear the lies behind the words.

Not everyone was meant to be a warrior. Some must survive to tell the truth.

I have promised my body a massage if it will just hold together until this healing period with the new hip is over. LOL Poor little joints. Poor little muscles. All filled with aches and pains. I have apologized daily for all the crap I put it through, without conscience, when I was young. Back then, people lived forever. The reality of mortality was lax in my youth, but when it hit in my family, it hit hard, and I have never taken life for granted since.

Those last ten pounds of weight I kept trying to lose... gone, but not in a good way. Anesthesia always fries my taste buds. So far, the only thing I can taste with any enjoyment is warm, salty and cold, sweet. And then only in small bites.

Yesterday, my sweet daughter came to my house and made Thanksgiving dinner for us. Everything veggie for me. She knows what I like. Baked sweet potato...a scalloped potato casserole, buttered squash, fresh green beans sautéed in butter with a bit of scallion. Hot baked rolls, deviled eggs. I so enjoyed it...but I enjoyed even more that she was doing it here, so I wouldn't have to negotiate all the steps in her house.

The kitchen has always been the heart of a home for me, and she brought the meaning of the day home to me. She's been baking for days... She bakes and sells pecan pies and pumpkin rolls with cream cheese filling every year, and has them down to a science. They are so good. And this year she made one of Little Mama's favorite holiday cake recipes, too. A spice Bundt cake with brown butter icing drizzled over the top. She brought me a tiny piece of all three desserts, and I have enjoyed every bite that went in my mouth. Her Grand and her Grandma would be so proud.

She has a lot of her Grandma's old cook books, and we were laughing, remembering how Mother always wrote little notes in the margins, or somewhere on the recipe...Stuff like this. "Good one!, or "Awful. Don't make again., or "Delicious. Kids love it."

My mother loved baking. The holidays and her family were her joy. I am a lot like her in this way. I wish I could bring my Little Mama home with me, sit her in a kitchen, and let her watch, and laugh, and talk, and poke her finger in the batter, and lick the bowls. But those days are gone...even if I was healthy enough to do that, she is not. That time has passed for her, but she's left a legacy of bakers in her wake, and granddaughters, and great-granddaughters picking up the slack.

※

Who you are at this very moment, is who you created by your lifetime of words, actions, and deeds. The paths you took, the bridges you burned, the mistakes you made, the crises you survived, the goals you achieved... is by your hand and heart.

YOU.

Age changes only your personal appearance and physical abilities. Nothing inside you will ever age. The God-given soul that is you is forever young, but with each life you live, that soul grows and grows in understanding and love, until you are a light too bright to be looked upon without the barrier of your human body.

When we cower in fear, we hide our light. We don't want to be seen —to be found. But the longer we hide, the darker the world around us becomes, until the light that is you is too small to be seen.

Hide from nothing. Stand up to face your enemy. Stand strong against that which would bring you down. Step out of a path that has taken you into a life you do not want.

You always have the choice to walk either way on a path. The way you came, or the way you're going. There's nothing shameful in going back and starting over, especially if you were heading in the wrong direction. If the people in the world around you are on a path that is not yours, step off. You don't have to follow the crowd if its untrue to who you are.

I stepped out of the shadows.

I walked away from the beliefs of those who would cause harm.
I stand alone in what I think, and who I am.
My voice will not be lost, because I will not be trying to shout above a crowd.
I will be standing apart, speaking my truth.

Make peace with what is. The only thing that will, or can change, is how you receive it. If I could walk away from all that hurts and shocks me, and makes me feel nothing but despair, I would do it in a heartbeat. But what do you do when there's nowhere to go? Nowhere to hide? When it's everywhere, and you can't breathe for wanting to cry? You make peace with what is and know that God didn't do it, and He won't fix it because Man did it through free will, and all we can do is lean on Him for strength to get through it.
And that's the truth.

After all my huffing and puffing about wanting to make biscuits, I wound up only eating a half of one with a fried egg, and I was done. I gave the rest of them to Kathy and Scout this morning when she brought my groceries. We all like toasted leftover biscuits almost as much as we do fresh from the oven.

Last night I was having a dream in which I kept struggling and struggling to get my arms free, and then I heard a sweet, deep voice close to my ear say, "Sweetheart," and I woke, realized my arms were out from under the covers, and I was freezing. That's why I was dreaming that I couldn't get them free, because I was too cold to move. Bobby woke me up so I could get warm. I sighed...put them under the warm covers and said, 'thank you, baby,' and went back to sleep.
Love, the purest emotion, never fades, does not quit, does not die. Like the soul, it lives on long after the person you loved has passed to the other side.

It's why words that you read make you sigh—make you weep. Words are stories, and stories keep people alive in your heart, and in your head. It's why we share memories when we get together at holidays...because it is a family's way of bringing the ones we've loved and lost back to the table with us.

I use Grand's pickle dish every Christmas. I wear her aprons. I cook my food from the recipes she left behind...written in her own hand.

Just because you cannot see them anymore, does not mean they aren't still here. When you speak of them, when you remember and laugh, or remember with tears...they are there beside you, treasuring the knowledge that they did the right things in raising us...in loving us...in sharing part of their lives with us. We are their proof that a life wasn't wasted, and we owe it to them, no matter how sad or lonesome we are, to continue on...and to live the very best life that we can for ourselves, and for them, because they no longer have that choice.

The proof of a job well done is the quiet satisfaction at how sturdy it stands.

꽃

Saw on the news that a tropical storm they've named Alberto is brewing off the east coast of the U.S. along the southern shore. An odd parallel of life imitating art as I continue working on my story, Dark Water Rising...about a hurricane hitting the Houston area similar to where Hurricane Harvey hit.

Every day, I make a conscious effort to keep my opinions to myself, to not buy into someone else's battles, to believe that every adult deserves to exist within their own choices, even when their choices may be negative or harmful. If I do not have to live within that world, then it is not a part of me.

I have known destructive people. I have lived with negativity. And each time, I spent all of MY years trying to fix them. Trying to make THEM happy. It didn't work, because it wasn't me they were unhappy with. It was themselves.

This morning at Love church during Leslie Draper's message, she pointed this out to us... that everyone on this earth is broken in some way—some more than others. And she was talking about how broken people often let their brokenness become who they are—and how they hold onto the label of victim...that it becomes their identity. And, when those victims then take their wounds out daily, and display them to show that their pain is worse than your pain, and the stories of how life has hurt them, are far more devastating that how life has hurt you...then what they're doing is wounding others with their brokenness. Piercing hearts, slashing relationships, emotionally wounding others with the broken pieces of who they are.

Broken people can heal, and the image she painted of all of our broken pieces put back together again like a beautiful piece of art...like a mosaic, really spoke to me.

I see people for who they are without judgment. We are who we are. And the biggest injustice you can serve to yourself is to not only lie about who you are to others—but to also lie to yourself.

Flaws are the imperfections that make us all unique.

True beauty is not what's on the outside, but what shines from within.

I AM OPEN AND RECEPTIVE TO ALL GOOD.

There is something unique to each of us.

Something no one will ever know.

Our Thoughts.

Words are powerful. They hold energy, so whatever you speak is the energy with which you will walk for that day. Thoughts are silent, but can be just as powerful, because they color your mood.

People react to your mood as quickly as they would react to your words.

Think about how you want to be perceived.

Are you the easy-going, happy worker at your job?

Do you work through frustration by fixing the problem without comment, or are you the person who rants and curses all the way through the change of plans?

At the end of the day, are you going home satisfied with what you've done, or do you carry your anger and frustration home, and end the day the same way?

Think about it.

The day I stopped worrying about what other people thought about me, was the most freeing day of my life.

I'm not here to satisfy someone else's view of the world.

I don't dress to please others. I dress to please myself.

I seek comfort in clothes, not the latest fashions.

My body is just a vehicle. It serves a purpose that has nothing to do with conforming it to a certain shape and size to suit the fashion of the day.

I'm working hard on ridding myself of ego. If I don't bow down to fashion, or the need to surpass someone else's accomplishments, and just tend to me and follow my path, then I have lost my need for public approval.

Life is more than the culmination of the jobs we held, and the many hats we wore as child, woman, employee, wife, mother, daughter, friend.

I don't feel the need to leave some kind of legacy behind.

That's all wrapped up in ego.

My intention is to not hurt others in the pursuit of my own purposes.

Think about that, too.

I do.

Every day.

I am breaking myself of saying things like, "I have arthritis, I'm getting old, etc.", because these are things that have negative connotations. It's like I'm claiming those by saying them aloud. When the Universe hears us claiming physical pains and emotional complaints we utter daily, like, I'll never get ahead, or If I didn't have bad luck, I'd have no luck at all…all of that feel sorry for ourselves talk… then that's what we will get daily.

Why?

Because we are ALL spiritual beings first. We came from the Universe, and we are loved. So when the Universe hears us claiming those ailments, we are given more, because it is assumed that's what we want.

So I'm not hurting. I feel great. I am loved. And I love.

There are people who make the same mistakes over and over in life, because they keep fishing for a whale in the same little pond. If you stay in the same environment, living the same life, complaining daily, but still doing the same things over and over, you will continue to get the same thing, which is something you didn't want.

If you want a different life—a better life—then see beyond the horizon of where you are.

Don't pick a loser just because he gives you attention.

Nine times out of ten, all he's looking for is a place to sleep, and someone to feed him so he's not homeless on the streets.

Think about what you're doing. If you have children, think of the example you are setting for them.

You're showing them that it's okay to settle for less.

You're saying to yourself he's all I deserve.

You say it's better than nothing, but sister...I am here to tell you that is not the truth.

Being alone is far better than being with someone who hurts you. Someone who sucks the joy right out of your life. Someone who's just using you.

Never look for someone to love you, and think that will fix your life.

Love yourself first.

Be happy with you.

As the roots of a tree spread far beyond the shade of their branches, so does the power of the words we speak.

Do not joke about negating yourself or others. Even in jest, the Universe hears and obeys your requests.

Why you ask? Because the Universe does not have a sense of humor. Like a child who trusts everything he or she is told, the Universe reacts in the same way to you. There is no subtlety, no double entendre, no lying, no jesting.

You don't tell God..."oops... only kidding. I didn't really mean, I wish I was dead," when you're met at the proverbial Pearly Gates.

Language is for communication. It was not given to us to use as a weapon against others.

The Universe understands that words spoken in anger can never be taken back, and that while the wounds they might cause eventually fade, the scar they leave behind never will.

In all things, be thoughtful.

You came here, a perfect, beaming light.

We have all tarnished our souls in varying degrees, but like wiping off the dust on a mantle, so can you clean your soul of what you'd said and done.

Ask forgiveness FIRST from the people you have harmed.

In doing so, you have automatically shown the sincerity of your words, which the Universe has already heard.

Beautiful morning here. I'm bird watching, eating my breakfast, and as always, enjoying the quiet in my house as I begin my day. I never have the television on anymore unless I have down time, or if the weather is bad and I'm keeping up with that.

I know where my priorities are, and where my path leads, and I choose to focus on what I know, rather than the Muggle-wampus that passes for news stories.

So many great things are happening in the world, and we only hear the bad stuff. And we focus daily on the same bad stuff we heard about, until there's new bad stuff that happens, and that gives the Mugglewamps more dark to peddle.

So I'm watching birds fussing at the bird feeder, and eyeing the pine cones from my neighbor's tree that continue to fall in my back yard, and am grateful for the day.

Traveling out of town this morning to go see my niece, Crissy's, oldest daughter graduating high school. It's one of those days that always seemed like 'in the future' to Mom and Dad until it happened, and now they have a daughter full-grown, and one to be proud of, at that.

I know my sister, Diane, will be sitting at my side in spirit, proud of her girl and granddaughter, and I'll be her stand-in, just as I've been since Crissy was five. For a little girl who grew up without a mother, Crissy figured out early that the most important things her children would need, were her and her love. And they get it.

So... today is a day of retrospection for me.
Not wishing for what never happened...
Just grateful for my part in what did.
Be present in the lives of those you love.
They don't need what you buy them,
Half of much as they need you.
What I think and what I know are two different things.
Thinking is opinion, which is normal, and everyone has one.
Like thinking someone is nice, when someone else sees them in a different light.
Neither is wrong because our perceptions are also different.
Knowing is gut instinct, or what is YOUR learned truth.
Like knowing if you don't get out of the way of a moving car you are going to be hurt.
Knowing that a one dollar bill does not have as much value in buying power as a five dollar bill.
The problem is in using your personal opinion as indignation. Saying/writing things publicly that are opinion, and using them as fact, and using that power in a negative way.
While you are in the process of publicly attacking anyone, does it

ever occur to you what it would feel like to be on the other side of that? Would you welcome people doing that to you?

Then why do you do it?

You do realize that is adult bullying...don't you?

There is a huge wave against bullying now. We are horrified and indignant and empathetic when we see the end results of children being bullied in every aspect of their lives, and yet YOU do that every time you use your platform to attack others.

Bullies come in all shapes and sizes.

Some use pretty words with an underlying snap they call humor.

Some are blatantly rude and profane.

None of it is okay.

And when you are an adult...and you are still doing it... burning and slashing your way through life with word and deed to hurt or humiliate another, then we are left with but one assumption.

That you are nothing but a bully, with nothing important to say, and with no empathy for the humanity that surrounds you.

I would hope as we continue to move into a world of enlightenment, that what you say and do, does not hinder your ability to move with it.

I'm going to Love Church this morning. In that church I will not hear one word of shame or sinning. I will not be swamped with another peppering me with words of their opinion of righteousness.

I AM a lightworker. I honor God...the Great I AM...every day of my life. I know that is real. Because I have seen angels. I have heard the messages.

That is MY knowing.

This is my truth, not my opinion.

But my knowing, is also believing that you have a God-given right for your own choices and opinions.

What you don't have...is the right to force them on anyone else.

Bullying stops with you.

I woke up this morning with Purpose.

Purpose is a fine friend to have when you are awake, but trying to sleep with it is futile.

So... there are things to be said before I begin my day.

All things that can change shape and grow, in one way or another, are alive.

In the heart of the Great I AM... there aren't races of people with different colored skin and beliefs.

They are humanity.

Pieces of light that are part of I AM.

Light we call soul.

Souls choose who to be before they come here. For whatever reason or purpose...they chose the culture in which to exist, to do the work they came here to do.

In the Universe, they are all acknowledged as light beings...all living beings...all Source from I AM.

On this small blue ball in the vastness of the cosmos, in one tiny corner of a galaxy, they incarnate as human.

They have chosen a vehicle...a body...it is their mode of transportation for the time they are here. It is their means of communication for the time that they are here. It is a tool.

Many souls become bogged down by human rules, and human ways, and forget purpose as they live human ways. Catering to worship of that vehicle they chose, worshiping how their body looks. How it is clothed. Fighting a war with aging, and forgetting they came to learn, to teach, to grow.

For tens of thousands of years they have recycled, and recycled, and recycled themselves in many different incarnations, trying to get it right, and every time, they only wind up in human wars for human greed.

The Great I AM does not love them less, because light is but a part of the whole, but there comes a time when humanity has to be taken out of the picture, to be reminded of goal.

Humans think what they have, and how they do or don't worship is all that matters, while the truth is that IT HAS NOTHING TO DO WITH PURPOSE.

Think. Listen to something besides other people's opinions.

Find a subject matter other than squabbling over such things as religion, over skin color, over anything but things and appearance., to better yourself.

Time is infinite.

Our time here is not.

It does not matter one bit...NOT ONE BIT... if you don't believe me. Your soul's time here will end...and you will find out when you return, that once again, you let human greed and desire, and all of the human emotions that become deformed within the baseness of living life here...you let them run rampant over purpose.

Humanity is failing itself, and there is no one else to blame.

Even if you see all I've said in a different light, that is completely your right, part of the free choice that you were given as part of being human.

You can't pray this mess away, because God didn't make it. Humanity made its own mess with free choice.

God doesn't punish.

Humanity does.

Somewhere inside of all of us is the thread of memory that leads us to purpose. Search your heart...Look past your prejudice, because that isn't God light. Look past your greed for things you don't have— because that isn't God light. Look past judgment and revenge. Those emotions aren't part of God light.

Somewhere inside of you is the one thing you came here to do...to learn...even if it is a very small thing...like patience...or empathy for others...wherever you can find that purpose again...If ever there was a time to use it...to walk that path...the time is now.

In the past couple of days, several people have told me if posts on Social Media are too long, they just skip it. I call this Twitter brain.

About the only time I feel the need to shorten an explanation is if I'm about to yell FIRE.

These days, when people don't understand something, they're most likely going to attack you verbally, or ignore the message.

Either way, they're gonna miss the point and be all indignant and pissy when they're left behind.

So…in honor of Twitter brain…Here's your sign.

Read the fine print.

Pay attention to directions.

Use common sense as your road map in life, not someone else's opinion.

Happiness is available in all formats.

You can't end what's wrong in your life by always clicking Buy.

Try a free attitude adjustment of 'what the heck do you think you're doing' add a life-time supply of 'pay attention', then click Send.

My house is always so quiet.

It's not a sad quiet. It's a thoughtful quiet.

The kind of silence that comforts after a day of noise, and traffic, and people.

The silence of my childhood - when the only things making noise were cows, and birds…and sometimes the family dog yapping at a tortoise crossing the yard.

I miss the rhythm of family.

I really miss my Bobby. Even the sound of his pickup coming down the driveway toward the house quickened my heart. I knew there would be a big booming voice slashing through the quiet within me, and that all-engulfing hug that came with him.

So life changed, and I work every day not to get too comfortable within the silence of my life. I make myself do things just so I'll be out of the house. And such is the life of an introvert. Not very often lonely, just alone. Not bemoaning my life as it is, just accepting and finding comfort where it is offered.

It took me quite a few years of living to realize what a gift I've been given. To be able to adapt to life as it's dropped into my lap, is a learned behavior.

It comes from experiencing grief, learning hard lessons, and deciding to be the survivor, not the victim.

Everyone experiences disappointments, suffering, hard times and grief. But it's what you do with the lesson that marks your future path.

I never imagined I would be growing old alone...but then who does? What I am grateful for are the years I had raising my children, and the lessons I learned from the choices I made.

What you have to accept about loss, is that it isn't a personal attack on your happiness. It is just the end of someone's earthly journey. And when it's someone we hold dear, we go through shock, anger, and then grief, because of their absence in our lives.

They are fine...they are whole again...young again...they are home. The hardest thing I had to learn was trying to find me again. So much of my identity had been so wrapped up in their existence, that when they left, they took part of me with them.

And this is life.

Don't waste it.

It's not perfect But it's yours.

Own it.

This is a testimony to an act of angels. I have debated about sharing it for days, but I think it's too important to let it pass.

A week ago tomorrow my oldest granddaughter, Chelsea, was on one of the busy Dallas freeways going home, after having dinner with friends. It was dark, and the car in front of her suddenly swerved, which made her think something was in the highway, and so she swerved as well.

But she lost control when she did, and hit a concrete abutment beneath an overpass. She said, at that moment, she knew she was going to die, closed her eyes, and gave herself up.

She came to on the other side of the freeway, without having hit another car, or having any of them hit her.

Four lanes of speeding cars on a freeway, and she was still alive.

She said, in a very shaky voice, "Grandma, it's just like what happened to you. I get it. It just wasn't my time to die. It was angels, wasn't it?

And I said yes.

She's very bruised and sore, but her wounds are slight compared to what might have been.

She is without a car right now, but that is a small price to pay.

Such things are somehow provided.

She is forever changed by that experience.

She will be searching now, every day, wondering...what is it I'm supposed to do?

Why am I still here?

It's what all of us do, who have survived such things.

Nothing is ever taken for granted again, and gratitude is forever the word of the day.

Woke up to the sound of rain. Wasn't expecting that. Certainly changed my plans. I guess tomorrow will be the day I go put out Memorial Day flowers at cemeteries and not today. Kathy is going with me. My car is full of flowers, the back end is full, and the back seat, and floorboard all full, as well. I decorate the graves, because it pleases me to do so as a sign of remembrance, and because my elders taught me it was the thing to do.

The month is almost gone, and I'm not finished with the manuscript due June 1st.

Deadlines have their own level of anxiety.

I do not enjoy anxiety of any kind.

But I do enjoy solvency.

The way my life works now, one comes with the other.

I intend an easier way of living in abundance...without the anxiety, please, and thank you.

I closed my eyes last night, and immediately saw bright red flowing through black, like red silk spilling onto black velvet. I watched it like a movie, as the red morphed into a deep true turquoise color within the black, and then it morphed to blue, and then orange, and then green, and yellow...and then it all began to blend together and pull away from my sight as if I was now looking at it from above, and a long, long distance away.

I thought...galaxy...I had a glimpse of some far away galaxy.

I'd like to see that again.

Bought a handful of peaches from the supermarket this past week. Looked good. Even smelled like peaches. Taste was a huge disappointment. I can't remember the last time I ate fruit that tasted as it was supposed to taste. Ripened on the vine. On the tree. Not picked green, dumped in cold storage, and then gassed to make them look ripe, while they still tasted like fruit picked too soon. Hard inside, and green. Same with blackberries and raspberries. They look amazing, but have little to no taste.

It's like the food we're eating is fake, and we've been conditioned to buy on looks alone, and ignore the fact that we are being cheated out of the nutrition and enjoyment of food in its natural state. If I still lived on the farm, I would be growing my own food, and still enjoying fresh-picked fruits and vegetables.

Ah well, once upon a time I had the real thing, and it was good.

As you may have noticed, I have begun a new page separate from this called Creating Abundance and Prosperity. I have learned so much in the past couple of years and it has drastically changed my life, that I was led to share.

It's not me turning into someone else. It's just me, still being me.

Feel free to follow and I'll share what I know, and what I learned.

You know how I am...I always want to fix people's problems, help solve their troubles...This is just another way I can give back.

I share my life.

I share knowledge.

I share what I know about writing.

I share recipes, and I share tears.

I share experiences.

I share stories.

I share my family with you.

Giving is part of what makes me who I am.

Don't be afraid to show the world who you are.
Live in your truth.

🙢

What a day. I'm just happy to be home and standing upright. This morning before Kathy came, I was outside refilling the bird feeder. Stubbed my toe, caught myself by holding onto the bird feeder stand, and happily didn't fall. Wasn't going to tell anyone, and then Kathy arrived, and came outside to let me know she was there. She saw the back of my shirt and said, "Mom! What's all over the back of your shirt? It looks like—"

"It's bird seed," I said. "I might have fallen against the bird stand, but it was just a stumble."

She's muttering and brushing all of it off my shirt. It seems there was a lot on the back of my shirt, so I said… "might oughta check my hair, too."

"Oh good grief," she said, and started combing her fingers through my hair to get it out there, too.

After I was de-seeded, we headed toward Shawnee to pick up Crissy. Our first stop on the Memorial Day Express, was the Prague cemetery. Put flowers on Grandma and Grandpa Sala's grave, and put flowers on baby Sala, who died when he was six months old.

By now, Kathy has alerted Crissy that I nearly fell, so they're both afraid to let me wander too far away as we search for a grave site, finally found it, and I let the girls put the flowers on it, while I stayed in the car. (getting old is hysterical)

The marker I was looking for was my Smith grandparents, Vester and Katie, and I reminded Kathy that's the grandmother you were named for, Kathryn Ann… She grinned. "I know. I remember."

So then we drive farther down to where my Daddy, and my sister, Diane, are buried. They're side by side. They died within two months of each other. Crissy put the flowers on her mother's grave, and cried for the mother she doesn't remember, then put the flowers in the vase that's there on the stone. Kathy did most of Daddy's for me. I just stood and watched, remembering the time when my Grand began to fall a lot...and stumble...and how we all stayed close . Kathy used to run ahead of Grand, and move all the little twigs and rocks from in front of her when they were going to the chicken house, because she was afraid that Grand would fall.

So we finally head to Paden, decorate my little brother's grave and my Shero great-grandparents who are right beside him. His name was Eric Michael. He died the same day he was born. Then we drive further up to where my Aunt Jane and Uncle Baxter Davis were buried, then up the hill to my Grand and Grampy, then my Aunt Lorraine and Uncle Ralph Stone.

Little Mama's headstone has been in place right beside her parents for more than 30 years. We always have a little laugh at how LM had to be in charge of everything...including her death, which has yet to happen. Had one bouquet of flowers leftover, and Crissy and Kathy put it in the vase on LM's headstone. They said they'd been looking at this little headstone for as long as they could remember, and it always looks bare and lonesome without flowers, so now it's decorated, too.

If Little Mama could only remember us, she would so get a kick out of that.

Finally, we have all of the flowers done, and we're walking back to the car, when I stepped in a hole, and started falling forward. Kathy was too far away to catch me, when out of left field comes Crissy Carol, like she was shot out of a gun. She grabbed my arm just before I went down, and saved me from yet another fall. Scared the crap out of both of the girls, but I was just irked. I have new glasses. They are bifocals. I've always had the kind that never had a line, but these do, and my depth perception...at this point and time...is not great.

I will adjust...and I will not hurt myself in the meantime. I refuse.

I'm home now. Hot (it was 91 degrees), tired, (can't imagine why), hungry but not cooking a dang thing, and ready to put my feet up and write, which involves sitting on my butt and doing what I do best... telling stories.

Be safe on this Memorial Day weekend.

Love to all of you.

Taking a parachute with me next time I leave the house.

I worked until after 1:30 a.m.
 I kept thinking, "I'm going to bed as soon as I finish this scene, and then I'd finish it. I'd look at the clock and think... Not yet. Not yet, and kept writing.

It was a quarter to two when I finally turned everything off and headed to my bedroom. I was already ready for bed and had been writing in my nightgown...so I mostly just turned out lights in there and crawled into bed.

I said my prayers...then kept staring at the ceiling. Finally closed my eyes and rolled over...the angst feeling still with me, and at straight up 2:00 a.m. Little Mama's care center called to tell me that she'd fallen again, and hit her head. It wasn't a bad fall. There was no knot and nothing was bleeding, but they're required to tell me. I just said, "Bless her heart, thank you for calling." But the moment I was back in bed, that feeling was gone.

The waiting feeling that wouldn't let me sleep, was her imminent fall.

This is my life. This is who I am, and how I came into this world. I reject nothing about it. And so it is.

I had a phrase come into my head so strongly this morning, that I knew it was meant to share.

Now is the time for tending your sheep.

I know it means that if you aren't doing it now, to begin.

Do what needs to be done.

Apologize if the need is there.

Make peace within your family.

I know this sounds very Star Wars...but walk away from the dark in your life. It does not serve your purpose.

Gather those around you who you love, to be reminded of what it means to be connected by heart and by blood.

Clean house...which means getting rid of what no longer fits in your life, as well as within the place where you live. The past way of life is no longer working.

Do one thing a day that gives you joy.

❧

When you give all of your focus to family and job, without care for your own welfare and needs, you are starving yourself.

A body can move long after the spirit within has been broken.

The old saying, running on empty, is the perfect analogy.

When you get to that point, all it will take to come apart is one complaint too many, one criticism you've heard a thousand times before, but on this day it will be your final straw.

And it will be no one's fault but yours.

You enslaved yourself.

You gave away so much of yourself, that you forgot you also hold the key to your release.

There is no reward for being a martyr.

All you've done is taught the people around you that you have no value, which gives them permission to view your existence as none of their concern.

If you want to break free of the yoke you've put on yourself, but don't know how to let it be known that you are changing the rules, go buy some doormats, and put them down in front of every bedroom in the house, and when your family asks you what those are for, then tell them. "I am resigning from the job of doormat in this family, and that is your replacement."

Every day, you show people how to treat you, by what you let be said or done in your presence.

If you are offended, it is your job to say so.

And to remember:

I AM OPEN AND RECEPTIVE TO ALL GOOD.

❧

Going to get a massage this morning. It will be my morning meditation...if I don't fall asleep.

Getting my hour of reflexology directly afterward...Why?

Not because I'm spoiling myself.

It's because my spirit needs healing, too.

Both of these ancient techniques are well known for releasing stress, and through no fault of my own, I live with that 24-7.

We are all stronger than we have been taught to believe.

Growing up, I heard, "You can't do that" more often than getting a pat on the back for what I did do.

I was told..."Girls aren't supposed to do that. That's a job for boys." So I learned at an early age to suppress what my instincts were telling me was right.

And at the same time, I heard adults telling boys, that's a girl's job, when they had been happy at their task until they were chastised for something they were capable of doing and happy to do so.

We let ourselves be controlled in every aspect of our lives growing up, and then we find ourselves out in the world with one skill set, when we really needed two.

How many generations will it take us to figure out that our power is our own?

It belongs to no one else but you.

Yes, you can give it away, but it can't be taken.

You either stand by what you know, or you falter.

There is no right or wrong here...It's part of the free will we came with.

It is your choice.

꙳

I dread going to see my Little Mama this morning with her new wounds and old scars, and when she's cognizant enough to know I'm someone she used to know...seeing the confusion in her eyes...wondering if I have the answer to where she is...and why she's still there.

She is half of what she weighed before the downhill slide...tiny bones with clothing hanging on her body... like a little scarecrow dressed in someone else's clothing, wanting to get away from the crows, but stuck in place, right where the farmer's daughter put her.

There are always answers in life. They're just not always what we wanted to hear.

Your choice, in these cases, is to stay put and stagnate,

Or make the change needed and put out new feelers...those hair-fine feathery growths that you see on the sides of old roots.

They are like advance scouts, sending riders in all directions, looking for water, which is the destination that they seek.

Like those little scouts, you will also grow feelers that will tell you without words, what direction you are meant to grow. Where you can find the water you need to flourish.

Trust the process.

God doesn't make mistakes.

Mother Earth is healing herself.

Ridding herself of the poison humanity has pumped into her, thrown on her, fouling her water, her land, her air, everything that God put here that grows.

We have killed off animals to the point of extinction, polluted drinking water, pumped waste chemicals, and wastes of all kinds into the vast spaces below earth, and let it out as noxious fumes into the sky. We have destroyed the balance of living things in the oceans.

There are no excuses for any of it. There are no longer ways to fix it.

Mother Earth is doing it for herself.

We see the devastation brought about by volcanic activity, by hurricanes, tornadoes, floods, and fires, and we throw our hands up to the Lord and say, "Save us."

He already tried, when He said "Do unto others, what you would have them do unto you."

We have no food, we cry. Feed us.

He already showed us how to feed each other, but do we? No. We burn crops in the field. We drop prices so that food growers cannot even afford to harvest what they have grown.

We foul the water, even when an entire nation of people...our First People here...the Native Americans marched...and held firm on their ground to save water not just for them, but for all of us. And yet we turned away from them, unaware and uncaring that they wintered in extreme conditions, were beaten, jailed, shot, and some died in their efforts for all of us.

We have watched it all...and said a meaningless prayer for people we did not know, and went out to dinner, and shopped for new things...and spent money we had, without further thought for what was happening to those who had nothing.

Mother Earth has no more use for us.

And humanity is choosing sides.

There is no more in between.

There are people in the constant act of offending, hurting, lying, killing.

And there are people and Lightworkers—standing firm, fighting in their own way by staying in a constant state of peace, refusing to barter away what they believe in.

There is a shift in consciousness to stand in the God-light, not a spot-light.

There are vast numbers of people all over this planet who have been preparing for this for a long, long time, and knowing what all of this turmoil meant.

For thousands of years, we knew better but did not do better.

For hundreds of years, we saw signs and looked away.

Not us, we said. It will never happen to us, we said.

I don't care, we said. We'll be dead and gone before that happens, we said.

Talking time is over.

Making fun of people who call themselves Lightworkers is no longer a joke, because the joke will be on you.

You are either with the dark side who touts money, power, hate and greed.

Or you choose to stand in the light and make The Shift.

Mother Earth has made her choice.

Where are you?

※

People say all the time, I just want to be happy.

The thing is...no one can EVER give that to you.

Fancy cars, nice clothes, all the money in the world to spend, and it will never be enough to make someone happy.

HAPPINESS COMES FROM WITHIN.

You have to forgive yourself, and forget all those who have hurt you.

You have to accept yourself as you are, not how you want to be.

You have to love yourself first, before you can love anyone else.

You CAN satisfy someone else's comforts, wishes, and desires, but you can't even make THEM happy. They have to find that within themselves, as well.

You dwell for years on a betrayal. You hold that hate. You weep for the cruelty. You talk about it. You become THAT person. The one who was betrayed. You take that as your identity.

Just like when you lose a job.

You immediately see yourself as THAT person—one who is not worthy of being paid.

And then you take on the shame, and you continue to look for new work, but you have saddled yourself with baggage by believing you aren't good enough.

And guess what? That shows in your body language, in the sound of your voice, in the way you present yourself.

You are virtually daring someone to hire you. Then when they don't, it only reinforces your first belief. That you aren't any good.

So now you're not only a VICTIM of betrayal, but you must also be a LOSER, a scourge on society because you can't find work.

So now you have a great conversation starter.

You are THE ONE WHO COMPLAINS LOUDEST AND LONGEST.

And then to top it all off, you feel you are the most betrayed of all time, and the most put-upon ever. No one likes you. No one loves you. And so you begin to seek your tribe.

You now hate everyone who's not like you, and are looking for like-minded people.

Now, you are not only a VICTIM and a LOSER, but you have fallen into the CANT GET OUT hole, and there are so many others in here like you, that you crawl on over to the MIGHT AS WELL STAY hole.

And here you are.

Can you look back into this past and see where it first went wrong?

Can you see that it was your refusal to let go of misery that started it?

Open your eyes.

If you see yourself in this in any matter, shape, or form, then I have given you a road map out.

Today. Now. In this very moment...let go of the past.

You have the power.

Just turn it loose and don't look back.

Controversy, Fear, Anger, Grief.

These negative emotions are swamping the planet (not just here). And it's all part of the growing division on this planet. I said it the other day, and I'll say it again.

There is no more in-between for good and bad.

There aren't any more fences to ride.

And the media feeds all of the controversy, fear, anger, and grief to us, face-slap after face-slap, so that when one scandal begins to fade, they have more to keep people angry or afraid.

ANGER AND FEAR FEED NEGATIVITY.

And everything negative keeps the puppets jumping, which is the goal of behind the scene power brokers...

A good portion of our country buys into everything the media says, because it used to be a reliable source of news.

Newspapers, then television news, WERE the in-between.

They WERE the ones who verified facts before anything was broadcast, or went into print. But when "in-between" disappeared within the Shift, they chose a side.

The reason I'm pointing all of this out is to give you pause...to be able to step back, see the logic of what's happening to ALL OF US, and how we're being manipulated.

They don't want us to find ways to get along.

When the Whole is of one mindset...a mindset of peace for all, with the freedom to know this is the way it's supposed to be, then the Whole cannot be divided.

And if there is no way to divide a nation,

Then there is no way to control it.

Don't buy into the bullshit.

It can't be substantiated.

And it washes away when it rains.

❧

We have gathered together over the centuries, living in cities that grow larger and larger over time, until there's no way to find the in and out without a map.

There are people who are born in a city, and live their entire life without ever venturing even ten miles beyond where they were born.

What was this thing that called people to gather up in herds like the buffalo, and live behind walls? Safety in numbers... protection from weather... protection from the wild animals that clawed at their doors?

The more people that came, the less they were bothered by the animals. But there was another danger they never saw coming.

It came from man, himself.

From the neighbor who stole.

From the neighbor who told a lie about them out of jealousy.

From the man who cheated on his wife...and the wife who cheated on her husband...and the children who use to play together were taught not to associate anymore, because the parents were angry with each other, and the children were forbidden to associate, and they made up stories about why they were no good...and they began picking up the reasons why they should be run out of the city...they didn't look like everyone else... they didn't conform.

And no one realized the biggest danger they faced was from what they, themselves, had created.

This was not what God had made.

But it is what Man created.

The smaller your world...the smaller your understanding of everything else. You cannot see beyond your own doorstep. You are afraid of what's out there because you have not experienced it.

It isn't your fault. But it is how your world has evolved.

The biggest gift you could ever give yourself, is to step out of your comfort zone, and see how the rest of the world lives. You might be surprised to learn that every family wants the same thing—the means to take care of those they love, food for the table and a safe and comfortable place for all of you to be.

No matter the color of your skin, the way you dress, the language you speak, the land in which you live—THAT is universal.

Don't always look for what's different... look for what you understand.

A friend lost her father.

Another friend lost her job.

Yet another friend received an award from her work.

Scout received a big award at Boy Scout meeting last night.

Kathy's new car, less than a year old, has two recalls on it already.

I'm healing from hip surgery.

I have another friend who's having knee surgery soon.

Someone lost their husband in a wreck yesterday. I saw the post.

And so my point in all of this is... life is happening as we live it.

Your life can change forever in the middle of a heartbeat. Some things we never see coming, some we do. But it does not change the hurt, or the damage it will do.

Some things are good...they lift us up when we need it most.

But no matter what is happening in your life, for the love of God...do not take it as some kind of punishment for you personally. That's not how life works and it's not how God works.

We aren't promised anything.

We come here as a blank slate with free will, and for all the days of our life we are writing on that slate, telling our story as it happens by word or deed.

What many people don't understand is that it is not our job to write on someone else's life. We were not set up to judge. We did not come here as a tool to force others to our way of belief and living.

We are also not meant to live in herds.

That free will we came with means we can step out at any time and pursue what calls us.

Just because you might be afraid to try something new doesn't apply to everyone else.

Free will.

Your choice.

Choose wisely today.

It will affect how life treats you tomorrow.

Upheaval. Turmoil. Even when we don't like it...it's part of change.

We are in the midst of great change. All over the world. Not just here. Some of it is heartbreaking. Some of it shocking. But I was reminded in my prayers, that we aren't in charge. I was reminded that God has a plan. He's always had a plan. Sometimes we screwed it up with our free will, but He always has a way of realigning us...realigning what must be.

What's happening now is our realignment.

We have to trust that the Universe is already all over it...that they've got this, and we just don't see the path yet.

I've lived my whole life on trust.

Sometimes in the worst upheaval.

Sometimes in the saddest of times.

Sometimes not knowing how I will ever wade through what just happened to me, and yet somehow it always worked out. Somehow I learned to adjust, and sometimes, I could look back and see that the change was for the better.

This is what I remembered this morning.

This is what 'they' want you to know.

"They've got this."

You can't yet see the path.

But when it's time, it will be there.

So live your life. Do what you do. Go to work. Enjoy your families. Make love. Bake cookies. Help a stranger. Love your fellow man.

Just think of life as a muddy road. Be on it in joy, and if something knocks you off that path, then you get up, readjust your course, and keep moving. It's only when you stop that you start to sink.

⁂

Oh the dreams last night. They were endless and awful. I woke up once at 2:30 a.m. and had to get up and walk around to calm down. It is almost impossible to pull myself out of those kinds of dreams.

Wherever I was, I was there in spirit and wanted to leave, and still couldn't make it happen no matter how many orders I obeyed. I don't know how that plays out into real life, but being bullied isn't happening to me when I'm awake.

I don't take that anymore.

I am no longer the silent wife who takes the shouting.

I am not the first to back away, unless I deem the shouting worth addressing.

I. Fight. Back.

Denise has come and gone. My house is nice and clean again, and it smells wonderful. All ready for another Christmas and a week of baking, and prepping for Sunday dinner.

I get to set the dinner table with my new Pioneer Woman Christmas dishes, and have all of my family in and out before the day is over.

First wave of them comes here for dinner at noon and opening presents.

Second wave is my son and family coming here for supper, and opening presents and spending the night. We'll pile them and two dogs in everywhere before the night is over. I'll be ready for a three day nap by the time they're all gone but it will be worth it.

If you have no influence to change that which troubles you, then you have to trust that the process is progress.

The outcome may not be what you desire, but it will be the outcome you get.

Your job is not to complain about it from that day forward.

Your job is to figure out how to live with it.

It's like the parents who had two children.

One died.

One lived.

They spent the rest of their lives bemoaning their loss. They stopped living and missed the fact that one precious child still lived. They wasted their opportunity to find joy again.

They missed their chance to move forward.

And the child who lived lost the parents he needed, all because they refused to acknowledge their fate.

The hardest loss of all is losing the ability to love.

Such a cold morning. In the single digits. I slept until 10:15 this morning. First morning I've had a chance to sleep in, in over a week. It was wonderful not to hear an alarm go off at 7:00 a.m. Makes for a very long day for me because I usually write until nearly midnight.

Kathy has always liked for things to look pretty, or look cute. Even when she was a teenager, and we'd be going through a salad bar somewhere for lunch, she'd come back to the table with a perfect little cherry tomato on top of her salad.

I'd ask. "Why do you always put a tomato on your salad when you don't even like to eat them?"

"Because it makes it look cute, Mama, and you always eat my tomatoes for me."

I had another dream, and in the dream we are waiting.

I woke up without knowing what was coming, but I felt it was a truth—a message.

So I am waiting to see what comes. Not just for our country...but for the world.

Whatever it is, it felt like the answer.

Open your hearts.

Do good in the world.

Much good is needed to grow light.

We cannot move forward without light by which to see.

Left untended, the first seed of doubt that creeps into your life, will grow in size and importance until it spreads too far to stop.

Just because you do not experience something, or believe in something, doesn't mean it did not happen. It just means you are blinded by doubt, and that's okay.

We all do what we need to do in this world to feel safe and secure, and sometimes taking a step out of that emotional place feels threatening...so we don't take the step. We don't even open the door and look at what's on the other side for fear of what we might see.

As a child I was afraid of the dark.

As a woman, if I was outside at night, I was still fearful.

As a mother, I let go of my fears in order to care for my children, walking darkened rooms at night to check on them. Running outside in the dark to look for a forgotten toy, or to look for a child too late coming home. As I grew older, I realized it wasn't really the dark I feared. It was my inability to trust in God.

I said prayers and then didn't believe they would be heard.

I felt like it was all on me to protect what was mine.

I finally learned that what you give out in the world, you will get back.

I have seen angels three times in my life, and each time when I was at my lowest. I doubt nothing now. All things ARE possible. AND, I also know that just because I ask for things, doesn't mean they are going to happen. Some things are not meant for me. Some things are not meant for you.

We all come with different tasks, and we come with the ability to complete them. We're the ones who choose. It has taken me a lifetime to understand that the choices I made created the world in which I have lived.

During my hip replacement surgery, something happened they hadn't expected...I woke up during surgery, and they had to give me a second kind of anesthetic, then when I was in recovery, they couldn't wake me up.

I had a choice that day to go home...to go with Bobby. There are no words to describe the joy of being rid of this earthly body. But I was reminded that I had not completed my task...and so I came back to do what I was sent here to do. That's not heroic. That's just being practical. Trust me. I don't ever want to have to come back to this earth again, and relive another human life to complete a task. I am tired of the pettiness of humanity.

I open myself to ridicule by telling you this but I don't care, because there's something you have to understand. I know that there will be someone who'll read this, and gain the courage to trust that it's not the dark they have to fear, but the doubt they have let grow in their hearts.

Writing last night. As always,

It was flowing...one of those gifted sections of time when the words were already there...and then accidentally hit some random key and THANK YOU WINDOWS 10, you sorry sucker...the last ten pages of perfect prose were gone and wouldn't recover.

I sat there a minute in disbelief...poked around on a few sites to see if I could recover it, and then thought, what the heck...and started over. And it didn't make me cry. I actually laughed.

I didn't make it to bed until almost one a.m. and I was up at six, because today is house cleaning. However, I, by gosh, not only rewrote those ten pages, but five pages more before I quit.

I will not be screwed with this year...not even by a stinking piece of technology.

My theory is...if I did it once, then I can certainly do it again only better. So I did.

Lesson learned? Don't create more drama when you're already neck deep and sinking.

Denise is here cleaning.

Lord but she is a blessed presence in my life.

Not only cleans my house, but makes me laugh. We share stories about our families all the time because she's been coming to my house since 2005, and is as much family, as the ones I was born with.

Some things are so precious in our memories that the longing to relive them is painful. That's how I feel about Bobby. I think of him, and then I want to hear his laugh. Or feel his arms around me. Or the soft brush of his mustache against my skin when he kissed me. Sometimes I still feel a touch against my face, like the back of someone's finger brushing against my cheek when I'm sitting still and writing, and I know it's him—doing the same thing he did when we were together...walking up behind me on the sofa, then leaning over and kissing my cheek or the back of my neck.

His physical absence is hard for me to live with, but I remind myself daily that I never really lost him. He's still here, but in a different way. He said he'd never leave me. He was a man who kept his word.

In all ways, I dislike winter most.

I don't do cold. We rarely have snow, although we got a little this past weekend. We usually have ice, and that's what's predicted for this coming weekend. As the weather man said., a weather event of massive proportions for a three state area, with Oklahoma smack dab in the middle of it. I don't want it. I reject it. I refuse to be without power again for days on end. It is not going to be in my future, so there.

One of my nieces fell on the ice yesterday as she was going to work. Hit her head really hard, and her boss called her parents to come get her and take her to ER. Scared them all to death, I think. Her daddy said one of her pupils was bigger than the other when they got her, but after a CT scan and x-rays, etc... she turned out okay. Just a really bad headache. Glad you have such a hard head, Destiny. I was sure worried about you.

As I've gone through life, I have learned that speaking up for myself and for others gets easier with age. I guess after you have lived through, and witnessed so many injustices, you finally reach that point where you say to yourself, enough is enough.

Sometimes I find myself in the midst of someone else's argument, and it is too ridiculous to remark upon. That's when I remove myself from them, and the sound of their voices, because talking to people who are willing to fight about something that petty aren't angry with each other. They're angry with themselves.

And then there are other times when you have to speak up about something, or you know you'll regret missing the chance for the rest of your life. Sometimes you will witness a personal struggle that is so pure and heartbreaking that you have to react.

Like the woman in the wheelchair at my physical therapy last week. She was far younger than I am, and it was obvious she'd suffered a stroke. She was trying so hard to make her fingers move, and to speak to answer the therapists questions. Every muscle she could make move was a reason to celebrate, and every time it happened, another tear ran down her cheek. It was the most uplifting celebration of human spirit I have ever witnessed, and the most painful.

For now, she is trapped inside a body that will no longer respond. And the whole time she's struggling, I have the strongest urge to go wrap my arms around her. But I didn't know her, and was afraid she would take it the wrong way.

I finished my therapy and was gathering up my things to leave, and the whole time I hear this voice inside me saying, go back, go back. I was halfway across the room when I stopped and obeyed.

There a look of pain on her face as I walked up. I put my hand on her shoulder and gave it a slight squeeze."I'm sorry to bother you, but my heart kept telling me not to leave without saying what a good job you are doing."

The look on her face said it all. It was the right thing to do.

And I left.

I've thought about her off and on since, wondering what her life was like before, and what will happen to her now? We never think about being helpless until we are, and then the monumental task of finding our way through a life forever changed is frightening. All I can do for her is pray...but on that day our paths crossed, and she will be a point of light for me forever because she was refusing to quit.

That's what life comes down to...a refusal to quit.

Daily mantra/intention:
I AM OPEN AND RECEPTIVE TO ALL GOOD.

I didn't want to get up.

Worked all night in my sleep.

I'm tired, but now that I'm up, am getting into rhythm.

I used to dream all the time about being in a house with many, many, rooms and no doors. No matter how many rooms I searched looking for a way out, I never found it before I woke up. It was a horrible, frustrating dream.

I dream about the FHA house my parents built when I was 10. It was an L-shaped house that I thought was large and beautiful. I see it when I'm back in that area, and I see it's truth. It was a small, two-bed, one bath home. Probably about 1000 square feet, but it had electricity and water in the house. After living the first ten years of my life in old houses without power, or indoor plumbing, or indoor water, the new house was our mansion.

I dream about the first house I lived in with my ex, before we built my dream home. Only when I dream about it now, there are no floors, only grass, and too many people in it to find my family, and I'm always hiding from a tornado.

I dream now about places without walls. But I'm still not at peace in the dreams, and I am working, working, all night long.

Once this past week I dreamed I was with Bobby, but it wasn't a peaceful dream, it was him, and it was me after he died, all mixed up together.

I will never be free of that nightmare until I am in spirit, and with him again. I think it is behind me. I don't dwell on it at all. And then I close my eyes, and there I am. So...it is not behind me. It is just buried beneath my waking responsibilities.

Ever since intelligent life has lived on this earth, there have been troubles, disasters, hard times and death. But in the middle, when we're living the life, there has also been laughter and joy, relief and rescue, and successes.

From the time of hunting to survive, to now when people drive somewhere, for someone else to feed them, nothing that's happening is new. It's just being presented to us now in different ways.

So why does knowing this matter?

It matters because, in all these thousands of years, we haven't changed what mattered.

And that fact, in itself, is not a thing to brag about.

Technology has changed. Modes of transportation, ways to heal, availability of foods, comfortable clothing...all of these things making us more comfortable.

But humanity is, sadly, still the same.
We're still fighting each other. Judging each other, Hiding behind greed and deceit. Betraying, hurting, killing.
That is not only ridiculous, but it's also appalling.
Don't be mad at each other.
Recognize that we are all being played.
And know this.
Verbal wars are just as divisive and harmful as physical wars.
If you want to live in peace, it has to start with you.

Had an electrician out this morning to repair a loose socket on one of the can lights in my ceiling. They've come and gone, and I have a light back in working order. Yay!

The time it takes to rage and gripe about something someone said or did to you, is triple the negative energy it takes to let it go. Say a silent blessing for them so your own heart is no longer bothered, and, as my mother always said, consider the source.
Some people are missing filters.
The cool part is, that you aren't.
I want to heal the world.
I want to fix people's troubles.
I want everyone to be happy.
The thing is...it's not my path to do any of that.
But what my empathy does impact, is the sufferer's need for solace.
I am a good hugger. Not nearly as good as Bobby was, but good enough.
I will cry with you, and laugh with you.
I will see your need to be heard and listen.
I will give you a helping hand up, if you are down.
I will feed you.
I will say prayers for you.
I will care about your welfare, long after your need for help has come and gone.

Some people call Empaths "do-gooders".

But that's because they fear showing their emotions, so they make fun of people who do, and that's okay, because I also feel your fear of getting too close.

Life did that to you.

But if you want to change, you have only to ask. Or, if you're afraid of the sound of your own voice, just hold out your hand.

One of those do-gooders will take it, and hold on as tight as you need to be held, until you are strong enough to walk on your own.

⁂

I was reminded of a line in the 23rd Psalm as I woke those morning...

"Yea though I walk through the Valley of Death...I will fear no evil..."

Because all night long I dreamed in peril. I dreamed of danger. I dreamed of turmoil and flight from oncoming hordes...And right beside me, everywhere I was...my son would appear...never speaking, but there, putting himself between me, and whatever was threatening me. I have no words to explain the strength his presence gave me in each instance, only that I knew he was there for me.

I'm not sure why I keep dreaming of this huge apocalyptic failing of humanity, but it is unsettling.

I don't have any explanations for my son's continuing appearance in those dreams, and there are many words I could use to describe him, but only one that holds the most of his truth. He is steadfast. A good and honest man who holds close to his heart those he loves most. I view it as a heroic thing, that even in sleep he follows me into another dimension to keep me safe.

With God's love, and with the love of my family, I fear no evil.

When you think of how others see you, what do you think they see?

Some will not see past the outward appearance. They are the

people who are merely passing through your life. In the long run, they will not matter.

Some will hear only the words you speak, without looking into the reasons why they were spoken. They will cause discord and spread gossip. Set them aside and move on.

Some will see past the way you look, past the words you speak, to the heart of who you are and why you hurt.

Why you distrust.

And who you love.

Gather those around you.

They will be strength when yours has faltered.

They will be the comfort you seek when life has pulled you down.

They matter to you.

Make sure you return the favor.

I've been reading so many sad posts.

I know holidays like Valentine's Day, or Mother's Day are hard when you're missing loved ones, or when you're too ill to enjoy it yourself.

Just know that being sad is actually okay. Humans are full of emotions and that's just one of them.

We can't enjoy glad as we should, until we've been where it's sad.

Sending all of you love.

Cry and be done.

Glad is waiting.

Joy is right around the corner.

You don't need a holiday to make you happy.

All you have to do is let go, and let love in.

It's always there...waiting for you to open that door.

I turned on television and scanned the shows. They were about to make hot tub chicken on the Food Network. I thought that sounded a little wonky, like the guy I once knew who ran out of propane for his cook stove, and thought he could heat up a can of beans in the dishwasher. It exploded. They never did use that dishwasher again, and hot tub chicken didn't sound any more promising.

So I changed the channel and scrolled down to movies.

I've seen them all so many times, or they were the ones I don't ever want to see, and then I get down to the last one on the list, and there's Beer For My Horses, starring country singers Willie Nelson, and Toby Keith.

Between hot tub chicken, and Beer For My Horses, I had a full moment of redneck ecstasy, because I am one, and then thought, naw.

As Bobby used to say... I CAN'T WANT IT.

I turned it off. I'm listening to the Louise Hay, Receiving Prosperity, CD instead.

Called to check on Little Mama this morning. She's up and walking around like her usual self...picking things up...which means in her mind, the house is messy. They'll never find the stuff she's moving around. I know that from experience.

Still writing. My publisher gave me an extra week on the deadline because of the week I lost running back and forth with all of Little Mama's falls. That was a huge relief.

You know this feeling most of you have inside you right now because it's almost Christmas? The one where you smile at strangers, and hold the doors open for people with their hands full of kids and packages? That feeling you call "the holiday spirit"?

So...did you know there's a way to feel that year 'round? And you don't need pine-scented candles, and Christmas music playing. You don't need stores overflowing with products, and sales, either.

In fact... you don't need stuff to get that feeling.

It comes with patience and understanding, a calm way of looking at the world, and the willingness to let everyone be who they were meant to be.

🙢

The light of a new day is ever brighter than the darkness into which it is born.

We don't ever die.

It's like going away to school, and when it's over, we pack up and go home.

Another new year is imminent.

What will you make of it?

I hope it's not a list. Like last year—and the year before.

Act upon what you don't like.

Grow out of the rut you are in.

Be prepared to pursue what you want.

What matters most is never given, it is earned.

Life lessons are never graded.

But you will repeat them, over and over until you get it right.

🙢

Had a cool thing happen when I was running errands this morning. I always write down what I want to manifest today, and Leslie Draper told me at my last counseling session to try something different...make it fun, she said.

So today I wrote that my intention was to manifest a big laugh with a stranger. That's pretty random, right? If I can manifest that, then I'm getting there, so to speak.

I drove to the south side of the city to the newest Wal-Mart to finish up my errands, and as I was walking in, a woman was going out. She stared at me, and then stopped and asked me if I was Sharon Sala. I said, yes, and she said, "I'm Regina, (she's in the online Actualization of Prosperity class I'm in that Leslie Draper is teaching, but I'd never met her.) She said..."I set my intention this week to meet you, and now I have. I'm so happy."

We talked and laughed at how awesome it is to be learning how to draw things to us that we want. She was on her way out the door before it hit me that I'd just manifested my daily intention today in sharing a laugh with a stranger.

How awesome is that? Without knowing it...we had become each other's manifested intention.

I'm still smiling and I know she is, too.

Leslie Draper, what you're teaching us about prosperity in life, is just the most amazing experience. As you keep saying, it's not all about money.

I wish I'd been taught this growing up.

I wish we'd all been taught this.

To appreciate our family and life, and not just money, as our personal prosperity.

What a different world this would have been!!

꿎

Empathy for others is a gift, even though it is often a painful one. I would not want to be immune to someone else's tears.

I have this daydream of a kind of reunion, where all of us who I talk to daily on Facebook, get together for one big day of fun, food, and visiting. Telling stories, taking pictures, and flooding Social Media for days with pictures of the reunion. I always imagine what it would be like, and who would click with who, and in the midst of it all, someone would find out that they were actually related to someone else who was there.

Yes, this is how writer's thoughts work. Always a 'what if?' Always wondering, dreaming, always giving a happy ever after in our thoughts to something that would never work out in real life.

I am well aware that one day this WILL actually happen, except it won't be on this plane...but on another just a heartbeat away.

Thinking about life and its full circle moments yesterday.

Someone became a grandfather for the first time, and someone else buried the love of their life, and someone got fired, and someone else got a new job, and someone's child learned to walk ,and someone's child was sent to jail, and someone was abused, and someone else received an engagement ring.

Life for one person becomes a tragedy, at the same time someone else is celebrating. That's how it works. And in the midst of it all, there are some of us who will fall on the side of grief and celebration at the same time...because that's ALSO how life works.

What have to do is figure out how to navigate it with empathy, kindness, love, and understanding. And, we are certainly allowed disgust, dismay, and disappointment, too, because that's also how life works. Our job is to learn how to walk in both worlds without alienation, and to know when it's time to abandon ship. Some relationships aren't worth saving.

Funny email from Sears,
  Just got a Happy Anniversary message from them.
  I didn't know we were married.
  I didn't even know we'd hooked up.
  However... according to them we've been together for 20 years now, so where the heck are my anniversary gifts? Not one Christmas present.
  Not even a birthday present.
  What kind of relationship is that?
  I feel used.
  Dear Sears... I think it's best we don't see each other anymore.
  Don't take it wrong. It's me...not you.

ଈ

It is a new day and you feel worn out and used up?
  Then the first thing that must change is you.
  Part of it is attitude.

We FEEL the rut we're in.
We FEEL being unappreciated.
We FEEL emotionally drained or abused.

In this case...you have given away your power to external interference.

You let a job, a boss, a husband/wife, your children, aging parents control YOU.

Demands coming from every direction are made at you.

And what do you do?

You comply.

You might argue, but you cave in.

You might suffer it silently, but the weight of being unappreciated in every aspect of your life is physically sickening.

You think you have no choices.

BUT YOU DO.

Whether you are a man or a woman, you deserve respect, and when you are not getting it from the people closest to you, then it is your job...your right...to demand it.

I figured out a long time ago that MY husband could put a load of clothes in the washer or the dryer as well as I could.

I found out that a package of cookies from the store was just as sweet as the homemade ones that had been expected—NO—demanded of me.

I found out that saying NO to constant requests for my precious free time was not as hard as I once thought.

The first time I left the kids with my husband (now ex), and went to an afternoon movie by myself, they thought the world was coming to an end. No one wanted to go with me, so I drove 30 miles to the next town to the movie theater by myself. Just me and a radio and my dreams. I sat in the dark watching magic come to life...watching happy ever after at the end while eating popcorn and my ever-present Diet Dr. Pepper. I drove home renewed...Yes, I walked back into the same chaos because I hadn't begun to work on them.

I was still working on me, but I could handle it.

It's the little things... one leads to the other... from a movie...to a lunch out with a friend...to telling the ladies at the church I couldn't serve food at a certain event, because I was going to my child's basketball game, to making your family a priority over petty demands from others.

It's about sorting through priorities...and picking what matters most, which is YOU.

YOU cannot be the best partner, the best parent, the best employee, unless you feel like you are already the best YOU that you can be.

And don't tell me you can't do this, because I did not need to spend money to change me. It all came from within.

It's about picking what matters, and learning to say no.

Respect yourself. Demand it from others, and that worn out, used up person you were becomes renewed. And this is how the new you begins.

Re-assessing.
    Re-evaluating.
    Renewed.

I'm home.

Those words mean the world to me.

And yet... The past few days I have been spending with my writing tribe have refilled the creative well of my soul. Being around people like me, who see the world in stories... and who are driven to write them down, is comfortable for an introvert like me. Being able to share them with people who love to read is truly the best part of this life.

Meeting them is the icing on the cake.

I know the writers I met for the first time see me as old, and in one aspect I am, but I don't feel old. I feel like a survivor, and in a way, that's what life is about... surviving wrecks.

Purpose is what you set out to do in life.

Then life interferes, and purpose is wrecked.

Losing a job, then struggling through uncertainty is a wreck.

You survive it by finding another, and taking that deep breath as your life finds a new level.

The chaos of a broken marriage, or the death of people you hold dear is a wreck, and with this kind of wreck, also comes grief.

Surviving this is often complicated by a feeling of having been uprooted. You still function in one aspect, but you have no safe place of refuge to go home to again.

And so you survive this by putting one foot in front of the other, and don't stop.

Ttaking life one day at a time, until you awake one day to the realization that you are on the other side of the pain.

Every time you reset purpose, you will be challenged.

What you have to remember is that you are also learning how resilient you have become, and how strong you can be when the need arises.

And so time passes with you facing one challenge after another, shifting paths, skipping hurdles, walking through grief, changing worlds, living a purpose-driven life, already confident that whatever happens you will figure it out.

You know this, because you have already survived many wrecks.

You know how to walk away still breathing.

I take all of this to heart every time I look in a mirror.

I do not bemoan gray hair and wrinkles, or sagging flesh that was once taut and toned. I am not old.

Not really.

What you see are just scars from all the wrecks that have been my life.

So pack a few Band-Aids and a sense of humor as you go through life, take a seat and hold on to something sturdy...like your faith.

The ride is wild.

There will be wrecks.

And there will be scars.

But you've got this.

Yesterday was a busy day in miserable heat. So many errands to run. The farthest place I go today is outside to water the plants. I don't know why I still do this because they're all gonna be fried by the time I get back from conference anyway.

Every day you choose an attitude.

You have the option to be happy, simply by saying to yourself that is how you choose to spend the day. No matter how frustrating things become as a day progresses, if you have chosen not to let it bother you, then by the end of the day you will be tired and ready to rest, but with a lighter heart.

Anger is a heavy emotion. It weighs you down emotionally, and after a while, it manifests in a physical way as well, pulling your shoulders down, causing pain in your body, and pulling facial features down into lines that grow deeper with the years.

Grief saps every ounce of joy you possess, and it comes to all of us. Having suffered this enough to know what I'm talking about, I have to say that for me, the only way to get through it was to feel it. You have to acknowledge what you lost, before you learn how to go on without them. But you do go on. It is part of the lesson. How you do that, comes from the choices you make. I just remind myself every day of the years I had with someone...rather than counting the years of loss. That was my lesson learned.

Today I am able to delight in the years I had in their presence, rather than concentrating on the absence.

I stood in a room last night trying to remember what I was after, then laughed out loud and told Bobby I hoped he was getting a kick out of me growing old, because I was driving myself nuts.

I live alone...but I am not alone. It is a matter of faith that brings me to that conclusion...that and paying attention. Recognizing the signs... acknowledging the assistance that comes when I ask for it.

Lost my Kindle (in the house) the other day. I almost never use it, so I couldn't remember where I'd put it. I stomped through the house muttering to myself for a good hour, looking in drawers, shelves, etc...trying to remember when I'd had it last. April I think, when I flew to Milwaukee. So I finally stopped fuming...took a deep breath and said aloud..."I need help. Please help me find my Kindle."

Then I turned around, staring at the furniture in my bedroom. I had looked in every drawer multiple times, but this time was different. I had asked for help, and so I started over, looking again because I had faith I would find it now. And I did., second drawer I opened...it was on top of everything in it. With the charger cord. Waiting for me to pick it up.

"Thank you!" I said aloud, and put it with the stuff I'm packing to take to Orlando.

As Tony Soprano would say... "bada boom."

I am making a cake today for Kathy to take to Scout's Boy Scout troop meeting tonight. It's a big event...awards, etc. and Scout is moving up another notch on his way to Eagle Scout. Kathy has meetings after school every day this week, so I volunteered to pick Scout up from school instead of her or Ash trying to make time to get him. And that's why I am making a cake for a household of bakers who could easily do one better. LOL No one has time to do that but me.

I coughed a good portion of the night. Still don't have much of a voice, and I'm worn out from not enough sleep. Thank you Mother Nature for sharing the pollen of your flowering plants so freely this Spring. Wish I could return the favor. Hmm, I wonder what happens if Mother Nature had to sneeze? A sudden down burst of hail?

A pelting of pine cones? A ration of shit?

Ah well, I've been chatty enough.

Now I will patty cake, patty cake, and pretend I am the baker man so I can bake Scout a cake as fast as I can.

It's Monday.

It's the perfect day to change your attitude to happy.

Change your expression to a smile.

Begin something that you consider fun.

It should not always be about work.

If you don't stop and take time to find your joy, you will wake up one day to find yourself too old for chasing dreams.

Why work three jobs just so you can buy a second house you think you need, and then travel to it just to have fun?

Have fun no matter where you're living. Fun isn't about geography, and doesn't cost a dime.

❦

Last night there were my analogies for life in my dreams. Without going into endless detail about what I saw, and what it meant, the bottom line was "see their truths."

In other words, look beyond what I see and hear, to the reasons for what's being said and done.

Don't take offense at hurtful words.

Don't take things personally because the anger in which things are said and done in my presence, come from other sources, and not from something I caused.

I will be the 'whipping boy" so to speak, because I will see the pain from which their words are spoken, and understand and forgive. It won't hurt me personally, even though I might hurt for them.

So, I can do that. I've done it countless times my whole life without thinking about it.

You do it. We all do it.

It's when someone you love says something hurtful to you, but because we love them, and if we are paying attention to what's going on in their lives, we understand why things are said, and love them anyway.

It's the child screaming out, "I hate you." It's the teenager calling you an ugly name when in fact they're only accusing you of something they already feel. They're the ones who feel mean. They hate themselves, but because they trust us enough to keep loving them anyway, the bad words get said.

The deal is, you have to be adult enough not to scream back.

Words spoken are alive.

They will live among the people who heard them forever. If they were negative words... and if there's not someone among the listeners who knows how to love and forgive, the words will take on a life of their own.

They can ruin friendships, tear families apart, destroy marriages and jobs and lives. All because of something said in anger and haste.

Know this... the next time something hurtful is said to me or about me, you are already forgiven.

Scout's allergies are on the march again. Poor sweetie, all he does is cough, cough, cough. He has meds now and his mama said he will be back in school tomorrow regardless.

I'm sleepy. It's the kind of sleepy where you would happily crawl under a table somewhere and go to sleep, as long as you were out of the line of traffic. I've worked at jobs when I felt that way. I know it's allergies for me, too. Sometimes that's how I feel when they're starting up. So I'm going to take a nap and I'll write later. Just talked to Kathy, she was on her planning period and running home to check on him. Ah the worries of a working mother. Your heart is always with your family first, and yet you're never able to be in two places at once. It always helps when there are aunties or grannies, etc., to fill the gap.

I dreamed all night long. Once again trying to get somewhere. Every mode of transportation I chose let me down. Finally I started out on foot, and I was almost at the destination when I woke up. So...the analogy I took from that was, don't depend on others to get you where you need to be in life.

It doesn't matter how you want your life to be. It's not going to change the facts of it. Right now, in this moment, you are exactly where your choices took you.

You know the drill.

If you don't like it, choose another path.

FROM THE AUTHOR

I hope you've enjoyed this book, but more importantly, I pray you find answers and ways to be at peace with yourself, and your world.

I will be doing other books in the future from the posts I've been saving.

The next one will be posts about my childhood, and my journey to this destination.

You'll recognize the next book, because I'll be smiling at you from the cover again, waiting to welcome you back into my world.

Made in the USA
Lexington, KY
26 August 2018